the beginning God created the heavens and t

empty, and darkness covered the deep waters. And the Spirit of God was

hovering over the surface of the waters. Then God said, "Let there be

t," and there was light. And God saw that the light was good. Then he

rated the light from the darkness. God called the light "day" and the dark

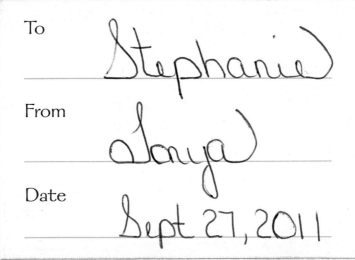

To **Stephanie**

From **Tonya**

Date **Sept 27, 2011**

In the beginning God created the heavens

and the earth. The earth was formless and empty, and darkness covered

deep waters. And the Spirit of God was hovering over the surface of

the waters. Then God said, "Let there be light," and there was light.

And God saw that the light was good. Then he separated the light from

THE
BIBLE
IN 366 DAYS

FOR WOMEN

CHRISTIAN ART
PUBLISHERS

Originally published by Christelike Uitgewersmaatskappy
under the title *Die Bybel in 366 dae vir vroue*

© 2009

English edition
© 2010 Christian Art Publishers
PO Box 1599, Vereeniging, 1930, RSA

First edition 2010

Cover designed by Christian Art Publishers

Image © Lukas Skarits, 2009
Used under license from Shutterstock.com

Scripture taken from the *Holy Bible*,
New Living Translation, second edition,
copyright © 1996, 2004. Used by permission of
Tyndale House Publishers, Inc., Carol Stream,
Illinois 60188. All rights reserved.

Set in 9 on 12 pt Arial
by Christian Art Publishers

Printed in China

ISBN 978-1-77036-441-7

11   12   13   14   15   16   17   18   19   20   –   14   13   12   11   10   9   8   7   6   5

Dedicated to all the women in my family and
circle of friends – may the Word always be
new and wonderful to you;
may it always be a living Word from the
mouth of a loving Father;
may this always
be a Word of comfort and power,
through the working of the Holy Spirit.
And may your lives still be a beautiful
answer to His Word.

The word of the Lord remains forever.

~ *1 Peter 1:25*

January

Let There Be Light!

God's first words at creation were, "Let there be light." After He made light, He created the expanse; the land, sun, moon and stars, the seas, trees and plants, birds, fish and animals. And God saw that it was good.

[1]In the beginning God created the heavens and the earth. [3]Then God said, "Let there be light," and there was light. [4]And God saw that the light was good. Then he separated the light from the darkness.

[9]Then God said, "Let the waters beneath the sky flow together into one place, so dry ground may appear." And that is what happened.

[14]Then God said, "Let lights appear in the sky to separate the day from the night. Let them mark off the seasons, days, and years. [15]Let these lights in the sky shine down on the earth." And that is what happened. [16]God made two great lights—the larger one to govern the day, and the smaller one to govern the night. He also made the stars.

[20]Then God said, "Let the waters swarm with fish and other life. Let the skies be filled with birds of every kind." [21]So God created great sea creatures and every living thing that scurries and swarms in the water, and every sort of bird—each producing offspring of the same kind. And God saw that it was good. [22]Then God blessed them, saying, "Be fruitful and multiply. Let the fish fill the seas, and let the birds multiply on the earth."

[24]Then God said, "Let the earth produce every sort of animal, each producing offspring of the same kind—livestock, small animals that scurry along the ground, and wild animals." And that is what happened. [25]God made all sorts of wild animals, livestock, and small animals, each able to produce offspring of the same kind. And God saw that it was good.

~ Genesis 1:1, 3-4, 9, 14-16, 20-22, 24-25

The Crown of Creation

God's last work of creation was making people in His image. He told the first two people to be fruitful and increase in number, and to rule over the earth. God saw that His handiwork was good in every sense.

1[26]God said, "Let us make human beings in our image, to be like ourselves. They will reign over the fish in the sea, the birds in the sky, the livestock, all the wild animals on the earth, and the small animals that scurry along the ground."

[27]So God created human beings in his own image. In the image of God he created them; male and female he created them.

[28]Then God blessed them and said, "Be fruitful and multiply. Fill the earth and govern it. Reign over the fish in the sea, the birds in the sky, and all the animals that scurry along the ground." [29]Then God said, "Look! I have given you every seed-bearing plant throughout the earth and all the fruit trees for your food. [30]And I have given every green plant as food for all the wild animals, the birds in the sky, and the small animals that scurry along the ground—everything that has life." And that is what happened. [31]Then God looked over all he had made, and he saw that it was very good! And evening passed and morning came, marking the sixth day.

2[1]So the creation of the heavens and the earth and everything in them was completed. [2]On the seventh day God had finished his work of creation, so he rested from all his work. [3]And God blessed the seventh day and declared it holy, because it was the day when he rested from all his work of creation.

[4]This is the account of the creation of the heavens and the earth.

~ Genesis 1:26-2:4

The Perfect Mate for Adam

Adam was lonely before God made him a companion, somebody to help and compliment him. "She is bone from my bone," declares Adam. God's will today is still for you to be the perfect mate for your husband and stand by him no matter what.

[18]Then the LORD God said, "It is not good for the man to be alone. I will make a helper who is just right for him." [19]So the LORD God formed from the ground all the wild animals and all the birds of the sky. He brought them to the man to see what he would call them, and the man chose a name for each one. [20]He gave names to all the livestock, all the birds of the sky, and all the wild animals. But still there was no helper just right for him.

[21]So the LORD God caused the man to fall into a deep sleep. While the man slept, the LORD God took out one of the man's ribs and closed up the opening. [22]Then the LORD God made a woman from the rib, and he brought her to the man. [23]"At last!" the man exclaimed. "This one is bone from my bone, and flesh from my flesh! She will be called 'woman,' because she was taken from 'man.'"

[24]This explains why a man leaves his father and mother and is joined to his wife, and the two are united into one. [25]Now the man and his wife were both naked, but they felt no shame.

~ Genesis 2:18-25

Sin Enters the World

When the snake tempted Eve, she not only succumb-
ed to temptation, but she also involved Adam. Then
sin entered the world and the first people were alien-
ated from God. We still suffer because of the consequences of Eve's wrong decision.

¹The serpent was the shrewdest of all the wild animals the LORD God had made. One day he asked the woman, "Did God really say you must not eat the fruit from any of the trees in the garden?"

²"Of course we may eat fruit from the trees in the garden," the woman replied. ³"It's only the fruit from the tree in the middle of the garden that we are not allowed to eat. God said, 'You must not eat it or even touch it; if you do, you will die.'"

⁴"You won't die!" the serpent replied to the woman. ⁵"God knows that your eyes will be opened as soon as you eat it, and you will be like God, knowing both good and evil."

⁶The woman was convinced. She saw that the tree was beautiful and its fruit looked delicious, and she wanted the wisdom it would give her. So she took some of the fruit and ate it. Then she gave some to her husband, who was with her, and he ate it, too. ⁷At that moment their eyes were opened, and they suddenly felt shame at their nakedness. So they sewed fig leaves together to cover themselves.

⁸When the cool evening breezes were blowing, the man and his wife heard the LORD God walking in the garden. So they hid from the LORD God among the trees. ⁹Then the LORD God called to the man, "Where are you?" ¹⁰He replied, "I heard you walking in the garden, so I hid. I was afraid because I was naked."

¹¹"Who told you that you were naked?" the LORD God asked. "Have you eaten from the tree whose fruit I commanded you not to eat?"

~ Genesis 3:1-11

Punishment for Sin

God never lets sin go unpunished. He punished Adam and Eve severely for their disobedience. However, God promised that one day Someone will come to undo the work of Satan and to bring people back to God again.

¹²The man replied, "It was the woman you gave me who gave me the fruit, and I ate it." ¹³Then the LORD God asked the woman, "What have you done?"

"The serpent deceived me," she replied. "That's why I ate it." ¹⁴Then the LORD God said to the serpent, "Because you have done this, you are cursed more than all animals. You will crawl on your belly, groveling in the dust as long as you live. ¹⁵And I will cause hostility between you and the woman, and between your offspring and her offspring. He will strike your head, and you will strike his heel."

¹⁶Then he said to the woman, "I will sharpen the pain of your pregnancy, and in pain you will give birth. And you will desire to control your husband, but he will rule over you."

¹⁷And to the man he said, "Since you listened to your wife and ate from the tree whose fruit I commanded you not to eat, the ground is cursed because of you. All your life you will struggle to scratch a living from it.

¹⁹"By the sweat of your brow will you have food to eat until you return to the ground from which you were made. For you were made from dust, and to dust you will return."

²²Then the LORD God said, "Look, the human beings have become like us, knowing both good and evil. What if they reach out, take fruit from the tree of life, and eat it? Then they will live forever!" ²³So the LORD God banished them from the Garden of Eden, and he sent Adam out to cultivate the ground from which he had been made.

~ Genesis 3:12-17, 19, 22-23

Violence Enters the World

Cain murdered his brother Abel because God accepted Abel's offering, but not his. God spared Cain's life but banned him from the land.

¹Adam had sexual relations with his wife, Eve, and she became pregnant. When she gave birth to Cain, she said, "With the LORD's help, I have produced a man!" ²Later she gave birth to his brother and named him Abel. When they grew up, Abel became a shepherd, while Cain cultivated the ground. ³When it was time for the harvest, Cain presented some of his crops as a gift to the LORD. ⁴Abel also brought a gift—the best of the firstborn lambs from his flock. The LORD accepted Abel and his gift, ⁵but he did not accept Cain and his gift. This made Cain very angry.

⁶"Why are you so angry?" the LORD asked Cain. ⁷"You will be accepted if you do what is right. But if you refuse to do what is right, then watch out! Sin is crouching at the door, eager to control you. But you must subdue it and be its master."

⁸One day Cain suggested to his brother, "Let's go out into the fields." And while they were in the field, Cain attacked his brother, Abel, and killed him. ⁹Afterward the LORD asked Cain, "Where is Abel?"

"I don't know," Cain responded. "Am I my brother's guardian?"

¹⁰But the LORD said, "What have you done? Listen! Your brother's blood cries out to me from the ground! ¹¹Now you are cursed and banished from the ground, which has swallowed your brother's blood. ¹²From now on you will be a homeless wanderer on the earth." ¹³Cain replied to the LORD, "My punishment is too great for me to bear! ¹⁴You have banished me from the land and from your presence; you have made me a homeless wanderer."

~ Genesis 4:1-14

Noah Obeys God

God gave Noah an impossible task – to put a pair of every animal inside the ark. And Noah did exactly what God asked. When God gives you an impossible task He will help you to make it possible. You only need to obey and trust Him.

[1]When everything was ready, the LORD said to Noah, "Go into the boat with all your family, for among all the people of the earth, I can see that you alone are righteous. [2]Take with you seven pairs—male and female—of each animal I have approved for eating and for sacrifice, and take one pair of each of the others. [3]Also take seven pairs of every kind of bird. There must be a male and a female in each pair to ensure that all life will survive on the earth after the flood. [4]Seven days from now I will make the rains pour down on the earth. And it will rain for forty days and forty nights, until I have wiped from the earth all the living things I have created." [5]So Noah did everything as the LORD commanded him.

[17]For forty days the floodwaters grew deeper, covering the ground and lifting the boat high above the earth. [18]As the waters rose higher and higher above the ground, the boat floated safely on the surface. [19]Finally, the water covered even the highest mountains on the earth, [20]rising more than twenty-two feet above the highest peaks. [21]All the living things on earth died— birds, domestic animals, wild animals, small animals that scurry along the ground, and all the people. [22]Everything that breathed and lived on dry land died. [23]God wiped out every living thing on the earth—people, livestock, small animals that scurry along the ground, and the birds of the sky. All were destroyed. The only people who survived were Noah and those with him in the boat. [24]And the floodwaters covered the earth for 150 days.

~ Genesis 7:1-5, 17-24

A Rainbow of Promise

Because Noah obeyed God, He saved his family and made him a promise: the rainbow is the sign of this promise. Every time you see a rainbow let it remind you that God always keeps His promises.

8¹⁸So Noah, his wife, and his sons and their wives left the boat. ¹⁹And all of the large and small animals and birds came out of the boat, pair by pair. ²⁰Then Noah built an altar to the LORD, and there he sacrificed as burnt offerings the animals and birds that had been approved for that purpose. ²¹And the LORD was pleased with the aroma of the sacrifice and said to himself, "I will never again curse the ground because of the human race, even though everything they think or imagine is bent toward evil from childhood. I will never again destroy all living things. ²²As long as the earth remains, there will be planting and harvest, cold and heat, summer and winter, day and night."

9⁸Then God told Noah and his sons, ⁹"I hereby confirm my covenant with you and your descendants, ¹⁰and with all the animals that were on the boat with you—the birds, the livestock, and all the wild animals—every living creature on earth. ¹¹Yes, I am confirming my covenant with you. Never again will flood-waters kill all living creatures; never again will a flood destroy the earth." ¹²Then God said, "I am giving you a sign of my covenant with you and with all living creatures, for all generations to come. ¹³I have placed my rainbow in the clouds. It is the sign of my covenant with you and with all the earth. ¹⁴When I send clouds over the earth, the rainbow will appear in the clouds, ¹⁵and I will remember my covenant with you and with all living creatures. Never again will the floodwaters destroy all life. ¹⁶When I see the rainbow in the clouds, I will remember the eternal covenant between God and every living creature on earth."

~ Genesis 8:18-22, 9:8-16

The Call of Abram

Abram obeyed God's command to leave his land. Then God made a covenant with him. God promised him that his offspring would be as many as the stars. God would also give them a land to live in.

12¹The Lord had said to Abram, "Leave your native country, your relatives, and your father's family, and go to the land that I will show you. ²I will make you into a great nation. I will bless you and make you famous, and you will be a blessing to others. ³I will bless those who bless you and curse those who treat you with contempt. All the families on earth will be blessed through you." ⁴So Abram departed as the Lord had instructed, and Lot went with him. Abram was seventy-five years old when he left Haran. ⁵He took his wife, Sarai, his nephew Lot, and all his wealth—his livestock and all the people he had taken into his household at Haran—and headed for the land of Canaan.

⁷Then the Lord appeared to Abram and said, "I will give this land to your descendants." And Abram built an altar there and dedicated it to the Lord, who had appeared to him.

15¹Some time later, the Lord spoke to Abram in a vision and said to him, "Do not be afraid, Abram, for I will protect you, and your reward will be great."

⁵Then the Lord took Abram outside and said to him, "Look up into the sky and count the stars if you can. That's how many descendants you will have!" ⁶And Abram believed the Lord, and the Lord counted him as righteous because of his faith.

¹⁸So the Lord made a covenant with Abram that day and said, "I have given this land to your descendants, all the way from the border of Egypt to the great Euphrates River.

~ Genesis 12:1-5, 7; 15:1, 5-6, 18

A Son for Abraham

Years passed without God's promise of many descendants coming true for Abraham. Only when it was humanly impossible for Abraham to have children, did God sent three visitors to him with the message that his wife would have a son within a year's time. Nothing is impossible with God.

¹One day Abraham was sitting at the entrance to his tent during the hottest part of the day. ²He looked up and noticed three men standing nearby. When he saw them, he ran to meet them and welcomed them, bowing low to the ground.

³"My lord," he said, "if it pleases you, stop here for a while. ⁴Rest in the shade of this tree while water is brought to wash your feet. ⁵And since you've honored your servant with this visit, let me prepare some food to refresh you before you continue on your journey."

"All right," they said.

⁹"Where is Sarah, your wife?" the visitors asked. "She's inside the tent," Abraham replied.

¹⁰Then one of them said, "I will return to you about this time next year, and your wife, Sarah, will have a son!" Sarah was listening to this conversation from the tent. ¹¹Abraham and Sarah were both very old by this time, and Sarah was long past the age of having children.

¹²So she laughed silently to herself and said, "How could a worn-out woman like me enjoy such pleasure, especially when my master—my husband—is also so old?" ¹³Then the LORD said to Abraham, "Why did Sarah laugh? Why did she say, 'Can an old woman like me have a baby?' ¹⁴Is anything too hard for the LORD? I will return about this time next year, and Sarah will have a son."

~ Genesis 18:1-5, 9-14

A Test of Abraham's Faith

When Abraham's long-awaited son had finally been born, God commanded the inexplicable: Abraham had to give his only son as an offering to God. Abraham did what God asked. Only when he was about to kill Isaac did God provide a lamb in his place. Abraham passed his test of faith – what about you?

¹Some time later, God tested Abraham's faith. "Abraham!" God called. "Yes," he replied. "Here I am."

²"Take your son, your only son—yes, Isaac, whom you love so much—and go to the land of Moriah. Go and sacrifice him as a burnt offering on one of the mountains, which I will show you."

³The next morning Abraham got up early. He saddled his donkey and took two of his servants with him, along with his son, Isaac. Then he chopped wood for a fire for a burnt offering and set out for the place God had told him about.

⁹When they arrived at the place where God had told him to go, Abraham built an altar and arranged the wood on it. Then he tied his son, Isaac, and laid him on the altar on top of the wood. ¹⁰And Abraham picked up the knife to kill his son as a sacrifice. ¹¹At that moment the angel of the LORD called to him from heaven, "Abraham! Abraham!" "Yes," Abraham replied. "Here I am!" ¹²"Don't lay a hand on the boy!" the angel said. "Do not hurt him in any way, for now I know that you truly fear God. You have not withheld from me even your son, your only son."

¹³Then Abraham looked up and saw a ram caught by its horns in a thicket. So he took the ram and sacrificed it as a burnt offering in place of his son. ¹⁴Abraham named the place Yahweh-Yireh (which means "the LORD will provide"). To this day, people still use that name as a proverb: "On the mountain of the LORD it will be provided."

~ Genesis 22:1-3, 9-14

Jacob Meets God

At the Jabbok River, Jacob wrestled with a man and refused to let go until he blessed him. "Your name will no longer be Jacob," the man told him. "From now on you will be called Israel, because you have fought with God and with men and have won." Jacob's eleven sons became the ancestors of Israel, God's people.

¹As Jacob started on his way again, angels of God came to meet him. ²When Jacob saw them, he exclaimed, "This is God's camp!" So he named the place Mahanaim.

²²During the night Jacob got up and took his two wives, his two servant wives, and his eleven sons and crossed the Jabbok River with them. ²³After taking them to the other side, he sent over all his possessions.

²⁴This left Jacob all alone in the camp, and a man came and wrestled with him until the dawn began to break. ²⁵When the man saw that he would not win the match, he touched Jacob's hip and wrenched it out of its socket. ²⁶Then the man said, "Let me go, for the dawn is breaking!" But Jacob said, "I will not let you go unless you bless me."

²⁷"What is your name?" the man asked. He replied, "Jacob."

²⁸"Your name will no longer be Jacob," the man told him. "From now on you will be called Israel, because you have fought with God and with men and have won." ²⁹"Please tell me your name," Jacob said.

"Why do you want to know my name?" the man replied. Then he blessed Jacob there. ³⁰Jacob named the place Peniel (which means "face of God"), for he said, "I have seen God face to face, yet my life has been spared." ³¹The sun was rising as Jacob left Peniel, and he was limping because of the injury to his hip.

~ Genesis 32:1-2, 22-31

Joseph Is Sold as a Slave

Because his father favored Joseph, his brothers hated
him and sold him as a slave. They told their father
that a wild animal had killed him. Joseph's life was
filled with undeserved suffering, but God never left
his side. God is with you too when you suffer.

¹⁸When Joseph's brothers saw him coming, they recognized
him in the distance. As he approached, they made plans to kill
him. ²⁰"Come on, let's kill him and throw him into one of these
cisterns. We can tell our father, 'A wild animal has eaten him.'"
²¹But when Reuben heard of their scheme, he came to Joseph's
rescue. "Let's not kill him," he said. ²²"Why should we shed any
blood? Let's just throw him into this empty cistern here in the
wilderness. Then he'll die without our laying a hand on him."
Reuben was secretly planning to rescue Joseph and return him
to his father.

²³When Joseph arrived, his brothers ripped off the beautiful
robe he was wearing. ²⁴Then they grabbed him and threw him
into the cistern. ²⁵Then, just as they were sitting down to eat,
they looked up and saw a caravan of camels in the distance
coming toward them.

²⁸When the Ishmaelites, who were Midianite traders, came
by, Joseph's brothers pulled him out of the cistern and sold him
to them for twenty pieces of silver. And the traders took him to
Egypt.

³¹Then the brothers killed a young goat and dipped Joseph's
robe in its blood. ³²They sent the beautiful robe to their father
with this message: "Look at what we found. Doesn't this robe belong to your son?"

³³"Yes," he said, "it is my son's robe. A wild animal must have
eaten him." ³⁴Then Jacob tore his clothes and dressed himself
in burlap. He mourned deeply for his son for a long time.

~ Genesis 37:18, 20-25, 28, 31-34

The Lord Is with Joseph

Despite the unfair treatment Joseph had to endure, God was with him and cared for him. Sometimes God uses suffering so that you can experience His presence.

[1]When Joseph was taken to Egypt by the Ishmaelite traders, he was purchased by Potiphar, an Egyptian officer. [2]The LORD was with Joseph, so he succeeded in everything he did as he served in the home of his Egyptian master. [3]Potiphar noticed this and realized that the LORD was with Joseph, giving him success in everything he did. [4]This pleased Potiphar, so he soon made Joseph his personal attendant.

[6]Joseph was a very handsome and well-built young man, [7]and Potiphar's wife soon began to look at him lustfully. "Come and sleep with me," she demanded. [8]But Joseph refused. "Look," he told her, "my master trusts me with everything in his entire household. [9]He has held back nothing from me except you, because you are his wife. It would be a great sin against God."

[11]One day, however, no one else was around when he went in to do his work. [12]She came and grabbed him by his cloak, demanding, "Come on, sleep with me!" Joseph tore himself away, but he left his cloak in her hand as he ran from the house. [16]She kept the cloak with her until her husband came home.

[19]Potiphar was furious when he heard his wife's story about how Joseph had treated her. [20]So he took Joseph and threw him into the prison where the king's prisoners were held, and there he remained. [21]But the LORD was with Joseph in the prison and showed him his faithful love.

~ Genesis 39:1-4, 6-9, 11-12, 16, 19-21

God's Plan

When Joseph was released from prison and interpreted Pharaoh's dream, he became the ruler of all Egypt. He also made a plan to end the famine and eventually his brothers had to buy grain from him. Joseph's sufferings didn't make him bitter, but allowed him to discover God's plan for his life.

3"I am Joseph!" he said to his brothers. "Is my father still alive?" But his brothers were speechless! 4"Please, come closer," he said to them. "I am Joseph, your brother, whom you sold into slavery in Egypt. 5But don't be upset, and don't be angry with yourselves for selling me to this place. It was God who sent me here ahead of you to preserve your lives. 7God has sent me ahead of you to keep you and your families alive and to preserve many survivors. 8It was God who sent me here, not you! And he is the one who made me an adviser to Pharaoh—the manager of his entire palace and the governor of all Egypt.

9"Now hurry back to my father and tell him, 'This is what your son Joseph says: God has made me master over all the land of Egypt. So come down to me immediately! 11I will take care of you there, for there are still five years of famine ahead of us. Otherwise you, your household, and all your animals will starve.'"

25They left Egypt and returned to their father, Jacob, in the land of Canaan. 26"Joseph is still alive!" they told him. "And he is governor of all the land of Egypt!" Jacob was stunned at the news—he couldn't believe it. 27But when they repeated to Jacob everything Joseph had told them, and when he saw the wagons Joseph had sent to carry him, their father's spirits revived. 28Then Jacob exclaimed, "It must be true! My son Joseph is alive! I must go and see him before I die."

~ Genesis 45:3-5, 7-9, 11, 25-28

God Gives a Deliverer

The Israelites endured much suffering and hardship. They had to work very hard, and Pharaoh killed their infant sons. God saw their hardship and made a plan for Moses to be adopted by Pharaoh's daughter. The palace life prepared him to lead God's people out of Egypt.

¹A man and woman from the tribe of Levi got married. ²The woman became pregnant and gave birth to a son. She saw that he was a special baby and kept him hidden for three months. ³But when she could no longer hide him, she got a basket made of papyrus reeds and waterproofed it with tar and pitch. She put the baby in the basket and laid it among the reeds along the bank of the Nile River. ⁴The baby's sister then stood at a distance, watching to see what would happen to him.

⁵Soon Pharaoh's daughter came down to bathe in the river, and her attendants walked along the riverbank. When the princess saw the basket among the reeds, she sent her maid to get it for her. ⁶When the princess opened it, she saw the baby. The little boy was crying, and she felt sorry for him. "This must be one of the Hebrew children," she said. ⁷Then the baby's sister approached the princess. "Should I go and find one of the Hebrew women to nurse the baby for you?" she asked.

⁸"Yes, do!" the princess replied. So the girl went and called the baby's mother. ⁹"Take this baby and nurse him for me," the princess told the baby's mother. "I will pay you for your help." So the woman took her baby home and nursed him.

¹⁰Later, when the boy was older, his mother brought him back to Pharaoh's daughter, who adopted him as her own son. The princess named him Moses, for she explained, "I lifted him out of the water."

~ Exodus 2:1-10

God Speaks to Moses

God appeared to Moses in a burning bush and told him to notice the people's suffering and hear their cries. He asked Moses to lead the Israelites out of Egypt, and promised to be with Him.

¹One day Moses was tending the flock of his father-in-law, Jethro, the priest of Midian. He led the flock far into the wilderness and came to Sinai, the mountain of God. ²There the angel of the Lord appeared to him in a blazing fire from the middle of a bush. Moses stared in amazement. Though the bush was engulfed in flames, it didn't burn up.

⁴When the Lord saw Moses coming to take a closer look, God called to him from the middle of the bush, "Moses! Moses!" "Here I am!" Moses replied. ⁵"Do not come any closer," the Lord warned. "Take off your sandals, for you are standing on holy ground. ⁶I am the God of your father—the God of Abraham, the God of Isaac, and the God of Jacob." When Moses heard this, he covered his face because he was afraid to look at God.

⁷Then the Lord told him, "I have certainly seen the oppression of my people in Egypt. I have heard their cries of distress because of their harsh slave drivers. Yes, I am aware of their suffering. ⁸So I have come down to rescue them from the power of the Egyptians and lead them out of Egypt into their own fertile and spacious land. It is a land flowing with milk and honey. ¹⁰Now go, for I am sending you to Pharaoh. You must lead my people Israel out of Egypt."

¹¹But Moses protested to God, "Who am I to appear before Pharaoh? Who am I to lead the people of Israel out of Egypt?" ¹²God answered, "I will be with you. And this is your sign that I am the one who has sent you: When you have brought the people out of Egypt, you will worship God at this very mountain."

~ Exodus 3:1-2, 4-8, 10-12

Moses' Endless Excuses

Moses had many excuses as to why he could not follow God's instructions, but God assured him that He would help him. Are you prepared to obey God without excuses?

¹Moses protested again, "What if they won't believe me or listen to me? What if they say, 'The Lord never appeared to you'?" ²Then the Lord asked him, "What is that in your hand?"

"A shepherd's staff," Moses replied. ³"Throw it down on the ground," the Lord told him. So Moses threw down the staff, and it turned into a snake! Moses jumped back.

⁵"Perform this sign," the Lord told him. "Then they will believe that the Lord, the God of their ancestors—the God of Abraham, the God of Isaac, and the God of Jacob—really has appeared to you. ⁶Now put your hand inside your cloak." So Moses put his hand inside his cloak, and when he took it out again, his hand was white as snow with a severe skin disease. ⁷"Now put your hand back into your cloak," the Lord said. So Moses put his hand back in, and when he took it out again, it was as healthy as the rest of his body. ⁸The Lord said to Moses, ⁹"And if they don't believe you or listen to you even after these two signs, then take some water from the Nile River and pour it out on the dry ground. When you do, the water from the Nile will turn to blood on the ground."

¹⁰But Moses pleaded with the Lord, "O Lord, I'm not very good with words. I never have been, and I'm not now, even though you have spoken to me." ¹¹Then the Lord asked Moses, "Who makes a person's mouth? Who decides whether people speak or do not speak, hear or do not hear, see or do not see? Is it not I, the Lord? ¹²Now go! I will be with you as you speak, and I will instruct you in what to say."

~ Exodus 4:1-3, 5-12

The Parting of the Red Sea

Eventually Moses succeeded in getting the pharaoh's permission to let the Israelites leave Egypt. But then the pharaoh pursued them with his army and chariots. God parted the sea so His people could have safe passage, but all the Egyptians drowned when they tried to follow God's people through the water.

[15]The LORD said to Moses, "Why are you crying out to me? Tell the people to get moving! [16]Pick up your staff and raise your hand over the sea. Divide the water so the Israelites can walk through the middle of the sea on dry ground."

[21]Then Moses raised his hand over the sea, and the LORD opened up a path through the water with a strong east wind. The wind blew all that night, turning the seabed into dry land. [22]So the people of Israel walked through the middle of the sea on dry ground, with walls of water on each side! [23]Then the Egyptians—all of Pharaoh's horses, chariots, and charioteers—chased them into the middle of the sea.

[26]When all the Israelites had reached the other side, the LORD said to Moses, "Raise your hand over the sea again. Then the waters will rush back and cover the Egyptians and their chariots and charioteers." [27]So as the sun began to rise, Moses raised his hand over the sea, and the water rushed back into its usual place. The Egyptians tried to escape, but the LORD swept them into the sea.

[30]That is how the LORD rescued Israel from the hand of the Egyptians that day. And the Israelites saw the bodies of the Egyptians washed up on the seashore. [31]When the people of Israel saw the mighty power that the LORD had unleashed against the Egyptians, they were filled with awe before him. They put their faith in the LORD and in his servant Moses.

~ Exodus 14:15-16, 21-23, 26-27, 30-31

Food in the Desert

Before long the Israelites were complaining because they didn't have food to eat. God sent them manna from heaven, and quail, to satisfy their hunger. For forty years God provided for His people in the desert. God still undertakes to provide for you.

²The whole community of Israel complained about Moses and Aaron. ³"If only the LORD had killed us back in Egypt," they moaned. "There we sat around pots filled with meat and ate all the bread we wanted. But now you have brought us into this wilderness to starve us all to death."

⁴Then the LORD said to Moses, "Look, I'm going to rain down food from heaven for you. Each day the people can go out and pick up as much food as they need for that day. I will test them in this to see whether or not they will follow my instructions."

¹¹Then the LORD said to Moses, ¹²"I have heard the Israelites' complaints. Now tell them, 'In the evening you will have meat to eat, and in the morning you will have all the bread you want. Then you will know that I am the LORD your God.'"

¹³That evening vast numbers of quail flew in and covered the camp. And the next morning the area around the camp was wet with dew. ¹⁴When the dew evaporated, a flaky substance as fine as frost blanketed the ground. ¹⁵The Israelites were puzzled when they saw it. "What is it?" they asked each other. They had no idea what it was.

³¹The Israelites called the food manna. It was white like coriander seed, and it tasted like honey wafers.

³⁵So the people of Israel ate manna for forty years until they arrived at the land where they would settle. They ate manna until they came to the border of the land of Canaan.

~ Exodus 16:2-4, 11-15, 31, 35

God's Law

On Mount Sinai, God gave Moses Ten Commandments to give to His people so that they could follow God's Law. Jesus teaches us that His Law is valid even today. The essentials of the Law are love for God and love for others.

¹God gave the people all these instructions: ²"I am the LORD your God, who rescued you from the land of Egypt, the place of your slavery. ³"You must not have any other god but me.

⁵"You must not bow down to them or worship them, for I, the LORD your God, am a jealous God who will not tolerate your affection for any other gods. I lay the sins of the parents upon their children; the entire family is affected—even children in the third and fourth generations of those who reject me.

⁷"You must not misuse the name of the LORD your God. The LORD will not let you go unpunished if you misuse his name.

⁸"Remember to observe the Sabbath day by keeping it holy. ⁹You have six days each week for your ordinary work, ¹⁰but the seventh day is a Sabbath day of rest dedicated to the LORD your God. On that day no one in your household may do any work. ¹¹For in six days the LORD made the heavens, the earth, the sea, and everything in them; but on the seventh day he rested. That is why the LORD blessed the Sabbath day and set it apart as holy.

¹²"Honor your father and mother. Then you will live a long, full life in the land the LORD your God is giving you. ¹³You must not murder. ¹⁴You must not commit adultery. ¹⁵You must not steal. ¹⁶You must not testify falsely against your neighbor. ¹⁷You must not covet your neighbor's house. You must not covet your neighbor's wife, male or female servant, ox or donkey, or anything else that belongs to your neighbor."

~ Exodus 20:1-3, 5, 7-17

Water from a Rock

When the people didn't have water in the desert, God told Moses to speak to a rock until water came from it. But Moses struck the rock with his staff. This disobedient act resulted in Moses not being permitted to lead the people into Canaan.

¹In the first month of the year, the whole community of Israel arrived in the wilderness of Zin and camped at Kadesh. While they were there, Miriam died and was buried. ²There was no water for the people to drink at that place, so they rebelled against Moses and Aaron. ³The people blamed Moses and said, "If only we had died in the LORD's presence with our brothers!"

⁶Moses and Aaron turned away from the people and went to the entrance of the Tabernacle, where they fell face down on the ground. Then the glorious presence of the LORD appeared to them, ⁷and the LORD said to Moses, ⁸"You and Aaron must take the staff and assemble the entire community. As the people watch, speak to the rock over there, and it will pour out its water. You will provide enough water from the rock to satisfy the whole community and their livestock."

⁹So Moses did as he was told. He took the staff from the place where it was kept before the LORD. ¹⁰Then he and Aaron summoned the people to come and gather at the rock. "Listen, you rebels!" he shouted. "Must we bring you water from this rock?" ¹¹Then Moses raised his hand and struck the rock twice with the staff, and water gushed out. So the entire community and their livestock drank their fill. ¹²But the LORD said to Moses and Aaron, "Because you did not trust me enough to demonstrate my holiness to the people of Israel, you will not lead them into the land I am giving them!"

~ Numbers 20:1-3, 6-12

God Goes Out Before Israel

Although the Israelites endured hardships in the desert and complained often, God went out before them, defeated their enemies and carried them each day. God wants to carry you when you face hard times too.

[19]"Just as the LORD our God commanded us, we left Mount Sinai and traveled through the great and terrifying wilderness, as you yourselves remember, and headed toward the hill country of the Amorites. When we arrived at Kadesh-barnea, [20]I said to you, 'You have now reached the hill country of the Amorites that the LORD our God is giving us. [21]Look! He has placed the land in front of you. Go and occupy it as the LORD, the God of your ancestors, has promised you. Don't be afraid! Don't be discouraged!'

[26]"But you rebelled against the command of the LORD your God and refused to go in. [27]You complained in your tents and said, 'The LORD must hate us. That's why he has brought us here from Egypt—to hand us over to the Amorites to be slaughtered.'

[29]"But I said to you, 'Don't be shocked or afraid of them! [30]The LORD your God is going ahead of you. He will fight for you, just as you saw him do in Egypt. [31]And you saw how the LORD your God cared for you all along the way as you traveled through the wilderness, just as a father cares for his child. Now he has brought you to this place.' [32]But even after all he did, you refused to trust the LORD your God, [33]who goes before you looking for the best places to camp, guiding you with a pillar of fire by night and a pillar of cloud by day. [34]When the LORD heard your complaining, he became very angry. So he solemnly swore, [35]'Not one of you from this wicked generation will live to see the good land I swore to give your ancestors.'"

~ Deuteronomy 1:19-21, 26-27, 29-35

Speak to Your Children

After he presented God's commands to Israel – that they must love the Lord their God with all their heart, soul, and strength – Moses asked them to share the Law with their children too. God also asks from you to share His commandments with your children.

[1]"These are the commands, decrees, and regulations that the LORD your God commanded me to teach you. You must obey them in the land you are about to enter and occupy, [2]and you and your children and grandchildren must fear the LORD your God as long as you live. If you obey all his decrees and commands, you will enjoy a long life. [3]Listen closely, Israel, and be careful to obey. Then all will go well with you, and you will have many children in the land flowing with milk and honey, just as the LORD, the God of your ancestors, promised you.

[4]"Listen, O Israel! The LORD is our God, the LORD alone. [5]And you must love the LORD your God with all your heart, all your soul, and all your strength. [6]And you must commit yourselves wholeheartedly to these commands that I am giving you today. [7]Repeat them again and again to your children. Talk about them when you are at home and when you are on the road, when you are going to bed and when you are getting up. [8]Tie them to your hands and wear them on your forehead as reminders. [9]Write them on the doorposts of your house and on your gates.

[11]"The houses will be richly stocked with goods you did not produce. You will draw water from cisterns you did not dig, and you will eat from vineyards and olive trees you did not plant. When you have eaten your fill in this land, [12]be careful not to forget the LORD, who rescued you from slavery in the land of Egypt. [13]You must fear the LORD your God and serve him. When you take an oath, you must use only his name."

~ Deuteronomy 6:1-9, 11-13

God Is Completely Faithful

Moses impressed it on the people's hearts that God is a faithful God, and that He will honor His covenant with them and show them His unconditional love. God is still the same today, and His faithfulness and promises are still true for you.

6[20]"In the future your children will ask you, 'What is the meaning of these laws, decrees, and regulations that the LORD our God has commanded us to obey?' [21]Then you must tell them, 'We were Pharaoh's slaves in Egypt, but the LORD brought us out of Egypt with his strong hand. [22]The LORD did miraculous signs and wonders before our eyes, dealing terrifying blows against Egypt and Pharaoh and all his people. [23]He brought us out of Egypt so he could give us this land he had sworn to give our ancestors. [24]And the LORD our God commanded us to obey all these decrees and to fear him so he can continue to bless us and preserve our lives, as he has done to this day. [25]For we will be counted as righteous when we obey all the commands the LORD our God has given us.'

7[6]"For you are a holy people, who belong to the LORD your God. Of all the people on earth, the LORD your God has chosen you to be his own special treasure.

[7]"The LORD did not set his heart on you and choose you because you were more numerous than other nations, for you were the smallest of all nations! [8]Rather, it was simply that the LORD loves you, and he was keeping the oath he had sworn to your ancestors. That is why the LORD rescued you with such a strong hand from your slavery and from the oppressive hand of Pharaoh, king of Egypt. [9]Understand, therefore, that the LORD your God is indeed God. He is the faithful God who keeps his covenant for a thousand generations and lavishes his unfailing love on those who love him and obey his commands."

~ Deuteronomy 6:20-25, 7:6-9

God Provides for His Children

God looked after and provided for His people in the desert for forty years. He is still able to guide His children today and satisfy all their needs. Trust God in this!

[1]"Be careful to obey all the commands I am giving you today. Then you will live and multiply, and you will enter and occupy the land the Lord swore to give your ancestors. [2]Remember how the Lord your God led you through the wilderness for these forty years, humbling you and testing you to prove your character, and to find out whether or not you would obey his commands. [3]Yes, he humbled you by letting you go hungry and then feeding you with manna, a food previously unknown to you and your ancestors. He did it to teach you that people do not live by bread alone; rather, we live by every word that comes from the mouth of the Lord.

[6]"So obey the commands of the Lord your God by walking in his ways and fearing him. [7]For the Lord your God is bringing you into a good land of flowing streams and pools of water, with fountains and springs that gush out in the valleys and hills. [8]It is a land of wheat and barley; of grapevines, fig trees, and pomegranates; of olive oil and honey. [9]It is a land where food is plentiful and nothing is lacking. It is a land where iron is as common as stone, and copper is abundant in the hills. [10]When you have eaten your fill, be sure to praise the Lord your God for the good land he has given you. [11]But that is the time to be careful! Beware that in your plenty you do not forget the Lord your God and disobey his commands, regulations, and decrees that I am giving you today.

[18]"Remember the Lord your God. He is the one who gives you power to be successful, in order to fulfill the covenant he confirmed to your ancestors with an oath."

~ Deuteronomy 8:1-3, 6-11, 18

Serve God!

There is only one true God, and He still expects of His children today to serve only Him, honor Him, and obey His commands. God's children should love Him above all else. Do you love God with all your heart?

10¹²"And now, Israel, what does the LORD your God require of you? He requires only that you fear the LORD your God, and live in a way that pleases him, and love him and serve him with all your heart and soul. ¹³And you must always obey the LORD's commands and decrees that I am giving you today for your own good. ¹⁴Look, the highest heavens and the earth and everything in it all belong to the LORD your God.

¹⁵"Yet the LORD chose your ancestors as the objects of his love. And he chose you, their descendants, above all other nations, as is evident today. ¹⁶Therefore, change your hearts and stop being stubborn. ¹⁷For the LORD your God is the God of gods and Lord of lords. He is the great God, the mighty and awesome God, who shows no partiality and cannot be bribed. ¹⁸He ensures that orphans and widows receive justice. He shows love to the foreigners living among you and gives them food and clothing.

¹⁹"So you, too, must show love to foreigners, for you yourselves were once foreigners in the land of Egypt. ²⁰You must fear the LORD your God and worship him and cling to him. Your oaths must be in his name alone. ²¹He alone is your God, the only one who is worthy of your praise, the one who has done these mighty miracles that you have seen with your own eyes.

11¹You must love the LORD your God and obey all his requirements, decrees, regulations, and commands."

~ Deuteronomy 10:12-21; 11:1

Obey My Commands

When Israel, as a nation, undertook to obey God's commands, He promised to bless their land. But He also warned them that their sins would be punished.

¹¹"The land you will soon take over is a land of hills and valleys with plenty of rain—¹²a land that the LORD your God cares for.

¹³"If you carefully obey all the commands I am giving you today, and if you love the LORD your God and serve him with all your heart and soul, ¹⁴then he will send the rains in their proper seasons—the early and late rains—so you can bring in your harvests of grain, new wine, and olive oil. ¹⁵He will give you lush pastureland for your livestock, and you yourselves will have all you want to eat. ¹⁶But be careful. Don't let your heart be deceived so that you turn away from the LORD and serve and worship other gods. ¹⁷If you do, the LORD's anger will burn against you. He will shut up the sky and hold back the rain, and the ground will fail to produce its harvests. Then you will quickly die in that good land the LORD is giving you.

¹⁸"Commit yourselves wholeheartedly to these words of mine. Tie them to your hands and wear them on your forehead as reminders. ¹⁹Teach them to your children. Talk about them when you are at home and when you are on the road, when you are going to bed and when you are getting up. ²⁰Write them on the doorposts of your house and on your gates, ²¹so that as long as the sky remains above the earth, you and your children may flourish in the land the LORD swore to give your ancestors.

²⁶"Look, today I am giving you the choice between a blessing and a curse! ²⁷You will be blessed if you obey the commands of the LORD your God that I am giving you today. ²⁸But you will be cursed if you reject the commands of the LORD your God and turn away from him and worship gods you have not known before."

~ Deuteronomy 11:11-21; 26-28

Blessings and Punishment

God promised His blessing to Israel if they obeyed Him, but warned that He would punish disobedience. Today we obey God freely and not out of fear of being punished, because Christ endured the cross and His Spirit makes us new.

¹"If you fully obey the LORD your God and carefully keep all his commands that I am giving you today, the LORD your God will set you high above all the nations of the world. ²You will experience all these blessings if you obey the LORD your God:

³Your towns and your fields will be blessed. ⁴Your children and your crops will be blessed. The offspring of your herds and flocks will be blessed. ⁵Your fruit baskets and breadboards will be blessed. ⁶Wherever you go and whatever you do, you will be blessed.

⁹"If you obey the commands of the LORD your God and walk in his ways, the LORD will establish you as his holy people as he swore he would do. ¹⁰Then all the nations of the world will see that you are a people claimed by the LORD, and they will stand in awe of you. ¹¹The LORD will give you prosperity in the land he swore to your ancestors to give you, blessing you with many children, numerous livestock, and abundant crops. ¹²The LORD will send rain at the proper time from his rich treasury in the heavens and will bless all the work you do. You will lend to many nations, but you will never need to borrow from them. ¹³If you listen to these commands of the LORD your God that I am giving you today, and if you carefully obey them, the LORD will make you the head and not the tail, and you will always be on top and never at the bottom. ¹⁴You must not turn away from any of the commands I am giving you today, nor follow after other gods and worship them."

~ Deuteronomy 28:1-6, 9-14

Choose Life!

It is possible to obey God's commands. Moses told the people to choose life by loving God, obeying Him and doing what pleases Him. Have you chosen life?

[6]"The LORD your God will change your heart and the hearts of all your descendants, so that you will love him with all your heart and soul and so you may live! [7]The LORD your God will inflict all these curses on your enemies and on those who hate and persecute you. [8]Then you will again obey the LORD and keep all his commands that I am giving you today.

[9]"The LORD your God will then make you successful in everything you do. He will give you many children and numerous livestock, and he will cause your fields to produce abundant harvests, for the LORD will again delight in being good to you as he was to your ancestors. [10]The LORD your God will delight in you if you obey his voice and keep the commands and decrees written in this Book of Instruction, and if you turn to the LORD your God with all your heart and soul.

[11]"This command I am giving you today is not too difficult for you to understand, and it is not beyond your reach. [12]It is not kept in heaven, so distant that you must ask, 'Who will go up to heaven and bring it down so we can hear it and obey?' [13]It is not kept beyond the sea, so far away that you must ask, 'Who will cross the sea to bring it to us so we can hear it and obey?' [14]No, the message is very close at hand; it is on your lips and in your heart so that you can obey it.

[15]"Now listen! Today I am giving you a choice between life and death, between prosperity and disaster. [16]For I command you this day to love the LORD your God and to keep his commands, decrees, and regulations by walking in his ways. If you do this, you will live and multiply, and the LORD your God will bless you and the land you are about to enter and occupy."

~ Deuteronomy 30:6-16

God Goes with You

Moses encouraged the people not to lose heart, but to be strong because God would never leave them nor forsake them. God is always by His children's side, which means He is always with you too.

[1]When Moses had finished giving these instructions to all the people of Israel, [2]he said, "I am now 120 years old, and I am no longer able to lead you. The LORD has told me, 'You will not cross the Jordan River.' [3]But the LORD your God himself will cross over ahead of you. He will destroy the nations living there, and you will take possession of their land. Joshua will lead you across the river, just as the LORD promised.

[4]"The LORD will destroy the nations living in the land, just as he destroyed Sihon and Og, the kings of the Amorites. [5]The LORD will hand over to you the people who live there, and you must deal with them as I have commanded you. [6]So be strong and courageous! Do not be afraid and do not panic before them. For the LORD your God will personally go ahead of you. He will neither fail you nor abandon you."

[7]Then Moses called for Joshua, and as all Israel watched, he said to him, "Be strong and courageous! For you will lead these people into the land that the LORD swore to their ancestors he would give them. You are the one who will divide it among them as their grants of land. [8]Do not be afraid or discouraged, for the LORD will personally go ahead of you. He will be with you; he will neither fail you nor abandon you."

~ Deuteronomy 31:1-8

February

God Carries His Children

God is great and His works are perfect. Like an eagle carries its eaglets on its wings, God guided His people, and still carries His children today. We must not forget God, like Israel once did.

[1]"Listen, O heavens, and I will speak! Hear, O earth, the words that I say! [2]Let my teaching fall on you like rain; let my speech settle like dew. Let my words fall like rain on tender grass, like gentle showers on young plants. [3]I will proclaim the name of the LORD; how glorious is our God! [4]He is the Rock; his deeds are perfect. Everything he does is just and fair. He is a faithful God who does no wrong; how just and upright he is!

[10]"He found them in a desert land, in an empty, howling wasteland. He surrounded them and watched over them; he guarded them as he would guard his own eyes. [11]Like an eagle that rouses her chicks and hovers over her young, so he spread his wings to take them up and carried them safely on his pinions. [12]The LORD alone guided them; they followed no foreign gods.

[18]"You neglected the Rock who had fathered you; you forgot the God who had given you birth.

[39]"Look now; I myself am he! There is no other god but me! I am the one who kills and gives life; I am the one who wounds and heals; no one can be rescued from my powerful hand!"

~ Deuteronomy 32:1-4, 10-12, 18, 39

The Eternal God Is Our Refuge

God is always ready to help His children. He is a refuge for His children, His everlasting arms are always underneath us. God is available to you; in trying times He will be your hiding place.

¹This is the blessing that Moses, the man of God, gave to the people of Israel before his death:

²"The LORD came from Mount Sinai and dawned upon us from Mount Seir; he shone forth from Mount Paran and came from Meribah-kadesh with flaming fire at his right hand. ³Indeed, he loves his people; all his holy ones are in his hands. They follow in his steps and accept his teaching."

¹²Moses said this about the tribe of Benjamin: "The people of Benjamin are loved by the LORD and live in safety beside him. He surrounds them continuously and preserves them from every harm.

²⁶"There is no one like the God of Israel. He rides across the heavens to help you, across the skies in majestic splendor. ²⁷The eternal God is your refuge, and his everlasting arms are under you. He drives out the enemy before you; he cries out, 'Destroy them!'

²⁸"So Israel will live in safety, prosperous Jacob in security, in a land of grain and new wine, while the heavens drop down dew. ²⁹How blessed you are, O Israel! Who else is like you, a people saved by the LORD? He is your protecting shield and your triumphant sword! Your enemies will cringe before you, and you will stomp on their backs!"

~ Deuteronomy 33:1-3, 12, 26-29

Joshua Receives a Task

God gave Israel's new leader an assignment that had to be fulfilled in the lives of His children: Be strong and courageous, obey the Law, do as I command, and I will be with you. You don't have to be afraid, because Joshua's God is also your God.

¹After the death of Moses the LORD's servant, the LORD spoke to Joshua son of Nun, Moses' assistant. He said, ²"Moses my servant is dead. Therefore, the time has come for you to lead these people, the Israelites, across the Jordan River into the land I am giving them.

³"I promise you what I promised Moses: 'Wherever you set foot, you will be on land I have given you—⁴from the Negev wilderness in the south to the Lebanon mountains in the north, from the Euphrates River in the east to the Mediterranean Sea in the west, including all the land of the Hittites.' ⁵No one will be able to stand against you as long as you live. For I will be with you as I was with Moses. I will not fail you or abandon you.

⁶"Be strong and courageous, for you are the one who will lead these people to possess all the land I swore to their ancestors I would give them.

⁷"Be strong and very courageous. Be careful to obey all the instructions Moses gave you. Do not deviate from them, turning either to the right or to the left. Then you will be successful in everything you do. ⁸Study this Book of Instruction continually. Meditate on it day and night so you will be sure to obey everything written in it. Only then will you prosper and succeed in all you do. ⁹This is my command—be strong and courageous! Do not be afraid or discouraged. For the LORD your God is with you wherever you go."

~ Joshua 1:1-9

Joshua's Farewell Message

Joshua asked the people to love God and be faithful to Him, because God had kept all His promises. God still undertakes to make all His promises come true in your life. Therefore, you can surrender to God completely and serve only Him.

¹Joshua, who was now very old, ²called together all the elders, leaders, judges, and officers of Israel. He said to them, "I am now a very old man. ³You have seen everything the LORD your God has done for you during my lifetime. The LORD your God has fought for you against your enemies. ⁴I have allotted to you as your homeland all the land of the nations yet unconquered, as well as the land of those we have already conquered—from the Jordan River to the Mediterranean Sea in the west. ⁵This land will be yours, for the LORD your God will himself drive out all the people living there now. You will take possession of their land, just as the LORD your God promised you.

⁶"So be very careful to follow everything Moses wrote in the Book of Instruction. Do not deviate from it, turning either to the right or to the left. ⁷Make sure you do not associate with the other people still remaining in the land. Do not even mention the names of their gods, much less swear by them or serve them or worship them. ⁸Rather, cling tightly to the LORD your God as you have done until now.

⁹"For the LORD has driven out great and powerful nations for you, and no one has yet been able to defeat you. ¹⁰Each one of you will put to flight a thousand of the enemy, for the LORD your God fights for you, just as he has promised. ¹¹So be very careful to love the LORD your God.

¹⁴"Soon I will die, going the way of everything on earth. Deep in your hearts you know that every promise of the LORD your God has come true. Not a single one has failed!"

~ Joshua 23:1-11, 14

Make a Decision
Once and for All

Joshua gave the people a choice to make – they had to choose whom they wanted to serve. Joshua declared that he and his house would serve the Lord. The people chose God, but quickly forgot Whom they had chosen. Whom do you choose? And are you faithful to your decision?

¹Joshua summoned all the tribes of Israel to Shechem, including their elders, leaders, judges, and officers. So they came and presented themselves to God.

²Joshua said to the people, ¹⁴"Fear the Lord and serve him wholeheartedly. Put away forever the idols your ancestors worshiped when they lived beyond the Euphrates River and in Egypt. Serve the Lord alone. ¹⁵But if you refuse to serve the Lord, then choose today whom you will serve. Would you prefer the gods your ancestors served beyond the Euphrates? Or will it be the gods of the Amorites in whose land you now live? But as for me and my family, we will serve the Lord."

¹⁶The people replied, "We would never abandon the Lord and serve other gods. ¹⁷For the Lord our God is the one who rescued us and our ancestors from slavery in the land of Egypt. He performed mighty miracles before our very eyes. As we traveled through the wilderness among our enemies, he preserved us.

¹⁸"It was the Lord who drove out the Amorites and the other nations living here in the land. So we, too, will serve the Lord, for he alone is our God."

~ Joshua 24:1-2, 14-18

A Woman as Judge

In a time when women were not highly esteemed, God chose Deborah as His instrument. She convinced Barak to fight against Sisera, and Sisera's army was defeated. God wants to use you to let His Kingdom come on earth – He will go out before you.

⁴Deborah, the wife of Lappidoth, was a prophet who was judging Israel at that time. ⁶One day she sent for Barak son of Abinoam, who lived in Kedesh in the land of Naphtali. She said to him, "This is what the LORD, the God of Israel, commands you: Call out 10,000 warriors from the tribes of Naphtali and Zebulun at Mount Tabor. ⁷And I will call out Sisera, commander of Jabin's army, along with his chariots and warriors, to the Kishon River. There I will give you victory over him."

⁸Barak told her, "I will go, but only if you go with me."

⁹"Very well," she replied, "I will go with you. But you will receive no honor in this venture, for the LORD's victory over Sisera will be at the hands of a woman." So Deborah went with Barak to Kedesh.

¹²When Sisera was told that Barak son of Abinoam had gone up to Mount Tabor, ¹³he called for all 900 of his iron chariots and all of his warriors, and they marched from Harosheth-haggoyim to the Kishon River. ¹⁴Then Deborah said to Barak, "Get ready! This is the day the LORD will give you victory over Sisera, for the LORD is marching ahead of you." So Barak led his 10,000 warriors down the slopes of Mount Tabor into battle.

¹⁵When Barak attacked, the LORD threw Sisera and all his chariots and warriors into a panic. Sisera leaped down from his chariot and escaped on foot. ¹⁶Then Barak chased the chariots and the enemy army all the way to Harosheth-haggoyim, killing all of Sisera's warriors. Not a single one was left alive.

~ Judges 4:4, 6-9, 12-16

God Is with You

God asked Gideon to save Israel from the Midianites. But Gideon had so many excuses that he failed to listen. Finally God used a miracle to convince Gideon that He was with him. God still performs miracles today, especially in people's hearts.

¹¹The angel of the LORD came and sat beneath the great tree at Ophrah, which belonged to Joash of the clan of Abiezer. Gideon son of Joash was threshing wheat at the bottom of a winepress to hide the grain from the Midianites.

¹²The angel of the LORD appeared to him and said, "Mighty hero, the LORD is with you!"

¹³"Sir," Gideon replied, "if the LORD is with us, why has all this happened to us? And where are all the miracles our ancestors told us about? Didn't they say, 'The LORD brought us up out of Egypt'? But now the LORD has abandoned us and handed us over to the Midianites."

¹⁴Then the LORD turned to him and said, "Go with the strength you have, and rescue Israel from the Midianites. I am sending you!"

¹⁵"But Lord," Gideon replied, "how can I rescue Israel? My clan is the weakest in the whole tribe of Manasseh, and I am the least in my entire family!" ¹⁶The LORD said to him, "I will be with you. And you will destroy the Midianites as if you were fighting against one man."

¹⁷Gideon replied, "If you are truly going to help me, show me a sign to prove that it is really the LORD speaking to me. ¹⁸Don't go away until I come back and bring my offering to you." He answered, "I will stay here until you return."

~ Judges 6:11-18

God Performs a Miracle

With God's help, Gideon and only 300 men defeated the mighty Midianite army. God is still the same God He was in Gideon's time. He performs miracles in many different ways, but not always in ways we expect. Our eyes of faith need to be open at all times.

²The LORD said to Gideon, "You have too many warriors with you. If I let all of you fight the Midianites, the Israelites will boast to me that they saved themselves by their own strength. ³Therefore, tell the people, 'Whoever is timid or afraid may leave this mountain and go home.'" So 22,000 of them went home, leaving only 10,000 who were willing to fight. ⁴But the LORD told Gideon, "There are still too many! Bring them down to the spring, and I will test them to determine who will go with you and who will not."

⁵When Gideon took his warriors down to the water, the LORD told him, "Divide the men into two groups. In one group put all those who cup water in their hands and lap it up with their tongues like dogs. In the other group put all those who kneel down and drink with their mouths in the stream." ⁶Only 300 of the men drank from their hands. All the others got down on their knees and drank with their mouths in the stream.

⁷The LORD told Gideon, "With these 300 men I will rescue you and give you victory over the Midianites. Send all the others home." ⁸So Gideon collected the provisions and rams' horns of the other warriors and sent them home. But he kept the 300 men with him. The Midianite camp was in the valley just below Gideon.

²²When the 300 Israelites blew their ram's horns, the LORD caused the warriors in the camp to fight against each other with their swords.

~ Judges 7:2-8, 22

A Future for Naomi

Naomi felt that God had made life bitter and miserable for her. But God was busy planning a new future for her. Sometimes we also feel as if God is sending one disaster after the other our way – but it is often *then* that God is revealing His perfect plan for our lives.

⁸On the way, Naomi said to her two daughters-in-law, "Go back to your mothers' homes. And may the LORD reward you for your kindness to your husbands and to me. ⁹May the LORD bless you with the security of another marriage." Then she kissed them good-bye, and they all broke down and wept. ¹⁰"No," they said. "We want to go with you to your people."

¹⁴Again they wept together, and Orpah kissed her mother-in-law good-bye. But Ruth clung tightly to Naomi. ¹⁵"Look," Naomi said to her, "your sister-in-law has gone back to her people and to her gods. You should do the same."

¹⁶But Ruth replied, "Don't ask me to leave you and turn back. Wherever you go, I will go; wherever you live, I will live. Your people will be my people, and your God will be my God. ¹⁷Wherever you die, I will die, and there I will be buried. May the LORD punish me severely if I allow anything but death to separate us!"

¹⁹So the two of them continued on their journey. When they came to Bethlehem, the entire town was excited by their arrival. "Is it really Naomi?" the women asked.

²⁰"Don't call me Naomi," she responded. "Instead, call me Mara, for the Almighty has made life very bitter for me."

~ Ruth 1:8-10, 14-17, 19-20

To God be the Glory!

Naomi's life changed in an instant. God gave Ruth a husband to care for them, and Naomi even received a grandson. The women rightly said that all the glory belonged to God. When God changes your circumstances for the better, He should get all the glory.

⁹Boaz said to the elders and to the crowd standing around, "You are witnesses that today I have bought from Naomi all the property of Elimelech, Kilion, and Mahlon. ¹⁰And with the land I have acquired Ruth, the Moabite widow of Mahlon, to be my wife. This way she can have a son to carry on the family name of her dead husband and to inherit the family property here in his hometown. You are all witnesses today."

¹¹Then the elders and all the people standing in the gate replied, "We are witnesses! ¹²And may the LORD give you descendants by this young woman who will be like those of our ancestor Perez, the son of Tamar and Judah."

¹³So Boaz took Ruth into his home, and she became his wife. When he slept with her, the LORD enabled her to become pregnant, and she gave birth to a son. ¹⁴Then the women of the town said to Naomi, "Praise the LORD, who has now provided a redeemer for your family! May this child be famous in Israel. ¹⁵May he restore your youth and care for you in your old age. For he is the son of your daughter-in-law who loves you and has been better to you than seven sons!"

¹⁶Naomi took the baby and cuddled him to her breast. And she cared for him as if he were her own. ¹⁷The neighbor women said, "Now at last Naomi has a son again!" And they named him Obed. He became the father of Jesse and the grandfather of David.

~ Ruth 4:9-17

God Fulfills Hannah's Deepest Longing

Hannah poured out her heart before God. With her prayer she expressed the desire of every childless woman. In the temple, Eli assured her that God would give her what she asked for. Trust God with your deepest longings.

²Elkanah had two wives, Hannah and Peninnah. Peninnah had children, but Hannah did not. ⁵And though he loved Hannah, he would give her only one choice portion because the LORD had given her no children. ⁶So Peninnah would taunt Hannah and make fun of her because the LORD had kept her from having children. ⁷Year after year it was the same—Peninnah would taunt Hannah as they went to the Tabernacle. Each time, Hannah would be reduced to tears and would not even eat.

⁹Once after a sacrificial meal at Shiloh, Hannah got up and went to pray. Eli the priest was sitting at his customary place beside the entrance of the Tabernacle. ¹⁰Hannah was in deep anguish, crying bitterly as she prayed to the LORD. ¹¹And she made this vow: "O LORD of Heaven's Armies, if you will look upon my sorrow and answer my prayer and give me a son, then I will give him back to you. He will be yours for his entire lifetime, and as a sign that he has been dedicated to the LORD, his hair will never be cut." ¹²As she was praying to the LORD, Eli watched her. ¹³Seeing her lips moving but hearing no sound, he thought she had been drinking. ¹⁴"Must you come here drunk?" he demanded. "Throw away your wine!" ¹⁵"Oh no, sir!" she replied. "I haven't been drinking wine or anything stronger. But I am very discouraged, and I was pouring out my heart to the LORD."

¹⁷"In that case," Eli said, "go in peace! May the God of Israel grant the request you have asked of him."

~ 1 Samuel 1:2, 5-7, 9-15, 17

A Covenant with God

God answered Hannah's plea and gave her the son she so longed for. And Hannah fulfilled her promise to God – she gave Samuel back to the Lord. Make sure to keep your promises to God like Hannah did.

¹⁹The entire family got up early the next morning and went to worship the Lord once more. Then they returned home to Ramah. When Elkanah slept with Hannah, the Lord remembered her plea, ²⁰and in due time she gave birth to a son. She named him Samuel, for she said, "I asked the Lord for him."

²¹The next year Elkanah and his family went on their annual trip to offer a sacrifice to the Lord. ²²But Hannah did not go. She told her husband, "Wait until the boy is weaned. Then I will take him to the Tabernacle and leave him there with the Lord permanently."

²³"Whatever you think is best," Elkanah agreed. "Stay here for now, and may the Lord help you keep your promise." So she stayed home and nursed the boy until he was weaned.

²⁴When the child was weaned, Hannah took him to the Tabernacle in Shiloh. They brought along a three-year-old bull for the sacrifice and a basket of flour and some wine. ²⁵After sacrificing the bull, they brought the boy to Eli.

²⁶"Sir, do you remember me?" Hannah asked. "I am the woman who stood here several years ago praying to the Lord. ²⁷I asked the Lord to give me this boy, and he has granted my request. ²⁸Now I am giving him to the Lord, and he will belong to the Lord his whole life." And they worshiped the Lord there.

~ 1 Samuel 1:19-28

Remember to Say Thanks!

After Hannah had left Samuel at the temple to serve God there, she sang a song of joy to the Lord. She praised and worshiped God because He answered her prayers. Remember to thank God when He answers your prayers.

[1]Then Hannah prayed: "My heart rejoices in the LORD! The LORD has made me strong. Now I have an answer for my enemies; I rejoice because you rescued me. [2]No one is holy like the LORD! There is no one besides you; there is no Rock like our God.

[6]"The LORD gives both death and life; he brings some down to the grave but raises others up. [7]The LORD makes some poor and others rich; he brings some down and lifts others up. [8]He lifts the poor from the dust and the needy from the garbage dump. He sets them among princes, placing them in seats of honor. For all the earth is the LORD's, and he has set the world in order.

[9]"He will protect his faithful ones, but the wicked will disappear in darkness. No one will succeed by strength alone. [10]Those who fight against the LORD will be shattered. He thunders against them from heaven; the LORD judges throughout the earth. He gives power to his king; he increases the strength of his anointed one."

[11]Then Elkanah returned home to Ramah without Samuel. And the boy served the LORD by assisting Eli the priest.

~ 1 Samuel 2:1-2, 6-11

A Listening Servant

When God spoke to Samuel, he didn't understand who was speaking to him at first. But when Eli told him what to do, Samuel said, "Speak, Lord, your servant is listening." God wants you to listen for His voice too, and we hear His voice most clearly in His Word.

¹Meanwhile, the boy Samuel served the Lord by assisting Eli. Now in those days messages from the Lord were very rare, and visions were quite uncommon. ²One night Eli, who was almost blind by now, had gone to bed. ³The lamp of God had not yet gone out, and Samuel was sleeping in the Tabernacle near the Ark of God.

⁴Suddenly the Lord called out, "Samuel!"

"Yes?" Samuel replied. "What is it?" ⁵He got up and ran to Eli. "Here I am. Did you call me?"

"I didn't call you," Eli replied. "Go back to bed." So he did.

⁶Then the Lord called out again, "Samuel!" Again Samuel got up and went to Eli. "Here I am. Did you call me?"

"I didn't call you, my son," Eli said. "Go back to bed." ⁷Samuel did not yet know the Lord because he had never had a message from the Lord before.

⁸So the Lord called a third time, and once more Samuel got up and went to Eli. "Here I am. Did you call me?" Then Eli realized it was the Lord who was calling the boy. ⁹So he said to Samuel, "Go and lie down again, and if someone calls again, say, 'Speak, Lord, your servant is listening.'" So Samuel went back to bed.

¹⁰The Lord came and called as before, "Samuel! Samuel!" And Samuel replied, "Speak, your servant is listening."

~ 1 Samuel 3:1-10

God Asks Obedience from Us

Because King Saul disobeyed God's commands, he was rejected as king of Israel. God still puts a high price on obedience – it is more important to Him than any offerings. Are you prepared to be completely obedient to God?

[19]"Why haven't you obeyed the LORD? Why did you rush for the plunder and do what was evil in the LORD's sight?"

[20]"But I did obey the LORD," Saul insisted. "I carried out the mission he gave me. I brought back King Agag, but I destroyed everyone else. [21]Then my troops brought in the best of the sheep, goats, cattle, and plunder to sacrifice to the LORD your God in Gilgal."

[22]But Samuel replied, "What is more pleasing to the LORD: your burnt offerings and sacrifices or your obedience to his voice? Listen! Obedience is better than sacrifice, and submission is better than offering the fat of rams. [23]Rebellion is as sinful as witchcraft, and stubbornness as bad as worshiping idols. So because you have rejected the command of the LORD, he has rejected you as king."

[24]Then Saul admitted to Samuel, "Yes, I have sinned. I have disobeyed your instructions and the LORD's command, for I was afraid of the people and did what they demanded. [25]But now, please forgive my sin and come back with me so that I may worship the LORD." [26]But Samuel replied, "I will not go back with you! Since you have rejected the LORD's command, he has rejected you as king of Israel."

[28]And Samuel said to him, "The LORD has torn the kingdom of Israel from you today and has given it to someone else—one who is better than you. [29]And he who is the Glory of Israel will not lie, nor will he change his mind, for he is not human that he should change his mind!"

~ 1 Samuel 15:19-26, 28-29

God Looks at Things Differently

When God sent Samuel to Bethlehem to anoint a new king from the sons of Jesse, Samuel believed that the respectable Eliab was God's obvious choice. But the Lord chose David. People's hearts are more important to God than their appearances.

⁴So Samuel did as the LORD instructed. When he arrived at Bethlehem, the elders of the town came trembling to meet him. "What's wrong?" they asked. "Do you come in peace?"

⁵"Yes," Samuel replied. "I have come to sacrifice to the LORD. Purify yourselves and come with me to the sacrifice." Then Samuel performed the purification rite for Jesse and his sons and invited them to the sacrifice, too.

⁶When they arrived, Samuel took one look at Eliab and thought, "Surely this is the LORD's anointed!" ⁷But the LORD said to Samuel, "Don't judge by his appearance or height, for I have rejected him. The LORD doesn't see things the way you see them. People judge by outward appearance, but the LORD looks at the heart."

¹⁰In the same way all seven of Jesse's sons were presented to Samuel. But Samuel said to Jesse, "The LORD has not chosen any of these." ¹¹Then Samuel asked, "Are these all the sons you have?" "There is still the youngest," Jesse replied. "But he's out in the fields watching the sheep and goats." "Send for him at once," Samuel said. "We will not sit down to eat until he arrives."

¹²So Jesse sent for him. He was dark and handsome, with beautiful eyes. And the LORD said, "This is the one; anoint him." ¹³So as David stood there among his brothers, Samuel took the flask of olive oil he had brought and anointed David with the oil. And the Spirit of the LORD came powerfully upon David from that day on.

~ 1 Samuel 16:4-7, 10-13

In the Name of the Lord!

With God's help the young David defeated the mighty giant Goliath with his slingshot, and all the Philistines fled. You can do anything, if you do it in the name of the Lord.

³²"Don't worry about this Philistine," David told Saul. "I'll go fight him! ³⁷The Lord who rescued me from the claws of the lion and the bear will rescue me from this Philistine!" Saul finally consented. "All right, go ahead," he said. "And may the Lord be with you!"

⁴¹Goliath walked out toward David with his shield bearer ahead of him, ⁴²sneering in contempt at this ruddy-faced boy. ⁴³"Am I a dog," he roared at David, "that you come at me with a stick?" And he cursed David by the names of his gods.

⁴⁵David replied to the Philistine, "You come to me with sword, spear, and javelin, but I come to you in the name of the Lord of Heaven's Armies—the God of the armies of Israel, whom you have defied. ⁴⁶Today the Lord will conquer you, and I will kill you and cut off your head. And then I will give the dead bodies of your men to the birds and wild animals, and the whole world will know that there is a God in Israel!"

⁴⁹Reaching into his shepherd's bag and taking out a stone, he hurled it with his sling and hit the Philistine in the forehead. The stone sank in, and Goliath stumbled and fell face down on the ground. ⁵⁰So David triumphed over the Philistine with only a sling and a stone, for he had no sword. ⁵¹Then David ran over and pulled Goliath's sword from its sheath. David used it to kill him and cut off his head.

~ 1 Samuel 17:32, 37, 41-43, 45-46, 49-51

Friendship's Worth

David and Jonathan's friendship was legendary.
Jonathan was disobedient to his father, and put his
own life in danger to save David's life. The worth of
true friendship cannot be measured.

⁸"Show me this loyalty as my sworn friend—for we made a solemn pact before the LORD—or kill me yourself if I have sinned
against your father. But please don't betray me to him!"

⁹"Never!" Jonathan exclaimed. "You know that if I had the
slightest notion my father was planning to kill you, I would tell
you at once."

¹⁰Then David asked, "How will I know whether or not your
father is angry?"

¹¹"Come out to the field with me," Jonathan replied. And they
went out there together.

¹²Then Jonathan told David, "I promise by the LORD, the God
of Israel, that by this time tomorrow, or the next day at the latest,
I will talk to my father and let you know at once how he feels
about you. If he speaks favorably about you, I will let you know.
¹³But if he is angry and wants you killed, may the LORD strike
me and even kill me if I don't warn you so you can escape and
live. May the LORD be with you as he used to be with my father.
¹⁴And may you treat me with the faithful love of the LORD as long
as I live. But if I die, ¹⁵treat my family with this faithful love, even
when the LORD destroys all your enemies from the face of the
earth."

¹⁶So Jonathan made a solemn pact with David, saying,
"May the LORD destroy all your enemies!" ¹⁷And Jonathan made
David reaffirm his vow of friendship again, for Jonathan loved
David as he loved himself.

~ 1 Samuel 20:8-17

David Succumbs to Temptation

When David saw Uriah's beautiful wife, he slept with her and arranged for her husband to be killed in battle. But God saw David's sins. We cannot hide anything from God; therefore we must sincerely confess our sins to God so that we can receive His forgiveness.

[2]Late one afternoon, after his midday rest, David got out of bed and was walking on the roof of the palace. As he looked out over the city, he noticed a woman of unusual beauty taking a bath. [3]He sent someone to find out who she was, and he was told, "She is Bathsheba, the daughter of Eliam and the wife of Uriah the Hittite." [4]Then David sent messengers to get her; and when she came to the palace, he slept with her. She had just completed the purification rites after having her menstrual period. Then she returned home. [5]Later, when Bathsheba discovered that she was pregnant, she sent David a message, saying, "I'm pregnant." [6]Then David sent word to Joab: "Send me Uriah the Hittite." So Joab sent him to David.

[8]Then he told Uriah, "Go on home and relax." David even sent a gift to Uriah after he had left the palace. [9]But Uriah didn't go home. He slept that night at the palace entrance with the king's palace guard.

[14]So the next morning David wrote a letter to Joab and gave it to Uriah to deliver. [15]The letter instructed Joab, "Station Uriah on the front lines where the battle is fiercest. Then pull back so that he will be killed." [17]And when the enemy soldiers came out of the city to fight, Uriah the Hittite was killed along with several other Israelite soldiers.

~ 2 Samuel 11:2-6, 8-9, 14-15, 17

God Punishes Sin

God sent the prophet Nathan to David, to reveal his sins to him and announce his judgment. David showed remorse and received God's forgiveness. Our sins are forgiven through Christ's death on the cross. By repenting our sins and accepting Christ's salvation, we are forgiven.

¹So the LORD sent Nathan the prophet to tell David this story: "There were two men in a certain town. One was rich, and one was poor. ²The rich man owned a great many sheep and cattle. ³The poor man owned nothing but one little lamb he had bought. He raised that little lamb, and it grew up with his children. It ate from the man's own plate and drank from his cup. He cuddled it in his arms like a baby daughter.

⁴One day a guest arrived at the home of the rich man. But instead of killing an animal from his own flock or herd, he took the poor man's lamb and killed it and prepared it for his guest."

⁵David was furious. "As surely as the LORD lives," he vowed, "any man who would do such a thing deserves to die! ⁶He must repay four lambs to the poor man for the one he stole and for having no pity."

⁷Then Nathan said to David, "You are that man! The LORD, the God of Israel, says: I anointed you king of Israel and saved you from the power of Saul. ⁹Why, then, have you despised the word of the LORD and done this horrible deed? For you have murdered Uriah the Hittite with the sword of the Ammonites and stolen his wife."

¹³Then David confessed to Nathan, "I have sinned against the LORD." Nathan replied, "Yes, but the LORD has forgiven you, and you won't die for this sin. ¹⁴Nevertheless, because you have shown utter contempt for the LORD by doing this, your child will die."

~ 2 Samuel 12:1-7, 9, 13-14

God Gives Light

In 2 Samuel 22, David expressed his faith and trust in God which gave him victory over his enemies. God also wants to be the light in your dark circumstances. He wants to be your rock and safe shelter.

¹David sang this song to the LORD on the day the LORD rescued him from all his enemies and from Saul. ²He sang: "The LORD is my rock, my fortress, and my savior; ³my God is my rock, in whom I find protection. He is my shield, the power that saves me, and my place of safety. He is my refuge, my savior, the one who saves me from violence.

⁷"But in my distress I cried out to the LORD; yes, I cried to my God for help. He heard me from his sanctuary; my cry reached his ears.

¹⁷"He reached down from heaven and rescued me; he drew me out of deep waters. ²⁰He led me to a place of safety; he rescued me because he delights in me.

²⁹"O LORD, you are my lamp. The LORD lights up my darkness. ³⁰In your strength I can crush an army; with my God I can scale any wall.

³¹"God's way is perfect. All the LORD's promises prove true. He is a shield for all who look to him for protection. ³²For who is God except the LORD? Who but our God is a solid rock? ³³God is my strong fortress, and he makes my way perfect. ³⁴He makes me as surefooted as a deer, enabling me to stand on mountain heights."

~ 2 Samuel 22:1-3, 7, 17, 20, 29-34

A Request for Wisdom

When God asked Solomon what he wanted, he asked for wisdom. God then also gave him wealth, esteem and a long life. If you lack wisdom you can ask God, and He will give it to you.

³Solomon loved the LORD and followed all the decrees of his father, David, except that Solomon, too, offered sacrifices and burned incense at the local places of worship.

⁵That night the LORD appeared to Solomon in a dream, and God said, "What do you want? Ask, and I will give it to you!" ⁶Solomon replied, "You showed faithful love to your servant my father, David, because he was honest and true and faithful to you. And you have continued your faithful love to him today by giving him a son to sit on his throne. ⁷Now, O LORD my God, you have made me king instead of my father, David, but I am like a little child who doesn't know his way around. ⁸And here I am in the midst of your own chosen people, a nation so great and numerous they cannot be counted! ⁹Give me an understanding heart so that I can govern your people well and know the difference between right and wrong. For who by himself is able to govern this great people of yours?"

¹⁰The Lord was pleased that Solomon had asked for wisdom. ¹¹So God replied, "Because you have asked for wisdom in governing my people with justice and have not asked for a long life or wealth or the death of your enemies—¹²I will give you what you asked for! I will give you a wise and understanding heart such as no one else has had or ever will have! ¹³And I will also give you what you did not ask for—riches and fame! No other king in all the world will be compared to you for the rest of your life! ¹⁴And if you follow me and obey my decrees and my commands as your father, David, did, I will give you a long life."

~ 1 Kings 3:3, 5-14

The Story of Two Mothers

Solomon could point out the rightful mother of a living child, because he could see her love for her child in her actions. Even two prostitutes realized that Solomon's exceptional wisdom came from God.

¹⁶Some time later two prostitutes came to the king to have an argument settled. ¹⁷"Please, my lord," one of them began, "this woman and I live in the same house. I gave birth to a baby while she was with me in the house. ¹⁸Three days later this woman also had a baby. We were alone; there were only two of us in the house. ¹⁹But her baby died during the night when she rolled over on it. ²⁰Then she got up in the night and took my son from beside me while I was asleep. She laid her dead child in my arms and took mine to sleep beside her."

²²Then the other woman interrupted, "It certainly was your son, and the living child is mine."

"No," the first woman said, "the living child is mine, and the dead one is yours." And so they argued back and forth before the king. ²³Then the king said, "Let's get the facts straight. Both of you claim the living child is yours, and each says that the dead one belongs to the other. ²⁴All right, bring me a sword." So a sword was brought to the king. ²⁵Then he said, "Cut the living child in two, and give half to one woman and half to the other!"

²⁶Then the woman who was the real mother of the living child, and who loved him very much, cried out, "Oh no, my lord! Give her the child—please do not kill him!" But the other woman said, "All right, he will be neither yours nor mine; divide him between us!" ²⁷Then the king said, "Do not kill the child, but give him to the woman who wants him to live, for she is his mother!" ²⁸When all Israel heard the king's decision, the people were in awe of the king, for they saw the wisdom God had given him for rendering justice.

~ 1 Kings 3:16-20, 22-28

Solomon's Prayer

Solomon praised God for staying true to His covenant and fulfilling all the promises He made to His people. Solomon also prayed that the people would listen to God, and asked Him to forgive their sins.

[22]Solomon stood before the altar of the LORD in front of the entire community of Israel. He lifted his hands toward heaven, [23]and he prayed, "O LORD, God of Israel, there is no God like you in all of heaven above or on the earth below. You keep your covenant and show unfailing love to all who walk before you in wholehearted devotion. [24]You have kept your promise to your servant David, my father. You made that promise with your own mouth, and with your own hands you have fulfilled it today.

[28]"Nevertheless, listen to my prayer and my plea, O LORD my God. Hear the cry and the prayer that your servant is making to you today.

[30]"May you hear the humble and earnest requests from me and your people Israel when we pray toward this place. Yes, hear us from heaven where you live, and when you hear, forgive.

[35]"If the skies are shut up and there is no rain because your people have sinned against you, and if they pray toward this Temple and acknowledge your name and turn from their sins because you have punished them, [36]then hear from heaven and forgive the sins of your servants, your people Israel. Teach them to follow the right path, and send rain on your land that you have given to your people as their special possession.

[39]"Hear from heaven where you live, and forgive. Give your people what their actions deserve, for you alone know each human heart."

~ 1 Kings 8:22-24, 28, 30, 35-36, 39

Solomon Blesses God's People

Solomon spoke to God's people, blessed them, and confirmed that God had kept all His promises toward them. God is still true to His children today, and therefore we can believe with our whole hearts that He will fulfill His promises.

[54] When Solomon finished making these prayers and petitions to the LORD, he stood up in front of the altar of the LORD, where he had been kneeling with his hands raised toward heaven. [55] He stood and in a loud voice blessed the entire congregation of Israel: [56] "Praise the LORD who has given rest to his people Israel, just as he promised. Not one word has failed of all the wonderful promises he gave through his servant Moses. [57] May the LORD our God be with us as he was with our ancestors; may he never leave us or abandon us. [58] May he give us the desire to do his will in everything and to obey all the commands, decrees, and regulations that he gave our ancestors.

[60] "Then people all over the earth will know that the LORD alone is God and there is no other. [61] And may you be completely faithful to the LORD our God. May you always obey his decrees and commands, just as you are doing today."

[65] Then Solomon and all Israel celebrated the Festival of Shelters in the presence of the LORD our God. A large congregation had gathered from as far away as Lebo-hamath in the north and the Brook of Egypt in the south. The celebration went on for fourteen days in all—seven days for the dedication of the altar and seven days for the Festival of Shelters. [66] After the festival was over, Solomon sent the people home. They blessed the king and went to their homes joyful and glad because the LORD had been good to his servant David and to his people Israel.

~ 1 Kings 8:54-58, 60-61, 65-66

The Lord Is God

While the prophets of Baal asked for fire but nothing happened, God answered Elijah's prayer. Fire from heaven devoured Elijah's offering as well as the altar. Only after this incident did God's people acknowledge Him as the only God.

²⁰Ahab summoned all the people of Israel and the prophets to Mount Carmel. ²¹Then Elijah stood in front of them and said, "How much longer will you waver, hobbling between two opinions? If the LORD is God, follow him! But if Baal is God, then follow him!" But the people were completely silent.

²²Then Elijah said to them, "I am the only prophet of the LORD who is left, but Baal has 450 prophets. ²³Now bring two bulls. The prophets of Baal may choose whichever one they wish and cut it into pieces and lay it on the wood of their altar, but without setting fire to it. I will prepare the other bull and lay it on the wood on the altar, but not set fire to it. ²⁴Then call on the name of your god, and I will call on the name of the LORD. The god who answers by setting fire to the wood is the true God!" And all the people agreed.

³⁶At the usual time for offering the evening sacrifice, Elijah the prophet walked up to the altar and prayed, "O LORD, God of Abraham, Isaac, and Jacob, prove today that you are God in Israel and that I am your servant. Prove that I have done all this at your command. ³⁷O LORD, answer me! Answer me so these people will know that you, O LORD, are God and that you have brought them back to yourself." ³⁸Immediately the fire of the LORD flashed down from heaven and burned up the young bull, the wood, the stones, and the dust. It even licked up all the water in the trench! ³⁹And when all the people saw it, they fell face down on the ground and cried out, "The LORD—he is God! Yes, the LORD is God!"

~ 1 Kings 18:20-24, 36-39

Elijah Feels Defeated

Elijah was scared when Jezebel threatened to kill him. He fled to Beersheba and fell asleep under a broom tree. An angel from God strengthened him, and Elijah heard God's whisper in the wind. God never leaves His children on their own when they're afraid.

²So Jezebel sent this message to Elijah: "May the gods strike me and even kill me if by this time tomorrow I have not killed you just as you killed them." ³Elijah was afraid and fled for his life. He went to Beersheba, a town in Judah, and he left his servant there. ⁴Then he went on alone into the wilderness, traveling all day. He sat down under a solitary broom tree and prayed that he might die. "I have had enough, LORD," he said. "Take my life, for I am no better than my ancestors who have already died."

⁵Then he lay down and slept under the broom tree. But as he was sleeping, an angel touched him and told him, "Get up and eat!" ⁶He looked around and there beside his head was some bread baked on hot stones and a jar of water! So he ate and drank and lay down again. ⁷Then the angel of the LORD came again and touched him and said, "Get up and eat some more, or the journey ahead will be too much for you."

⁸So he got up and ate and drank, and the food gave him enough strength to travel forty days and forty nights to Mount Sinai, the mountain of God. ⁹There he came to a cave, where he spent the night.

But the LORD said to him, "What are you doing here, Elijah?" ¹⁰Elijah replied, "I have zealously served the LORD God Almighty. But the people of Israel have broken their covenant with you, torn down your altars, and killed every one of your prophets. I am the only one left, and now they are trying to kill me, too."

~ 1 Kings 19:2-10

Just One God

The testimony of a young Israelite girl convinced Naaman to go to Elisha, and after he washed himself in the Jordan River, he was healed of leprosy. This miracle made the heathen Naaman realize that the God of Israel was the only true God. Your testimony is also of vital importance.

¹The king of Aram had great admiration for Naaman, the commander of his army, because through him the LORD had given Aram great victories. But though Naaman was a mighty warrior, he suffered from leprosy. ²At this time Aramean raiders had invaded the land of Israel, and among their captives was a young girl who had been given to Naaman's wife as a maid. ³One day the girl said to her mistress, "I wish my master would go to see the prophet in Samaria. He would heal him of his leprosy."

⁴So Naaman told the king what the young girl from Israel had said. ⁵"Go and visit the prophet," the king of Aram told him. "I will send a letter of introduction for you to take to the king of Israel." So Naaman started out, carrying as gifts 750 pounds of silver, 150 pounds of gold, and ten sets of clothing.

⁹So Naaman went with his horses and chariots and waited at the door of Elisha's house. ¹⁰But Elisha sent a messenger out to him with this message: "Go and wash yourself seven times in the Jordan River. Then your skin will be restored, and you will be healed of your leprosy."

¹⁴So Naaman went down to the Jordan River and dipped himself seven times, as the man of God had instructed him. And his skin became as healthy as the skin of a young child's, and he was healed!

~ 2 Kings 5:1-5, 9-10, 14

The Danger of Greediness

Elisha's servant tried to steal a gift that didn't belong to him. In the process he twisted the truth, but was caught and rebuked by Elisha. He was also struck with leprosy. Greed is not acceptable to God.

[19]"Go in peace," Elisha said. So Naaman started home again. [20]But Gehazi, the servant of Elisha, the man of God, said to himself, "My master should not have let this Aramean get away without accepting any of his gifts. As surely as the LORD lives, I will chase after him and get something from him."

[21]So Gehazi set off after Naaman. When Naaman saw Gehazi running after him, he climbed down from his chariot and went to meet him. "Is everything all right?" Naaman asked. [22]"Yes," Gehazi said, "but my master has sent me to tell you that two young prophets from the hill country of Ephraim have just arrived. He would like 75 pounds of silver and two sets of clothing to give to them." [23]"By all means, take twice as much silver," Naaman insisted. He gave him two sets of clothing, tied up the money in two bags, and sent two of his servants to carry the gifts for Gehazi. [24]But when they arrived at the citadel, Gehazi took the gifts from the servants and sent the men back. Then he went and hid the gifts inside the house.

[25]When he went in to his master, Elisha asked him, "Where have you been, Gehazi?" "I haven't been anywhere," he replied. [26]But Elisha asked him, "Don't you realize that I was there in spirit when Naaman stepped down from his chariot to meet you? Is this the time to receive money and clothing, olive groves and vineyards, sheep and cattle, and male and female servants? [27]Because you have done this, you and your descendants will suffer from Naaman's leprosy forever." When Gehazi left the room, he was covered with leprosy; his skin was white as snow.

~ 2 Kings 5:19-27

March

On God's Winning Side

Gehazi was afraid when he saw the mighty Aramean army, but Elisha prayed for his eyes to be opened. Gehazi then saw that the hillside around Elisha was filled with horses and chariots of fire sent by God. With God you are always on the winning side.

¹³"Go and find out where he is," the king commanded, "so I can send troops to seize him." And the report came back: "Elisha is at Dothan." ¹⁴So one night the king of Aram sent a great army with many chariots and horses to surround the city. ¹⁵When the servant of the man of God got up early the next morning and went outside, there were troops, horses, and chariots everywhere. "Oh, sir, what will we do now?" the young man cried to Elisha.

¹⁶"Don't be afraid!" Elisha told him. "For there are more on our side than on theirs!" ¹⁷Then Elisha prayed, "O LORD, open his eyes and let him see!" The LORD opened the young man's eyes, and when he looked up, he saw that the hillside around Elisha was filled with horses and chariots of fire. ¹⁸As the Aramean army advanced toward him, Elisha prayed, "O LORD, please make them blind." So the LORD struck them with blindness as Elisha had asked. ¹⁹Then Elisha went out and told them, "You have come the wrong way! This isn't the right city! Follow me, and I will take you to the man you are looking for." And he led them to the city of Samaria. ²⁰As soon as they had entered Samaria, Elisha prayed, "O LORD, now open their eyes and let them see." So the LORD opened their eyes, and they discovered that they were in the middle of Samaria. ²¹When the king of Israel saw them, he shouted to Elisha, "My father, should I kill them? Should I kill them?" ²²"Of course not!" Elisha replied. "Do we kill prisoners of war? Give them food and drink and send them home again to their master."

~ 2 Kings 6:13-22

Impossible Made Possible

Samaria stared severe famine in the face, and because the king believed that Elisha brought this suffering on them, he wanted to kill Elisha. But Elisha prophesied that food would be freely available the next day. God often saves in ways that appear impossible to people.

6 ²⁴Some time later, however, King Ben-hadad of Aram mustered his entire army and besieged Samaria. ²⁵As a result, there was a great famine in the city. ²⁶One day as the king of Israel was walking along the wall of the city, a woman called to him, "Please help me, my lord the king!" ²⁷He answered, "If the LORD doesn't help you, what can I do? I have neither food from the threshing floor nor wine from the press to give you." ²⁸But then the king asked, "What is the matter?" She replied, "This woman said to me: 'Come on, let's eat your son today, then we will eat my son tomorrow.' ²⁹So we cooked my son and ate him. Then the next day I said to her, 'Kill your son so we can eat him,' but she has hidden her son."

³⁰When the king heard this, he tore his clothes in despair. And as the king walked along the wall, the people could see that he was wearing burlap under his robe next to his skin. ³¹"May God strike me and even kill me if I don't separate Elisha's head from his shoulders this very day," the king vowed.

7 ¹Elisha replied, "Listen to this message from the LORD! This is what the LORD says: By this time tomorrow in the markets of Samaria, five quarts of choice flour will cost only one piece of silver, and ten quarts of barley grain will cost only one piece of silver." ²The officer assisting the king said to the man of God, "That couldn't happen even if the LORD opened the windows of heaven!" But Elisha replied, "You will see it happen with your own eyes, but you won't be able to eat any of it!"

~ 2 Kings 6:24-31; 7:1-2

God Gives a Way Out

Four lepers went to the Aramean army's camp and found it deserted. They told the people at the palace, which meant Elisha's prophecy was fulfilled. God can give a way out in any situation.

[3]There were four men with leprosy sitting at the entrance of the city gates. "Why should we sit here waiting to die?" they asked each other. [4]"We will starve if we stay here, but with the famine in the city, we will starve if we go back there. So we might as well go out and surrender to the Aramean army. If they let us live, so much the better. But if they kill us, we would have died anyway." [5]So at twilight they set out for the camp of the Arameans. But when they came to the edge of the camp, no one was there!

[6]For the Lord had caused the Aramean army to hear the clatter of speeding chariots and the galloping of horses and the sounds of a great army approaching. "The king of Israel has hired the Hittites and Egyptians to attack us!" they cried to one another. [7]So they panicked and ran into the night, abandoning their tents, horses, donkeys, and everything else, as they fled for their lives. [8]When the lepers arrived at the edge of the camp, they went into one tent after another, eating and drinking wine; and they carried off silver and gold and clothing and hid it. [9]Finally, they said to each other, "This is not right. This is a day of good news, and we aren't sharing it with anyone! If we wait until morning, some calamity will certainly fall upon us. Come on, let's go back and tell the people at the palace."

[10]So they went back to the city and told the gatekeepers what had happened.

~ 2 Kings 7:3-10

God Heals Disease

When King Hezekiah became very ill, he begged God to heal him. God answered his prayer and healed him. This, however, doesn't mean that God will heal all diseases, although it is in His power to do so. Sometimes God wants to teach you valuable life lessons through your sickness.

[1]About that time Hezekiah became deathly ill, and the prophet Isaiah son of Amoz went to visit him. He gave the king this message: "This is what the LORD says: Set your affairs in order, for you are going to die. You will not recover from this illness."

[2]When Hezekiah heard this, he turned his face to the wall and prayed to the LORD, [3]"Remember, O LORD, how I have always been faithful to you and have served you single-mindedly, always doing what pleases you." Then he broke down and wept bitterly.

[4]But before Isaiah had left the middle courtyard, this message came to him from the LORD: [5]"Go back to Hezekiah, the leader of my people. Tell him, 'This is what the LORD, the God of your ancestor David, says: I have heard your prayer and seen your tears. I will heal you, and three days from now you will get out of bed and go to the Temple of the LORD. [6]I will add fifteen years to your life, and I will rescue you and this city from the king of Assyria. I will defend this city for my own honor and for the sake of my servant David.'"

[7]Isaiah said, "Make an ointment from figs." So Hezekiah's servants spread the ointment over the boil, and Hezekiah recovered!

~ 2 Kings 20:1-7

The Prayer of Jabez

Jabez asked God to bless him, expand his territory, be with him in all that he did, and keep him from all trouble and pain. God listened to him and answered his prayer. You can also pray to God and present your requests to Him with a faithful and bold heart.

[9]There was a man named Jabez who was more honorable than any of his brothers. His mother named him Jabez because his birth had been so painful.

[10]He was the one who prayed to the God of Israel, "Oh, that you would bless me and expand my territory! Please be with me in all that I do, and keep me from all trouble and pain!" And God granted him his request.

~ 1 Chronicles 4:9-10

Sing a Song of Praise to God!

When the Ark of the Covenant was brought back to Jerusalem, Asaph and his choir sang a song of praise to God: The Lord is great, and He is most worthy of praise. Honor and majesty surround Him, and there is strength and joy in His dwelling. Now sing your own song of joy to God.

¹They brought the Ark of God and placed it inside the special tent David had prepared for it. And they presented burnt offerings and peace offerings to God.

⁷On that day David gave to Asaph and his fellow Levites this song of thanksgiving to the Lord:

⁸Give thanks to the Lord and proclaim his greatness. Let the whole world know what he has done. ⁹Sing to him; yes, sing his praises. Tell everyone about his wonderful deeds. ¹⁰Exult in his holy name; rejoice, you who worship the Lord. ¹¹Search for the Lord and for his strength; continually seek him.

²⁵Great is the Lord! He is most worthy of praise! He is to be feared above all gods. ²⁶The gods of other nations are mere idols, but the Lord made the heavens! ²⁷Honor and majesty surround him; strength and joy fill his dwelling.

³⁴Give thanks to the Lord, for he is good! His faithful love endures forever.

~ 1 Chronicles 16:1, 7-11, 25-27, 34

Everything Comes from God

When David received gifts for the temple, he praised God and confessed that everything belonged to God. All your possessions come from God and ultimately belong to Him. What are you doing today with God's property?

¹⁰Then David praised the Lord in the presence of the whole assembly: "O Lord, the God of our ancestor Israel, may you be praised forever and ever! ¹¹Yours, O Lord, is the greatness, the power, the glory, the victory, and the majesty. Everything in the heavens and on earth is yours, O Lord, and this is your kingdom. We adore you as the one who is over all things. ¹²Wealth and honor come from you alone, for you rule over everything. Power and might are in your hand.

¹³"O our God, we thank you and praise your glorious name! ¹⁴But who am I, and who are my people, that we could give anything to you? Everything we have has come from you, and we give you only what you first gave us! ¹⁵We are here for only a moment, visitors and strangers in the land as our ancestors were before us. Our days on earth are like a passing shadow, gone so soon without a trace.

¹⁶"O Lord our God, even this material we have gathered to build a Temple to honor your holy name comes from you! It all belongs to you! ¹⁷I know, my God, that you examine our hearts and rejoice when you find integrity there. You know I have done all this with good motives, and I have watched your people offer their gifts willingly and joyously.

¹⁸"O Lord, make your people always want to obey you. See to it that their love for you never changes. ¹⁹Give my son Solomon the wholehearted desire to obey all your commands, laws, and decrees, and to do everything necessary to build this Temple, for which I have made these preparations."

~ 1 Chronicles 29:10-19

God Will Never Leave You

Azariah told King Asa that God would be with them as long as they stayed true to Him, but that God would leave them if they abandoned Him. The people then decided to renew their covenant with God, and experienced great joy and peace.

¹Then the Spirit of God came upon Azariah son of Oded, ²and he went out to meet King Asa as he was returning from the battle. "Listen to me, Asa!" he shouted. "Listen, all you people of Judah and Benjamin! The LORD will stay with you as long as you stay with him! Whenever you seek him, you will find him. But if you abandon him, he will abandon you.

³"For a long time Israel was without the true God, without a priest to teach them, and without the Law to instruct them. ⁴But whenever they were in trouble and turned to the LORD, the God of Israel, and sought him out, they found him.

⁵"During those dark times, it was not safe to travel. Problems troubled the people of every land."

¹⁰The people gathered at Jerusalem in late spring, during the fifteenth year of Asa's reign. ¹¹On that day they sacrificed to the LORD 700 cattle and 7,000 sheep and goats from the plunder they had taken in the battle. ¹²Then they entered into a covenant to seek the LORD, the God of their ancestors, with all their heart and soul. ¹³They agreed that anyone who refused to seek the LORD, the God of Israel, would be put to death—whether young or old, man or woman.

¹⁴They shouted out their oath of loyalty to the LORD with trumpets blaring and rams' horns sounding. ¹⁵All in Judah were happy about this covenant, for they had entered into it with all their heart. They earnestly sought after God, and they found him. And the LORD gave them rest from their enemies on every side.

~ 2 Chronicles 15:1-5, 10-15

Victory Belongs to God

Jahaziel prophesied that God would give His people victory over the heathen army. King Jehoshaphat and his army came against the enemies with people singing God's praises. God's people saw with their own eyes how the enemy started fighting against each other and killed each other. The victory was God's.

¹³As all the men of Judah stood before the LORD with their little ones, wives, and children, ¹⁴the Spirit of the LORD came upon one of the men standing there. His name was Jahaziel.

¹⁵He said, "Listen, all you people of Judah and Jerusalem! Listen, King Jehoshaphat! This is what the LORD says: Do not be afraid! Don't be discouraged by this mighty army, for the battle is not yours, but God's. ¹⁶Tomorrow, march out against them. You will find them coming up through the ascent of Ziz at the end of the valley that opens into the wilderness of Jeruel. ¹⁷But you will not even need to fight. Take your positions; then stand still and watch the LORD's victory. He is with you, O people of Judah and Jerusalem. Do not be afraid or discouraged. Go out against them tomorrow, for the LORD is with you!"

¹⁸Then King Jehoshaphat bowed low with his face to the ground. And all the people of Judah and Jerusalem did the same, worshiping the LORD.

²¹After consulting the people, the king appointed singers to walk ahead of the army, singing to the LORD and praising him for his holy splendor. This is what they sang: "Give thanks to the LORD; his faithful love endures forever!"

²²At the very moment they began to sing and give praise, the LORD caused the armies to start fighting among themselves. ²³The armies turned against their allies and killed every one of them. After they had destroyed the army of Seir, they began attacking each other.

~ 2 Chronicles 20:13-18, 21-23

Nehemiah Prays for the People

When Nehemiah heard that Jerusalem lay in ruins, he felt dismayed and surrendered himself to God through prayer and fasting. He confessed his own sins and that of the people, and reminded God that He promised to bring them back to their land.

¹In late autumn, in the month of Kislev, in the twentieth year of King Artaxerxes' reign, I was at the fortress of Susa. ²Hanani, one of my brothers, came to visit me with some other men who had just arrived from Judah. I asked them about the Jews who had returned there from captivity and about how things were going in Jerusalem.

³They said to me, "Things are not going well for those who returned to the province of Judah. They are in great trouble and disgrace. The wall of Jerusalem has been torn down, and the gates have been destroyed by fire."

⁴When I heard this, I sat down and wept. In fact, for days I mourned, fasted, and prayed to the God of heaven. ⁵Then I said, "O Lᴏʀᴅ, God of heaven, the great and awesome God who keeps his covenant of unfailing love with those who love him and obey his commands, ⁶listen to my prayer! Look down and see me praying night and day for your people Israel. I confess that we have sinned against you. Yes, even my own family and I have sinned!

⁷"We have sinned terribly by not obeying the commands, decrees, and regulations that you gave us through your servant Moses. ⁸Please remember what you told your servant Moses: 'If you are unfaithful to me, I will scatter you among the nations. ⁹But if you return to me and obey my commands and live by them, then even if you are exiled to the ends of the earth, I will bring you back to the place I have chosen for my name to be honored.'"

~ Nehemiah 1:1-9

Pray First, Then Act

Nehemiah asked the king if he could rebuild the walls of Jerusalem, but first he asked God to make his plans successful. The king gave his consent and Nehemiah left for Jerusalem where the citizens agreed to help him rebuild the wall.

4The king asked, "Well, how can I help you?" With a prayer to the God of heaven, 5I replied, "If it please the king, and if you are pleased with me, your servant, send me to Judah to rebuild the city where my ancestors are buried."

6The king, with the queen sitting beside him, asked, "How long will you be gone? When will you return?" After I told him how long I would be gone, the king agreed to my request.

16The city officials did not know I had been out there or what I was doing, for I had not yet said anything to anyone about my plans. I had not yet spoken to the Jewish leaders—the priests, the nobles, the officials, or anyone else in the administration.

17But now I said to them, "You know very well what trouble we are in. Jerusalem lies in ruins, and its gates have been destroyed by fire. Let us rebuild the wall of Jerusalem and end this disgrace!"

18Then I told them about how the gracious hand of God had been on me, and about my conversation with the king. They replied at once, "Yes, let's rebuild the wall!" So they began the good work.

~ Nehemiah 2:4-6, 16-18

With God's Help

With God's help, Nehemiah and his helpers finished rebuilding the wall in a record time. Their enemies were astounded and realized that God had helped them. Then Ezra read from the Book of the Law and the people praised God. When God helps you with your work, you will succeed.

6[15]So on October 2 the wall was finished—just fifty-two days after we had begun. [16]When our enemies and the surrounding nations heard about it, they were frightened and humiliated. They realized this work had been done with the help of our God.

7[1]After the wall was finished and I had set up the doors in the gates, the gatekeepers, singers, and Levites were appointed.

8In October, when the Israelites had settled in their towns, [8:1]all the people assembled with a unified purpose at the square just inside the Water Gate. They asked Ezra the scribe to bring out the Book of the Law of Moses, which the LORD had given for Israel to obey.

[6]Then Ezra praised the LORD, the great God, and all the people chanted, "Amen! Amen!" as they lifted their hands. Then they bowed down and worshiped the LORD with their faces to the ground.

[9]Then Nehemiah the governor, Ezra the priest and scribe, and the Levites who were interpreting for the people said to them, "Don't mourn or weep on such a day as this! For today is a sacred day before the LORD your God." For the people had all been weeping as they listened to the words of the Law.

[10]And Nehemiah continued, "Go and celebrate with a feast of rich foods and sweet drinks, and share gifts of food with people who have nothing prepared. This is a sacred day before our Lord. Don't be dejected and sad, for the joy of the LORD is your strength!"

~ Nehemiah 6:15-16; 7:1; 8:1, 6, 9-10

Vashti Refuses

When King Xerxes sent for his beautiful wife, Queen Vashti, to come before him so he could show her off to his friends, she refused. This courageous act resulted in Vashti losing her title as queen. In this way the path was being paved for Esther to become the next queen.

[10]On the seventh day of the feast, when King Xerxes was in high spirits because of the wine, he told the seven eunuchs who attended him [11]to bring Queen Vashti to him with the royal crown on her head. He wanted the nobles and all the other men to gaze on her beauty, for she was a very beautiful woman. [12]But when they conveyed the king's order to Queen Vashti, she refused to come. This made the king furious, and he burned with anger. [13]He immediately consulted with his wise advisers, who knew all the Persian laws and customs, for he always asked their advice.

[15]"What must be done to Queen Vashti?" the king demanded. "What penalty does the law provide for a queen who refuses to obey the king's orders, properly sent through his eunuchs?"

[19]"So if it please the king, we suggest that you issue a written decree, a law of the Persians and Medes that cannot be revoked. It should order that Queen Vashti be forever banished from the presence of King Xerxes, and that the king should choose another queen more worthy than she. [20]When this decree is published throughout the king's vast empire, husbands everywhere, whatever their rank, will receive proper respect from their wives!"

[21]The king and his nobles thought this made good sense, so he followed Memucan's counsel.

~ Esther 1:10-13, 15, 19-21

Esther Is Chosen as Queen

The king was looking for a new wife, and he chose the beautiful Esther, an orphan adopted by her cousin Mordecai. Esther was completely unaware of the fact that God would use her to save His people.

⁵At that time there was a Jewish man in the fortress of Susa whose name was Mordecai. ⁷This man had a very beautiful and lovely young cousin, Hadassah, who was also called Esther. When her father and mother died, Mordecai adopted her into his family and raised her as his own daughter.

⁸As a result of the king's decree, Esther, along with many other young women, was brought to the king's harem at the fortress of Susa and placed in Hegai's care. ⁹Hegai was very impressed with Esther and treated her kindly. He quickly ordered a special menu for her and provided her with beauty treatments. He also assigned her seven maids specially chosen from the king's palace, and he moved her and her maids into the best place in the harem.

¹²Before each young woman was taken to the king's bed, she was given the prescribed twelve months of beauty treatments—six months with oil of myrrh, followed by six months with special perfumes and ointments.

¹⁵When it was Esther's turn to go to the king, she accepted the advice of Hegai, the eunuch in charge of the harem. She asked for nothing except what he suggested, and she was admired by everyone who saw her.

¹⁶Esther was taken to King Xerxes at the royal palace in early winter of the seventh year of his reign. ¹⁷And the king loved Esther more than any of the other young women. He was so delighted with her that he set the royal crown on her head and declared her queen instead of Vashti.

~ Esther 2:5, 7-9, 12, 15-17

Esther Saves the People

Mordecai told Esther that Xerxes had been bribed to annihilate all the Jews, and he asked Esther to beg the king for mercy. Esther agreed, even though it was very dangerous, and asked the people to pray for her. Through her courageous act the Jewish people were saved.

⁵Then Esther sent for Hathach, one of the king's eunuchs who had been appointed as her attendant. She ordered him to go to Mordecai and find out what was troubling him and why he was in mourning.

⁷Mordecai told him the whole story, including the exact amount of money Haman had promised to pay into the royal treasury for the destruction of the Jews. ⁸Mordecai gave Hathach a copy of the decree issued in Susa that called for the death of all Jews. He asked Hathach to show it to Esther and explain the situation to her. He also asked Hathach to direct her to go to the king to beg for mercy and plead for her people.

¹³Mordecai sent this reply to Esther: "Don't think for a moment that because you're in the palace you will escape when all other Jews are killed. ¹⁴If you keep quiet at a time like this, deliverance and relief for the Jews will arise from some other place, but you and your relatives will die. Who knows if perhaps you were made queen for just such a time as this?"

¹⁵Then Esther sent this reply to Mordecai: ¹⁶"Go and gather together all the Jews of Susa and fast for me. Do not eat or drink for three days, night or day. My maids and I will do the same. And then, though it is against the law, I will go in to see the king. If I must die, I must die." ¹⁷So Mordecai went away and did everything as Esther had ordered him.

~ Esther 4:5, 7-8, 13-17

At the Receiving End of Disaster

Job lost all his possessions and his children. Still he managed to praise God and not blame Him. Will you stay true to God under such severe circumstances?

[8]The LORD asked Satan, "Have you noticed my servant Job? He is the finest man in all the earth. He is blameless—a man of complete integrity. He fears God and stays away from evil."

[9]Satan replied to the LORD, "Yes, but Job has good reason to fear God. [10]You have made him prosper in everything he does. [11]But reach out and take away everything he has, and he will surely curse you to your face!"

[12]"All right, you may test him," the LORD said to Satan. "Do whatever you want with everything he possesses, but don't harm him physically." So Satan left the LORD'S presence.

[14]A messenger arrived at Job's home with this news: [15]"The Sabeans raided us. They stole all the animals and killed all the farmhands. [16]While he was still speaking, another messenger arrived with this news: "The fire of God has fallen from heaven and burned up your sheep and all the shepherds." [17]While he was still speaking, a third messenger arrived with this news: "Three bands of Chaldean raiders have stolen your camels and killed your servants."

[18]While he was still speaking, another messenger arrived with this news: "Your sons and daughters were feasting in their oldest brother's home. [19]Suddenly, a powerful wind swept in from the wilderness and hit the house on all sides. The house collapsed, and all your children are dead."

[20]Job stood up and tore his robe in grief. He shaved his head and fell to the ground to worship. [21]He said, "The LORD gave me what I had, and the LORD has taken it away. Praise the name of the LORD!"

[22]In all of this, Job did not sin by blaming God.

~ Job 1:8-12, 14-22

Sickness and Adversity

The loss of his children and possessions were a big shock to Job. So too was his deteriorating health. His wife told him to curse God, but Job maintained that he had to accept the good and bad from God's hand. What would you have done?

¹One day the members of the heavenly court came again to present themselves before the LORD, and the Accuser, Satan, came with them. ²"Where have you come from?" the LORD asked Satan. Satan answered the LORD, "I have been patrolling the earth, watching everything that's going on."

³Then the LORD asked Satan, "Have you noticed my servant Job? He is the finest man in all the earth. He is blameless—a man of complete integrity. He fears God and stays away from evil. And he has maintained his integrity, even though you urged me to harm him without cause." ⁴Satan replied to the LORD, "Skin for skin! A man will give up everything he has to save his life. ⁵But reach out and take away his health, and he will surely curse you to your face!"

⁶"All right, do with him as you please," the LORD said to Satan. "But spare his life." ⁷So Satan left the LORD's presence, and he struck Job with terrible boils from head to foot.

⁸Job scraped his skin with a piece of broken pottery as he sat among the ashes. ⁹His wife said to him, "Are you still trying to maintain your integrity? Curse God and die."

¹⁰But Job replied, "You talk like a foolish woman. Should we accept only good things from the hand of God and never anything bad?" So in all this, Job said nothing wrong.

~ Job 2:1-10

Job's Friends Support Him

When Job's friends heard about all his afflictions, they sat with him for a whole week without saying a word. Only after the week had passed did Job manage to talk about his woes. Your friends need your support very much during tough times – you can even support them without saying a word.

2[11]When three of Job's friends heard of the tragedy he had suffered, they got together and traveled from their homes to comfort and console him. Their names were Eliphaz the Temanite, Bildad the Shuhite, and Zophar the Naamathite.

[12]When they saw Job from a distance, they scarcely recognized him. Wailing loudly, they tore their robes and threw dust into the air over their heads to show their grief. [13]Then they sat on the ground with him for seven days and nights. No one said a word to Job, for they saw that his suffering was too great for words.

3[1]At last Job spoke, and he cursed the day of his birth. [2]He said:

[11]"Why wasn't I born dead? Why didn't I die as I came from the womb?

[25]"What I always feared has happened to me. What I dreaded has come true. [26]I have no peace, no quietness. I have no rest; only trouble comes."

~ Job 2:11-3:2, 11, 25-26

God Tests Your Faith

Job wanted to share his hardships with God. He recognized his own insignificance. When you endure hardship, it helps to talk to God about it. You can tell God how you feel – He is often testing your faith when times are tough for you.

6"My days fly faster than a weaver's shuttle. They end without hope. 7O God, remember that my life is but a breath, and I will never again feel happiness. 8You see me now, but not for long. You will look for me, but I will be gone. 9Just as a cloud dissipates and vanishes, those who die will not come back. 10They are gone forever from their home—never to be seen again.

11"I cannot keep from speaking. I must express my anguish. My bitter soul must complain. 12Am I a sea monster or a dragon that you must place me under guard? 13I think, 'My bed will comfort me, and sleep will ease my misery,' 14but then you shatter me with dreams and terrify me with visions. 15I would rather be strangled—rather die than suffer like this. 16I hate my life and don't want to go on living. Oh, leave me alone for my few remaining days.

17"What are people, that you should make so much of us, that you should think of us so often? 18For you examine us every morning and test us every moment. 19Why won't you leave me alone, at least long enough for me to swallow!

20"If I have sinned, what have I done to you, O watcher of all humanity? Why make me your target? Am I a burden to you? 21Why not just forgive my sin and take away my guilt? For soon I will lie down in the dust and die. When you look for me, I will be gone."

~ Job 7:6-21

Face-to-Face

Even though Job reeled under his afflictions, he knew that he would see God face-to-face one day. He asked God to feel pity for him. Job acknowledged that his Redeemer lived, despite the suffering he endured.

[7]"I cry out, 'Help!' but no one answers me. I protest, but there is no justice. [8]God has blocked my way so I cannot move. He has plunged my path into darkness.

[21]"Have mercy on me, my friends, have mercy, for the hand of God has struck me. [22]Must you also persecute me, like God does? Haven't you chewed me up enough?

[23]"Oh, that my words could be recorded. Oh, that they could be inscribed on a monument, [24]carved with an iron chisel and filled with lead, engraved forever in the rock.

[25]"But as for me, I know that my Redeemer lives, and he will stand upon the earth at last. [26]And after my body has decayed, yet in my body I will see God! [27]I will see him for myself. Yes, I will see him with my own eyes. I am overwhelmed at the thought!"

~ Job 19:7-8, 21-27

When God Is Silent

Job wanted very much to know the reasons for his suffering, but God kept quiet when Job called to Him. Job's life consisted only of hardship at that moment. In really tough times we also feel that God is not answering us when we call to Him, but God is always there for us.

[20]"I cry to you, O God, but you don't answer. I stand before you, but you don't even look. [21]You have become cruel toward me. You use your power to persecute me. [22]You throw me into the whirlwind and destroy me in the storm. [23]And I know you are sending me to my death—the destination of all who live.

[24]"Surely no one would turn against the needy when they cry for help in their trouble. [25]Did I not weep for those in trouble? Was I not deeply grieved for the needy? [26]So I looked for good, but evil came instead. I waited for the light, but darkness fell.

[27]"My heart is troubled and restless. Days of suffering torment me. [28]I walk in gloom, without sunlight. I stand in the public square and cry for help. [29]Instead, I am considered a brother to jackals and a companion to owls. [30]My skin has turned dark, and my bones burn with fever. [31]My harp plays sad music, and my flute accompanies those who weep."

~ Job 30:20-31

God Speaks Through Suffering

Elihu assured Job that God sometimes spoke to people through suffering and pain, but that He is always willing to help. God would save Job so that his life would be filled with light again. When you suffer, listen carefully to what God wants to tell you through your suffering.

[14]"For God speaks again and again, though people do not recognize it. [15]He speaks in dreams, in visions of the night, when deep sleep falls on people as they lie in their beds.

[16]"He whispers in their ears and terrifies them with warnings. [17]He makes them turn from doing wrong; he keeps them from pride. [18]He protects them from the grave, from crossing over the river of death.

[19]"Or God disciplines people with pain on their sickbeds, with ceaseless aching in their bones.

[26]"When he prays to God, he will be accepted. And God will receive him with joy and restore him to good standing. [27]He will declare to his friends, 'I sinned and twisted the truth, but it was not worth it. [28]God rescued me from the grave, and now my life is filled with light.'"

~ Job 33:14-19, 26-28

To Keep Quiet Is Best

Job asked God dozens of "Why?" questions. In the end he realized that a person shouldn't accuse God, and confessed that he spoke when he should've kept quiet. It is best to rather be still and wait on God when things happen that you don't understand.

40¹Then the LORD said to Job, ²"Do you still want to argue with the Almighty? You are God's critic, but do you have the answers?"

³Then Job replied to the LORD, ⁴"I am nothing—how could I ever find the answers? I will cover my mouth with my hand. ⁵I have said too much already. I have nothing more to say."

⁶Then the LORD answered Job from the whirlwind: ⁷"Brace yourself like a man, because I have some questions for you, and you must answer them. ⁸Will you discredit my justice and condemn me just to prove you are right?

42¹Then Job replied to the LORD: ²"I know that you can do anything, and no one can stop you. ³You asked, 'Who is this that questions my wisdom with such ignorance?' It is I—and I was talking about things I knew nothing about, things far too wonderful for me. ⁵I had only heard about you before, but now I have seen you with my own eyes."

~ Job 40:1-8; 42:1-3, 5

Find Joy in God's Commandments

Women who find their joy and hope in God's Word and spend enough time studying it, are like trees planted along streams of water. They yield fruit in season, and they prosper in whatever they do.

[1]Oh, the joys of those who do not follow the advice of the wicked, or stand around with sinners, or join in with mockers. [2]But they delight in the law of the LORD, meditating on it day and night.

[3]They are like trees planted along the riverbank, bearing fruit each season. Their leaves never wither, and they prosper in all they do.

[4]But not the wicked! They are like worthless chaff, scattered by the wind. [5]They will be condemned at the time of judgment. Sinners will have no place among the godly.

[6]For the LORD watches over the path of the godly, but the path of the wicked leads to destruction.

~ Psalm 1

God Crowns You with Glory and Honor!

It is almost unfathomable that the almighty Creator spends so much time thinking about us. He has crowned our heads with glory and honor, and made us the rulers over everything He has made. Let's be responsible in this worthy calling.

¹O LORD, our Lord, your majestic name fills the earth! Your glory is higher than the heavens. ²You have taught children and infants to tell of your strength, silencing your enemies and all who oppose you.

³When I look at the night sky and see the work of your fingers—the moon and the stars you set in place—⁴what are mere mortals that you should think about them, human beings that you should care for them? ⁵Yet you made them only a little lower than God and crowned them with glory and honor.

⁶You gave them charge of everything you made, putting all things under their authority—⁷the flocks and the herds and all the wild animals, ⁸the birds in the sky, the fish in the sea, and everything that swims the ocean currents.

⁹O LORD, our Lord, your majestic name fills the earth!

~ Psalm 8

When God Feels Far Away

Sometimes in crisis situations it feels like God is far away and doesn't hear us when we call for help. But this can *never* happen. He knows about the people who mistreat you, He sees your problems and is more than ready to help you. Trust God with your whole heart!

¹O LORD, why do you stand so far away? Why do you hide when I am in trouble?

¹²Arise, O LORD! Punish the wicked, O God! Do not ignore the helpless! ¹³Why do the wicked get away with despising God? They think, "God will never call us to account." ¹⁴But you see the trouble and grief they cause. You take note of it and punish them. The helpless put their trust in you. You defend the orphans.

¹⁵Break the arms of these wicked, evil people! Go after them until the last one is destroyed. ¹⁶The LORD is king forever and ever! The godless nations will vanish from the land.

¹⁷LORD, you know the hopes of the helpless. Surely you will hear their cries and comfort them. ¹⁸You will bring justice to the orphans and the oppressed, so mere people can no longer terrify them.

~ Psalm 10:1, 12-18

Then You May Appear Before God

Nobody is holy and without sin, but as Christians we believe that Christ has saved us from death. And therefore we have free access to God's grace. Draw close to God with a sincere heart, and live like a person who has been saved.

¹Who may worship in your sanctuary, LORD? Who may enter your presence on your holy hill?

²Those who lead blameless lives and do what is right, speaking the truth from sincere hearts.

³Those who refuse to gossip or harm their neighbors or speak evil of their friends.

⁴Those who despise flagrant sinners, and honor the faithful followers of the LORD, and keep their promises even when it hurts.

⁵Those who lend money without charging interest, and who cannot be bribed to lie about the innocent. Such people will stand firm forever.

~ Psalm 15

Find Your Joy in the Lord

All good things come from God. Be glad and praise God every day because of this. In His presence is fullness of joy, and eternal pleasures are at His right hand. By God's side we are always safe.

[1]Keep me safe, O God, for I have come to you for refuge.

[2]I said to the LORD, "You are my Master! Every good thing I have comes from you."

[6]The land you have given me is a pleasant land. What a wonderful inheritance!

[7]I will bless the LORD who guides me; even at night my heart instructs me. [8]I know the LORD is always with me. I will not be shaken, for he is right beside me.

[9]No wonder my heart is glad, and I rejoice. My body rests in safety. [10]For you will not leave my soul among the dead or allow your holy one to rot in the grave.

[11]You will show me the way of life, granting me the joy of your presence and the pleasures of living with you forever.

~ Psalm 16:1-2, 6-11

God Is Your Rock

God wants to be your Rock, a safe refuge in times of distress. He will protect you from every danger because He loves you. His ways are perfect, and His words are flawless. God will arm you with strength and make your way perfect. Trust God for it!

¹I love you, Lord; you are my strength. ²The Lord is my rock, my fortress, and my savior; my God is my rock, in whom I find protection. He is my shield, the power that saves me, and my place of safety.

⁵The grave wrapped its ropes around me; death laid a trap in my path. ⁶But in my distress I cried out to the Lord; yes, I prayed to my God for help. He heard me from his sanctuary; my cry to him reached his ears.

¹⁶He reached down from heaven and rescued me; he drew me out of deep waters. ¹⁷He rescued me from my powerful enemies, from those who hated me and were too strong for me. ¹⁸They attacked me at a moment when I was in distress, but the Lord supported me. ¹⁹He led me to a place of safety; he rescued me because he delights in me.

²⁸You light a lamp for me. The Lord, my God, lights up my darkness. ²⁹In your strength I can crush an army; with my God I can scale any wall.

³⁰God's way is perfect. All the Lord's promises prove true. He is a shield for all who look to him for protection. ³¹For who is God except the Lord? Who but our God is a solid rock? ³²God arms me with strength, and he makes my way perfect. ³³He makes me as surefooted as a deer, enabling me to stand on mountain heights.

⁴⁶The Lord lives! Praise to my Rock! May the God of my salvation be exalted!

~ Psalm 18:1-2, 5-6, 16-19, 28-33, 46

The Glory of God

The heavens declare the glory of God, and the skies are the works of His hands. In His Word we learn about His greatness. His precepts give life, His Laws are more precious than gold. Ask the Lord to purify your thoughts so that they will be pleasing to His sight.

[1]The heavens proclaim the glory of God. The skies display his craftsmanship. [2]Day after day they continue to speak; night after night they make him known. [3]They speak without a sound or word; their voice is never heard. [4]Yet their message has gone throughout the earth, and their words to all the world. God has made a home in the heavens for the sun. [5]It bursts forth like a radiant bridegroom after his wedding. It rejoices like a great athlete eager to run the race. [6]The sun rises at one end of the heavens and follows its course to the other end. Nothing can hide from its heat.

[7]The instructions of the LORD are perfect, reviving the soul. The decrees of the LORD are trustworthy, making wise the simple. [8]The commandments of the LORD are right, bringing joy to the heart. The commands of the LORD are clear, giving insight for living. [9]Reverence for the LORD is pure, lasting forever. The laws of the LORD are true; each one is fair. [11]They are a warning to your servant, a great reward for those who obey them.

[12]How can I know all the sins lurking in my heart? Cleanse me from these hidden faults. [13]Keep your servant from deliberate sins! Don't let them control me. Then I will be free of guilt and innocent of great sin.

[14]May the words of my mouth and the meditation of my heart be pleasing to you, O LORD, my rock and my redeemer.

~ Psalm 19:1-9, 11-14

Can God Forsake You?

The psalmist felt that God had abandoned him, that He didn't answer his call for help. God left Jesus on the cross so that you would never be alone again. When times are tough, know that God is with you; He hears every cry.

[1]My God, my God, why have you abandoned me? Why are you so far away when I groan for help? [2]Every day I call to you, my God, but you do not answer. Every night you hear my voice, but I find no relief.

[6]But I am a worm and not a man. I am scorned and despised by all! [7]Everyone who sees me mocks me. They sneer and shake their heads, saying, [8]"Is this the one who relies on the LORD? Then let the LORD save him! If the LORD loves him so much, let the LORD rescue him!"

[9]Yet you brought me safely from my mother's womb and led me to trust you at my mother's breast. [10]I was thrust into your arms at my birth. You have been my God from the moment I was born.

[11]Do not stay so far from me, for trouble is near, and no one else can help me.

[19]O LORD, do not stay far away! You are my strength; come quickly to my aid!

[22]I will proclaim your name to my brothers and sisters. I will praise you among your assembled people.

[25]I will praise you in the great assembly. I will fulfill my vows in the presence of those who worship you.

~ Psalm 22:1-2, 6-11, 19, 22, 25

April

God Wants to be Your Shepherd

With God as the Shepherd of your life, you won't need anything. He cares for you. Even when you go through dark valleys He is with you. His goodness and love will be with you all the days of your life.

¹The LORD is my shepherd; I have all that I need. ²He lets me rest in green meadows; he leads me beside peaceful streams.

³He renews my strength. He guides me along right paths, bringing honor to his name.

⁴Even when I walk through the darkest valley, I will not be afraid, for you are close beside me. Your rod and your staff protect and comfort me.

⁵You prepare a feast for me in the presence of my enemies. You honor me by anointing my head with oil. My cup overflows with blessings.

⁶Surely your goodness and unfailing love will pursue me all the days of my life, and I will live in the house of the LORD forever.

~ Psalm 23

God Shows You the Path of Life

When people trust in God, He shows them which way they should go. He guides you in His truth and teaches you, because He is your Savior. He promises to forgive your sins, and He is always there to help you.

[1]O LORD, I give my life to you. [3]No one who trusts in you will ever be disgraced, but disgrace comes to those who try to deceive others.

[4]Show me the right path, O LORD; point out the road for me to follow. [5]Lead me by your truth and teach me, for you are the God who saves me. All day long I put my hope in you.

[8]The LORD is good and does what is right; he shows the proper path to those who go astray. [9]He leads the humble in doing right, teaching them his way. [10]The LORD leads with unfailing love and faithfulness all who keep his covenant and obey his demands.

[11]For the honor of your name, O LORD, forgive my many, many sins. [12]Who are those who fear the LORD? He will show them the path they should choose.

[13]They will live in prosperity, and their children will inherit the land. [14]The LORD is a friend to those who fear him. He teaches them his covenant. [15]My eyes are always on the LORD, for he rescues me from the traps of my enemies.

~ Psalm 25:1, 3-5, 8-15

God Gives You Courage

God is our light and refuge, we need not be afraid of anyone. When danger lurks, He will protect you. He teaches you how to live. Even if people threaten your life, you can trust in the Lord completely and be encouraged!

¹The LORD is my light and my salvation—so why should I be afraid? The LORD is my fortress, protecting me from danger, so why should I tremble?

³Though a mighty army surrounds me, my heart will not be afraid. Even if I am attacked, I will remain confident.

⁴The one thing I ask of the LORD—the thing I seek most—is to live in the house of the LORD all the days of my life, delighting in the LORD's perfections and meditating in his Temple. ⁵For he will conceal me there when troubles come; he will hide me in his sanctuary. He will place me out of reach on a high rock. ⁶Then I will hold my head high above my enemies who surround me. At his sanctuary I will offer sacrifices with shouts of joy, singing and praising the LORD with music.

⁷Hear me as I pray, O LORD. Be merciful and answer me! ⁸My heart has heard you say, "Come and talk with me." And my heart responds, "LORD, I am coming." ⁹Do not turn your back on me. Do not reject your servant in anger. You have always been my helper. Don't leave me now; don't abandon me, O God of my salvation! ¹⁰Even if my father and mother abandon me, the LORD will hold me close.

¹¹Teach me how to live, O LORD. Lead me along the right path, for my enemies are waiting for me. ¹³Yet I am confident I will see the LORD's goodness while I am here in the land of the living.

¹⁴Wait patiently for the LORD. Be brave and courageous. Yes, wait patiently for the LORD.

~ Psalm 27:1, 3-11, 13-14

Trade Your Sorrow for God's Joy

It is God who heals you and changes your present sorrow into abundant joy. His wrath is only momentary, but His grace is yours for eternity! Trade your sadness for God's lasting joy now, and continue to thank Him for everything.

¹I will exalt you, LORD, for you rescued me. You refused to let my enemies triumph over me. ²O LORD my God, I cried to you for help, and you restored my health. ³You brought me up from the grave, O LORD. You kept me from falling into the pit of death.

⁴Sing to the LORD, all you godly ones! Praise his holy name. ⁵For his anger lasts only a moment, but his favor lasts a lifetime! Weeping may last through the night, but joy comes with the morning.

⁶When I was prosperous, I said, "Nothing can stop me now!" ⁷Your favor, O LORD, made me as secure as a mountain. Then you turned away from me, and I was shattered.

⁸I cried out to you, O LORD. I begged the Lord for mercy, saying, ⁹"What will you gain if I die, if I sink into the grave? Can my dust praise you? Can it tell of your faithfulness? ¹⁰Hear me, LORD, and have mercy on me. Help me, O LORD."

¹¹You have turned my mourning into joyful dancing. You have taken away my clothes of mourning and clothed me with joy, ¹²that I might sing praises to you and not be silent. O LORD my God, I will give you thanks forever!

~ Psalm 30

A Rock of Refuge

God is a rock of refuge where you can take shelter from every danger. You can confidently place your entire life in His hands; He knows about all your problems and listens to your prayers. You can face each day with courage.

[1]O Lord, I have come to you for protection; don't let me be disgraced. Save me, for you do what is right. [2]Turn your ear to listen to me; rescue me quickly. Be my rock of protection, a fortress where I will be safe. [3]You are my rock and my fortress. For the honor of your name, lead me out of this danger.

[5]I entrust my spirit into your hand. Rescue me, Lord, for you are a faithful God.

[7]I will be glad and rejoice in your unfailing love, for you have seen my troubles, and you care about the anguish of my soul. [8]You have not handed me over to my enemies but have set me in a safe place.

[14]But I am trusting you, O Lord, saying, "You are my God!" [15]My future is in your hands. Rescue me from those who hunt me down relentlessly.

[19]How great is the goodness you have stored up for those who fear you. You lavish it on those who come to you for protection, blessing them before the watching world.

[22]In panic I cried out, "I am cut off from the Lord!" But you heard my cry for mercy and answered my call for help.

[24]So be strong and courageous, all you who put your hope in the Lord!

~ Psalm 31:1-3, 5, 7-8, 14-15, 19, 22, 24

Don't Keep Quiet about Your Sins!

Keeping quiet about your sins can make your zest for life disappear and your health deteriorate. Confess your sins before God so that He can forgive you. Then He will instruct you and show you which way you should go. He will watch over you so that you may live a joyful life.

[1]Oh, what joy for those whose disobedience is forgiven, whose sin is put out of sight! [2]Yes, what joy for those whose record the LORD has cleared of guilt, whose lives are lived in complete honesty!

[3]When I refused to confess my sin, my body wasted away, and I groaned all day long. [4]Day and night your hand of discipline was heavy on me. My strength evaporated like water in the summer heat.

[5]Finally, I confessed all my sins to you and stopped trying to hide my guilt. I said to myself, "I will confess my rebellion to the LORD." And you forgave me! All my guilt is gone.

[7]For you are my hiding place; you protect me from trouble. You surround me with songs of victory.

[8]The LORD says, "I will guide you along the best pathway for your life. I will advise you and watch over you. [9]Do not be like a senseless horse or mule that needs a bit and bridle to keep it under control."

[10]Many sorrows come to the wicked, but unfailing love surrounds those who trust the LORD. [11]So rejoice in the LORD and be glad, all you who obey him! Shout for joy, all you whose hearts are pure!

~ Psalm 32:1-5, 7-11

God Answers You

Praise God at all times for answering your prayers. When you look up to Him you can always be radiant with joy, even when the going gets tough. God hears His children crying out for help, and He helps those who are spiritually broken. He is with you during sad times.

[1]I will praise the LORD at all times. I will constantly speak his praises. [2]I will boast only in the LORD; let all who are helpless take heart. [3]Come, let us tell of the LORD's greatness; let us exalt his name together.

[4]I prayed to the LORD, and he answered me. He freed me from all my fears. [5]Those who look to him for help will be radiant with joy; no shadow of shame will darken their faces. [6]In my desperation I prayed, and the LORD listened; he saved me from all my troubles. [7]For the angel of the LORD is a guard; he surrounds and defends all who fear him.

[8]Taste and see that the LORD is good. Oh, the joys of those who take refuge in him! [9]Fear the LORD, you his godly people, for those who fear him will have all they need.

[17]The LORD hears his people when they call to him for help. He rescues them from all their troubles. [18]The LORD is close to the brokenhearted; he rescues those whose spirits are crushed.

~ Psalm 34:1-9, 17-18

Commit Your Life to God

Do not be upset by your circumstances. Stay calm and trust God to determine your life course. Even when you stumble, the Lord will help you get up again. With His commandments in your heart, you will know the right way to live.

³Trust in the LORD and do good. Then you will live safely in the land and prosper. ⁴Take delight in the LORD, and he will give you your heart's desires.

⁵Commit everything you do to the LORD. Trust him, and he will help you. ⁶He will make your innocence radiate like the dawn, and the justice of your cause will shine like the noonday sun.

⁷Be still in the presence of the LORD, and wait patiently for him to act. Don't worry about evil people who prosper or fret about their wicked schemes.

⁸Stop being angry! Turn from your rage! Do not lose your temper—it only leads to harm.

²³The LORD directs the steps of the godly. He delights in every detail of their lives. ²⁴Though they stumble, they will never fall, for the LORD holds them by the hand.

³¹They have made God's law their own, so they will never slip from his path.

~ Psalm 37:3-8, 23-24, 31

God Is Great!

God hears your cry for help and saves you. He sets your feet on a rock and gives you a new song of praise. He doesn't expect offerings from you, but He wants you to obey His will. Everyone who serves Him will come to know His greatness.

¹I waited patiently for the LORD to help me, and he turned to me and heard my cry. ²He lifted me out of the pit of despair, out of the mud and the mire. He set my feet on solid ground and steadied me as I walked along.

³He has given me a new song to sing, a hymn of praise to our God. Many will see what he has done and be amazed. They will put their trust in the LORD.

⁵O LORD my God, you have performed many wonders for us. Your plans for us are too numerous to list. You have no equal. If I tried to recite all your wonderful deeds, I would never come to the end of them.

⁶You take no delight in sacrifices or offerings. Now that you have made me listen, I finally understand—you don't require burnt offerings or sin offerings. ⁷Then I said, "Look, I have come. As is written about me in the Scriptures: ⁸I take joy in doing your will, my God, for your instructions are written on my heart."

¹¹LORD, don't hold back your tender mercies from me. Let your unfailing love and faithfulness always protect me.

¹⁷As for me, since I am poor and needy, let the Lord keep me in his thoughts. You are my helper and my savior. O my God, do not delay.

~ Psalm 40:1-3, 5-8, 11, 17

Longing for God

In each person's heart there is a longing for God. In times of sadness you sometimes wonder where God is. Place your hope in Him. Although life is sometimes hard, you can know for sure that God is your helper and that He is by your side constantly.

¹As the deer longs for streams of water, so I long for you, O God. ²I thirst for God, the living God. When can I go and stand before him? ³Day and night I have only tears for food, while my enemies continually taunt me, saying, "Where is this God of yours?"

⁵Why am I discouraged? Why is my heart so sad? I will put my hope in God! I will praise him again—my Savior and ⁶my God! Now I am deeply discouraged, but I will remember you—even from distant Mount Hermon, the source of the Jordan, from the land of Mount Mizar.

⁷I hear the tumult of the raging seas as your waves and surging tides sweep over me. ⁸But each day the Lᴏʀᴅ pours his unfailing love upon me, and through each night I sing his songs, praying to God who gives me life.

¹¹Why am I discouraged? Why is my heart so sad? I will put my hope in God! I will praise him again—my Savior and my God!

~ Psalm 42:1-3, 5-8, 11

God – Your Refuge

God is your refuge and is always ready to help you in any kind of situation. He is always with you. In times of trouble you can be still and know that He is God, that He will help you, and that He is your shelter.

¹God is our refuge and strength, always ready to help in times of trouble. ²So we will not fear when earthquakes come and the mountains crumble into the sea. ³Let the oceans roar and foam. Let the mountains tremble as the waters surge!

⁴A river brings joy to the city of our God, the sacred home of the Most High. ⁵God dwells in that city; it cannot be destroyed. From the very break of day, God will protect it.

⁶The nations are in chaos, and their kingdoms crumble! God's voice thunders, and the earth melts! ⁷The Lord of Heaven's Armies is here among us; the God of Israel is our fortress.

⁸Come, see the glorious works of the Lord: See how he brings destruction upon the world. ⁹He causes wars to end throughout the earth. He breaks the bow and snaps the spear; he burns the shields with fire.

¹⁰"Be still, and know that I am God! I will be honored by every nation. I will be honored throughout the world."

¹¹The Lord of Heaven's Armies is here among us; the God of Israel is our fortress.

~ Psalm 46:1-11

Everything Belongs to God

Everything in creation belongs to God – He doesn't need a thing from you. Yet, He promises to deliver you when you call on Him. Devote your life to Him out of gratitude for His redemptive work and be a witness to others about His salvation.

[1]The LORD, the Mighty One, is God, and he has spoken; he has summoned all humanity from where the sun rises to where it sets. [2]From Mount Zion, the perfection of beauty, God shines in glorious radiance.

[7]"O my people, listen as I speak. Here are my charges against you, O Israel: I am God, your God! [8]I have no complaint about your sacrifices or the burnt offerings you constantly offer.

[9]"But I do not need the bulls from your barns or the goats from your pens. [10]For all the animals of the forest are mine, and I own the cattle on a thousand hills. [11]I know every bird on the mountains, and all the animals of the field are mine.

[12]"If I were hungry, I would not tell you, for all the world is mine and everything in it. [13]Do I eat the meat of bulls? Do I drink the blood of goats? [14]Make thankfulness your sacrifice to God, and keep the vows you made to the Most High. [15]Then call on me when you are in trouble, and I will rescue you, and you will give me glory.

[23]"But giving thanks is a sacrifice that truly honors me. If you keep to my path, I will reveal to you the salvation of God."

~ Psalm 50:1-2, 7-15, 23

Cleanse Me from My Sins

In this gripping psalm, David pleads with God to have mercy on him and to take away his sins. He is aware of his transgressions, and longs for the happiness that only God can give. God forgives your sins through Jesus Christ, but you have to confess them first.

³For I recognize my rebellion; it haunts me day and night. ⁴Against you, and you alone, have I sinned; I have done what is evil in your sight. You will be proved right in what you say, and your judgment against me is just. ⁵For I was born a sinner—yes, from the moment my mother conceived me. ⁶But you desire honesty from the womb, teaching me wisdom even there.

⁷Purify me from my sins, and I will be clean; wash me, and I will be whiter than snow. ⁸Oh, give me back my joy again; you have broken me—now let me rejoice.

⁹Don't keep looking at my sins. Remove the stain of my guilt. ¹⁰Create in me a clean heart, O God. Renew a loyal spirit within me. ¹¹Do not banish me from your presence, and don't take your Holy Spirit from me.

¹²Restore to me the joy of your salvation, and make me willing to obey you. ¹³Then I will teach your ways to rebels, and they will return to you. ¹⁴Forgive me for shedding blood, O God who saves; then I will joyfully sing of your forgiveness.

¹⁸Look with favor on Zion and help her; rebuild the walls of Jerusalem. ¹⁹Then you will be pleased with sacrifices offered in the right spirit—with burnt offerings and whole burnt offerings. Then bulls will again be sacrificed on your altar.

~ Psalm 51:3-14, 18-19

God Counts Your Tears

In times of fear and sadness you can confidently hold fast to God's promises. He sees your afflictions and He keeps account of your tears. He saves you from death so that you can live in His light for the rest of your life.

³But when I am afraid, I will put my trust in you. ⁴I praise God for what he has promised. I trust in God, so why should I be afraid? What can mere mortals do to me?

⁸You keep track of all my sorrows. You have collected all my tears in your bottle. You have recorded each one in your book.

⁹My enemies will retreat when I call to you for help. This I know: God is on my side!

¹⁰I praise God for what he has promised; Yes, I praise the LORD for what he has promised. ¹¹I trust in God, so why should I be afraid? What can mere mortals do to me?

¹²I will fulfill my vows to you, O God, and will offer a sacrifice of thanks for your help. ¹³For you have rescued me from death; you have kept my feet from slipping. So now I can walk in your presence, O God, in your life-giving light.

~ Psalm 56:3-4, 8-13

God's Love Is Better than Life

It is good to yearn for God's presence, because His love for you is better than life itself. Think back on all the times in the past when He helped you and praise Him for it! Stay in the shadow of His wings.

[1] O God, you are my God; I earnestly search for you. My soul thirsts for you; my whole body longs for you in this parched and weary land where there is no water.

[2] I have seen you in your sanctuary and gazed upon your power and glory. [3] Your unfailing love is better than life itself; how I praise you!

[4] I will praise you as long as I live, lifting up my hands to you in prayer. [5] You satisfy me more than the richest feast. I will praise you with songs of joy.

[6] I lie awake thinking of you, meditating on you through the night. [7] Because you are my helper, I sing for joy in the shadow of your wings. [8] I cling to you; your strong right hand holds me securely.

[9] But those plotting to destroy me will come to ruin. They will go down into the depths of the earth. [10] They will die by the sword and become the food of jackals. [11] But the king will rejoice in God. All who trust in him will praise him, while liars will be silenced.

~ Psalm 63:1-11

God Is with You in Your Old Age

The older you get, the more you lose – either through death, or through the deterioration that comes with age. But you can never lose God. Because He stays with you, even in your old age, you can still be a miracle to many.

¹O LORD, I have come to you for protection; don't let me be disgraced. ²Save me and rescue me, for you do what is right. Turn your ear to listen to me, and set me free. ³Be my rock of safety where I can always hide. Give the order to save me, for you are my rock and my fortress.

⁵O Lord, you alone are my hope. I've trusted you, O LORD, from childhood. ⁶Yes, you have been with me from birth; from my mother's womb you have cared for me. No wonder I am always praising you!

⁷My life is an example to many, because you have been my strength and protection. ⁸That is why I can never stop praising you; I declare your glory all day long. ⁹And now, in my old age, don't set me aside. Don't abandon me when my strength is failing.

¹⁷O God, you have taught me from my earliest childhood, and I constantly tell others about the wonderful things you do. ¹⁸Now that I am old and gray, do not abandon me, O God. Let me proclaim your power to this new generation, your mighty miracles to all who come after me.

¹⁹Your righteousness, O God, reaches to the highest heavens. You have done such wonderful things. Who can compare with you, O God?

²³I will shout for joy and sing your praises, for you have ransomed me. ²⁴I will tell about your righteous deeds all day long, for everyone who tried to hurt me has been shamed and humiliated.

~ Psalm 71:1-3, 5-9, 17-19, 23-24

Remember What God Has Done

Although the psalmist prays to God, he receives no comfort. Then he remembers everything that God has done for him in the past. He realizes that God is the only God who can perform miracles, and the only God who guides and protects His people. God wants to do the same for you.

¹I cry out to God; yes, I shout. Oh, that God would listen to me! ²When I was in deep trouble, I searched for the Lord. All night long I prayed, with hands lifted toward heaven, but my soul was not comforted. ³I think of God, and I moan, overwhelmed with longing for his help.

⁴You don't let me sleep. I am too distressed even to pray! ⁵I think of the good old days, long since ended, ⁶when my nights were filled with joyful songs. I search my soul and ponder the difference now. ⁷Has the Lord rejected me forever? Will he never again be kind to me? ⁸Is his unfailing love gone forever? Have his promises permanently failed?

¹⁰And I said, "This is my fate; the Most High has turned his hand against me." ¹¹But then I recall all you have done, O LORD; I remember your wonderful deeds of long ago. ¹²They are constantly in my thoughts. I cannot stop thinking about your mighty works. ¹⁴You are the God of great wonders! You demonstrate your awesome power among the nations. ¹⁵By your strong arm, you redeemed your people.

¹⁶When the Red Sea saw you, O God, its waters looked and trembled! The sea quaked to its very depths. ¹⁸Your thunder roared from the whirlwind; the lightning lit up the world! The earth trembled and shook. ¹⁹Your road led through the sea, your pathway through the mighty waters—a pathway no one knew was there! ²⁰You led your people along that road like a flock of sheep, with Moses and Aaron as their shepherds.

~ Psalm 77:1-8, 10-12, 14-16, 18-20

Live Wisely

The life expectancy of most people is approximately seventy years, and that life is often filled with adversity. Even your best years are filled with hardship and sorrow and your sins lie bare before God. Ask Him to teach you how to use your days right so that you can receive wisdom.

¹Lord, through all the generations you have been our home! ²Before the mountains were born, before you gave birth to the earth and the world, from beginning to end, you are God.

⁴For you, a thousand years are as a passing day, as brief as a few night hours. ⁵You sweep people away like dreams that disappear. They are like grass that springs up in the morning. ⁶In the morning it blooms and flourishes, but by evening it is dry and withered.

⁷We wither beneath your anger; we are overwhelmed by your fury. ⁸You spread out our sins before you—our secret sins—and you see them all. ⁹We live our lives beneath your wrath, ending our years with a groan.

¹⁰Seventy years are given to us! Some even live to eighty. But even the best years are filled with pain and trouble; soon they disappear, and we fly away. ¹¹Who can comprehend the power of your anger? Your wrath is as awesome as the fear you deserve. ¹²Teach us to realize the brevity of life, so that we may grow in wisdom.

¹⁴Satisfy us each morning with your unfailing love, so we may sing for joy to the end of our lives. ¹⁵Give us gladness in proportion to our former misery! Replace the evil years with good.

~ Psalm 90:1-2, 4-12, 14-15

Your Guardian Angel

God is your Refuge and Protector against danger. Because He is with you, you are safe even in the midst of danger. He will command His angels to protect you so that you won't even hurt your foot on a stone. He will deliver you if you acknowledge His name.

¹Those who live in the shelter of the Most High will find rest in the shadow of the Almighty. ²This I declare about the LORD: He alone is my refuge, my place of safety; he is my God, and I trust him. ³For he will rescue you from every trap and protect you from deadly disease.

⁴He will cover you with his feathers. He will shelter you with his wings. His faithful promises are your armor and protection. ⁵Do not be afraid of the terrors of the night, nor the arrow that flies in the day.

⁶Do not dread the disease that stalks in darkness, nor the disaster that strikes at midday. ⁷Though a thousand fall at your side, though ten thousand are dying around you, these evils will not touch you.

⁹If you make the LORD your refuge, if you make the Most High your shelter, ¹⁰no evil will conquer you; no plague will come near your home. ¹¹For he will order his angels to protect you wherever you go. ¹²They will hold you up with their hands so you won't even hurt your foot on a stone. ¹³You will trample upon lions and cobras; you will crush fierce lions and serpents under your feet!

¹⁴The LORD says, "I will rescue those who love me. I will protect those who trust in my name. ¹⁵When they call on me, I will answer; I will be with them in trouble. I will rescue and honor them. ¹⁶I will reward them with a long life and give them my salvation."

~ Psalm 91:1-7, 9-16

Serve God with Joy

Everyone on earth needs to rejoice in God's honor and serve Him joyfully. Acknowledge that He created you and that you belong to Him. Thank Him and praise His name for as long as you live, because His faithful love endures forever.

[1]Shout with joy to the LORD, all the earth! [2]Worship the LORD with gladness. Come before him, singing with joy.

[3]Acknowledge that the LORD is God! He made us, and we are his. We are his people, the sheep of his pasture.

[4]Enter his gates with thanksgiving; go into his courts with praise. Give thanks to him and praise his name.

[5]For the LORD is good. His unfailing love continues forever, and his faithfulness continues to each generation.

~ Psalm 100

Praise the Lord

Praise the Lord and remember His wonderful deeds. He forgives sin and heals the sick. He delivers you from death, crowns you with love and compassion, and fills your life with good things. To Him be all the praise!

¹Let all that I am praise the LORD; with my whole heart, I will praise his holy name. ²Let all that I am praise the LORD; may I never forget the good things he does for me. ³He forgives all my sins and heals all my diseases. ⁴He redeems me from death and crowns me with love and tender mercies. ⁵He fills my life with good things. My youth is renewed like the eagle's!

⁶The LORD gives righteousness and justice to all who are treated unfairly.

⁸The LORD is compassionate and merciful, slow to get angry and filled with unfailing love. ⁹He will not constantly accuse us, nor remain angry forever. ¹⁰He does not punish us for all our sins; he does not deal harshly with us, as we deserve.

¹¹For his unfailing love toward those who fear him is as great as the height of the heavens above the earth. ¹²He has removed our sins as far from us as the east is from the west.

¹⁵Our days on earth are like grass; like wildflowers, we bloom and die. ¹⁶The wind blows, and we are gone—as though we had never been here. ¹⁷But the love of the LORD remains forever with those who fear him. His salvation extends to the children's children ¹⁸of those who are faithful to his covenant, of those who obey his commandments!

²²Praise the LORD, everything he has created, everything in all his kingdom. Let all that I am praise the LORD.

~ Psalm 103:1-6, 8-12, 15-18, 22

Meditate on God's Wonderful Deeds

God's acts of creation are great and wonderful. Everyone who delights in them should meditate on them. The Lord's deeds are glorious and majestic, and His faithfulness endures forever. Everything that He does is right and good, and all His instructions are trustworthy.

¹Praise the LORD! I will thank the LORD with all my heart as I meet with his godly people. ²How amazing are the deeds of the LORD! All who delight in him should ponder them.

³Everything he does reveals his glory and majesty. His righteousness never fails. ⁴He causes us to remember his wonderful works. How gracious and merciful is our LORD!

⁵He gives food to those who fear him; he always remembers his covenant. ⁶He has shown his great power to his people by giving them the lands of other nations.

⁷All he does is just and good, and all his commandments are trustworthy. ⁸They are forever true, to be obeyed faithfully and with integrity.

⁹He has paid a full ransom for his people. He has guaranteed his covenant with them forever. What a holy, awe-inspiring name he has! ¹⁰Fear of the LORD is the foundation of true wisdom. All who obey his commandments will grow in wisdom. Praise him forever!

~ Psalm 111

The Day That the Lord Has Made

This is the day that the Lord has made. Make use of every second, enjoy it, rejoice in it, and be glad about it! God shines His light on you. Be thankful toward God because He is good, and His goodness endures forever.

[1]Give thanks to the LORD, for he is good! His faithful love endures forever.

[5]In my distress I prayed to the LORD, and the LORD answered me and set me free.

[6]The LORD is for me, so I will have no fear. What can mere people do to me?

[7]Yes, the LORD is for me; he will help me. I will look in triumph at those who hate me. [8]It is better to take refuge in the LORD than to trust in people. [9]It is better to take refuge in the LORD than to trust in princes.

[14]The LORD is my strength and my song; he has given me victory. [15]Songs of joy and victory are sung in the camp of the godly. The strong right arm of the LORD has done glorious things! [23]This is the LORD's doing, and it is wonderful to see. [24]This is the day the LORD has made. We will rejoice and be glad in it.

[29]Give thanks to the LORD, for he is good! His faithful love endures forever.

~ Psalm 118:1, 5-9, 14-15, 23-24, 29

The Treasure of God's Word

God's commandments should be a song to you during your earthly pilgrimage. Meditate on each commandment and obey them all. The Lord's Word is a lamp for your feet, and a light for your path. Be as glad about it as someone who has discovered a treasure.

[4]You have charged us to keep your commandments carefully.

[9]How can a young person stay pure? By obeying your word.

[33]Teach me your decrees, O Lord; I will keep them to the end. [34]Give me understanding and I will obey your instructions; I will put them into practice with all my heart. [35]Make me walk along the path of your commands, for that is where my happiness is found.

[54]Your decrees have been the theme of my songs wherever I have lived.

[55]I reflect at night on who you are, O Lord; therefore, I obey your instructions.

[105]Your word is a lamp to guide my feet and a light for my path.

[112]I am determined to keep your decrees to the very end.

[130]The teaching of your word gives light, so even the simple can understand.

[162]I rejoice in your word like one who discovers a great treasure.

~ Psalm 119:4, 9, 33-35, 54-55, 105, 112, 130, 162

God Is Your Protector

God is always there to protect you; your help comes from Him. He keeps you from dangers and protects your life. He is always available because He never sleeps. He guards you – now and forevermore.

¹I look up to the mountains—does my help come from there? ²My help comes from the LORD, who made heaven and earth!

³He will not let you stumble; the one who watches over you will not slumber. ⁴Indeed, he who watches over Israel never slumbers or sleeps.

⁵The LORD himself watches over you! The LORD stands beside you as your protective shade. ⁶The sun will not harm you by day, nor the moon at night.

⁷The LORD keeps you from all harm and watches over your life. ⁸The LORD keeps watch over you as you come and go, both now and forever.

~ Psalm 121

God Changes Your Destiny

When God brought His people back to Jerusalem, it felt like a dream to them. They sang for joy, and the other nations saw that God did great things for them. God permanently changed their life course – and yours too – through Christ's crucifixion.

¹When the LORD brought back his exiles to Jerusalem, it was like a dream!

²We were filled with laughter, and we sang for joy. And the other nations said, "What amazing things the LORD has done for them." ³Yes, the LORD has done amazing things for us! What joy!

⁴Restore our fortunes, LORD, as streams renew the desert. ⁵Those who plant in tears will harvest with shouts of joy. ⁶They weep as they go to plant their seed, but they sing as they return with the harvest.

~ Psalm 126

Unless the Lord
Builds the House ...

Without God's blessing everything we do is in vain. Without God, parents can't raise their children properly, and all their hard work is wasted. Children are a gift from God, and blessed are those who receive them.

¹Unless the LORD builds a house, the work of the builders is wasted. Unless the LORD protects a city, guarding it with sentries will do no good.

²It is useless for you to work so hard from early morning until late at night, anxiously working for food to eat; for God gives rest to his loved ones.

³Children are a gift from the LORD; they are a reward from him. ⁴Children born to a young man are like arrows in a warrior's hands.

⁵How joyful is the man whose quiver is full of them! He will not be put to shame when he confronts his accusers at the city gates.

~ Psalm 127

God's Blessing

Psalm 128 teaches us that we have to serve God wholeheartedly if we want to experience His blessing. As the psalmist did in this Jewish benediction, we also acknowledge God as the Giver of all good things.

¹How joyful are those who fear the LORD—all who follow his ways! ²You will enjoy the fruit of your labor. How joyful and prosperous you will be!

³Your wife will be like a fruitful grapevine, flourishing within your home. Your children will be like vigorous young olive trees as they sit around your table. ⁴That is the LORD's blessing for those who fear him.

⁵May the LORD continually bless you from Zion. May you see Jerusalem prosper as long as you live. ⁶May you live to enjoy your grandchildren. May Israel have peace!

~ Psalm 128

Wait on the Lord

Be willing to wait on God in difficult situations. He forgives your sins, and you can place your hope in Him because He loves you. Stop worrying about things that you can do nothing about. The Lord will give you comfort and rest, like a baby in its mother's arms.

130¹From the depths of despair, O LORD, I call for your help. ²Hear my cry, O Lord. Pay attention to my prayer.

³LORD, if you kept a record of our sins, who, O Lord, could ever survive? ⁴But you offer forgiveness, that we might learn to fear you.

⁵I am counting on the LORD; yes, I am counting on him. I have put my hope in his word. ⁶I long for the Lord more than sentries long for the dawn, yes, more than sentries long for the dawn.

⁷O Israel, hope in the LORD; for with the LORD there is unfailing love. His redemption overflows. ⁸He himself will redeem Israel from every kind of sin.

131¹LORD, my heart is not proud; my eyes are not haughty. I don't concern myself with matters too great or too awesome for me to grasp.

²Instead, I have calmed and quieted myself, like a weaned child who no longer cries for its mother's milk. Yes, like a weaned child is my soul within me.

³O Israel, put your hope in the LORD—now and always.

~ Psalm 130; 131

Wonderfully Made

God knows everything about you – He knows what you are busy with, where you are in your life and what you think. He controls your life. You were fearfully and wonderfully made. God saw your unformed body long before your birth. All the days of your life are written in God's Book of Life.

¹O LORD, you have examined my heart and know everything about me. ²You know when I sit down or stand up. You know my thoughts even when I'm far away. ³You see me when I travel and when I rest at home. You know everything I do.

⁴You know what I am going to say before I say it, LORD. ⁵You go before me and follow me. You place your hand of blessing on my head. ⁶Such knowledge is too wonderful for me, too great for me to understand!

¹³You made all the delicate, inner parts of my body and knit me together in my mother's womb. ¹⁴Thank you for making me so wonderfully complex! Your workmanship is marvelous—how well I know it. ¹⁵You watched me as I was being formed in utter seclusion, as I was woven together in the dark of the womb. ¹⁶You saw me before I was born. Every day of my life was recorded in your book. Every moment was laid out before a single day had passed.

¹⁷How precious are your thoughts about me, O God. They cannot be numbered! ¹⁸I can't even count them; they outnumber the grains of sand! And when I wake up, you are still with me!

²³Search me, O God, and know my heart; test me and know my anxious thoughts. ²⁴Point out anything in me that offends you, and lead me along the path of everlasting life.

~ Psalm 139:1-6, 13-18, 23-24

May

Guard Your Tongue

God hears you when you call on Him. He accepts your prayers like a fragrant offering. Ask Him to guard your words and protect you against wrong desires. Fix your eyes on Him, because He is your safe refuge.

[1]O Lord, I am calling to you. Please hurry! Listen when I cry to you for help! [2]Accept my prayer as incense offered to you, and my upraised hands as an evening offering.

[3]Take control of what I say, O Lord, and guard my lips. [4]Don't let me drift toward evil or take part in acts of wickedness. Don't let me share in the delicacies of those who do wrong.

[5]Let the godly strike me! It will be a kindness! If they correct me, it is soothing medicine. Don't let me refuse it. But I pray constantly against the wicked and their deeds. [6]When their leaders are thrown down from a cliff, the wicked will listen to my words and find them true. [7]Like rocks brought up by a plow, the bones of the wicked will lie scattered without burial.

[8]I look to you for help, O Sovereign Lord. You are my refuge; don't let them kill me. [9]Keep me from the traps they have set for me, from the snares of those who do wrong.

[10]Let the wicked fall into their own nets, but let me escape.

~ Psalm 141

When You've Lost All Hope

Like the psalmist, you too can talk to God when you feel discouraged. Every morning He wants to tell you about His love and show you which road you should take. He will teach you to do His will so that you can live to glorify His name.

[1]Hear my prayer, O LORD; listen to my plea! Answer me because you are faithful and righteous. [2]Don't put your servant on trial, for no one is innocent before you.

[3]My enemy has chased me. He has knocked me to the ground and forces me to live in darkness like those in the grave.

[4]I am losing all hope; I am paralyzed with fear. [5]I remember the days of old. I ponder all your great works and think about what you have done. [6]I lift my hands to you in prayer. I thirst for you as parched land thirsts for rain.

[7]Come quickly, LORD, and answer me, for my depression deepens. Don't turn away from me, or I will die. [8]Let me hear of your unfailing love each morning, for I am trusting you. Show me where to walk, for I give myself to you.

[9]Rescue me from my enemies, LORD; I run to you to hide me. [10]Teach me to do your will, for you are my God. May your gracious Spirit lead me forward on a firm footing.

[11]For the glory of your name, O LORD, preserve my life. Because of your faithfulness, bring me out of this distress. [12]In your unfailing love, silence all my enemies and destroy all my foes, for I am your servant.

~ Psalm 143

Let Everything That Has Breath Praise God!

The whole of creation is summoned to give God praise: in His sanctuary, in His house, and under the heavens. Let us praise Him for His mighty deeds and infinite greatness. Praise Him with the sound of musical instruments. Let everything that has breath praise God together!

¹Praise the LORD! Praise God in his sanctuary; praise him in his mighty heaven! ²Praise him for his mighty works; praise his unequaled greatness!

³Praise him with a blast of the ram's horn; praise him with the lyre and harp! ⁴Praise him with the tambourine and dancing; praise him with strings and flutes!

⁵Praise him with a clash of cymbals; praise him with loud clanging cymbals. ⁶Let everything that breathes sing praises to the LORD! Praise the LORD!

~ Psalm 150

Where Wisdom Begins

Reverence for the Lord is the beginning of wisdom. Make an effort to understand this. Then you will know what it means to respect and know God. He grants wisdom – the kind of wisdom that will keep you from going the wrong way.

1 ⁷Fear of the Lord is the foundation of true knowledge, but fools despise wisdom and discipline.

2 ¹My child, listen to what I say, and treasure my commands. ²Tune your ears to wisdom, and concentrate on understanding. ³Cry out for insight, and ask for understanding.

⁴Search for them as you would for silver; seek them like hidden treasures. ⁵Then you will understand what it means to fear the Lord, and you will gain knowledge of God. ⁶For the Lord grants wisdom! From his mouth come knowledge and understanding.

⁹Then you will understand what is right, just, and fair, and you will find the right way to go. ¹⁰For wisdom will enter your heart, and knowledge will fill you with joy. ¹¹Wise choices will watch over you. Understanding will keep you safe.

¹²Wisdom will save you from evil people, from those whose words are twisted.

~ Proverbs 1:7; 2:1-6, 9-12

Cherish God's Commandments

Hold on to God's commandments, and you will live a full life. Put all your trust in Him, and don't rely on your own insight. Ask for His will in all that you do so that He can bless you and show you the path of life.

[1]My child, never forget the things I have taught you. Store my commands in your heart. [2]If you do this, you will live many years, and your life will be satisfying.

[3]Never let loyalty and kindness leave you! Tie them around your neck as a reminder. Write them deep within your heart. [4]Then you will find favor with both God and people, and you will earn a good reputation.

[5]Trust in the Lord with all your heart; do not depend on your own understanding. [6]Seek his will in all you do, and he will show you which path to take.

[7]Don't be impressed with your own wisdom. Instead, fear the Lord and turn away from evil. [8]Then you will have healing for your body and strength for your bones.

[9]Honor the Lord with your wealth and with the best part of everything you produce. [10]Then he will fill your barns with grain, and your vats will overflow with good wine.

[21]My child, don't lose sight of common sense and discernment. Hang on to them, [22]for they will refresh your soul. They are like jewels on a necklace.

~ Proverbs 3:1-10, 21-22

Search for Wisdom

If you are able to help someone, do it immediately. Search for wisdom and value it. Then it will bring you honor and crown you with prosperity. God will teach you about wisdom and guide you on the right road. Hold on to it, because it will enrich your life.

3 25You need not be afraid of sudden disaster or the destruction that comes upon the wicked, 26for the LORD is your security. He will keep your foot from being caught in a trap.

27Do not withhold good from those who deserve it when it's in your power to help them. 28If you can help your neighbor now, don't say, "Come back tomorrow, and then I'll help you."

29Don't plot harm against your neighbor, for those who live nearby trust you. 30Don't pick a fight without reason, when no one has done you harm.

31Don't envy violent people or copy their ways.

4 4My father taught me, "Take my words to heart. Follow my commands, and you will live. 5Get wisdom; develop good judgment. Don't forget my words or turn away from them. 6Don't turn your back on wisdom, for she will protect you. Love her, and she will guard you.

7"Getting wisdom is the wisest thing you can do! And whatever else you do, develop good judgment. 8If you prize wisdom, she will make you great. Embrace her, and she will honor you. 9She will place a lovely wreath on your head; she will present you with a beautiful crown."

10My child, listen to me and do as I say, and you will have a long, good life. 11I will teach you wisdom's ways and lead you in straight paths. 12When you walk, you won't be held back; when you run, you won't stumble.

~ Proverbs 3:25-31; 4:4-12

The Right Roadmap

Righteous people walk their road of life in the light, while the road that ungodly people walk is pitch dark. Be careful of what goes on in your heart, because your thoughts determine your actions. Do not deviate from what is right, and try to stay away from what is wrong.

[13]Take hold of my instructions; don't let them go. Guard them, for they are the key to life.

[18]The way of the righteous is like the first gleam of dawn, which shines ever brighter until the full light of day. [19]But the way of the wicked is like total darkness. They have no idea what they are stumbling over.

[20]My child, pay attention to what I say. Listen carefully to my words. [21]Don't lose sight of them. Let them penetrate deep into your heart, [22]for they bring life to those who find them, and healing to their whole body.

[23]Guard your heart above all else, for it determines the course of your life. [24]Avoid all perverse talk; stay away from corrupt speech.

[25]Look straight ahead, and fix your eyes on what lies before you. [26]Mark out a straight path for your feet; stay on the safe path. [27]Don't get sidetracked; keep your feet from following evil.

~ Proverbs 4:13, 18-27

Words of Wisdom

Kindness has a calming effect. Happiness shows on your face, while sadness makes you miserable. Think first, and act later. Speak the right words at the right time. Sparkly eyes bring joy, and good news brings good health. Don't ignore timely advice.

[1]A gentle answer deflects anger, but harsh words make tempers flare. [2]The tongue of the wise makes knowledge appealing, but the mouth of a fool belches out foolishness.

[3]The LORD is watching everywhere, keeping his eye on both the evil and the good. [4]Gentle words are a tree of life; a deceitful tongue crushes the spirit.

[13]A glad heart makes a happy face; a broken heart crushes the spirit.

[22]Plans go wrong for lack of advice; many advisers bring success. [23]Everyone enjoys a fitting reply; it is wonderful to say the right thing at the right time!

[26]The LORD detests evil plans, but he delights in pure words.

[28]The heart of the godly thinks carefully before speaking; the mouth of the wicked overflows with evil words.

[30]A cheerful look brings joy to the heart; good news makes for good health. [31]If you listen to constructive criticism, you will be at home among the wise.

[32]If you reject discipline, you only harm yourself; but if you listen to correction, you grow in understanding. [33]Fear of the LORD teaches wisdom; humility precedes honor.

~ Proverbs 15:1-4, 13, 22-23, 26, 28, 30-33

God has the Last Say

People can make their own plans, but God always has the last say. You can plan your course, but in the end God determines your destination. To gain wisdom is better than gaining silver. Each person who trusts in the Lord will prosper.

¹We can make our own plans, but the LORD gives the right answer. ²People may be pure in their own eyes, but the LORD examines their motives.

³Commit your actions to the LORD, and your plans will succeed. ⁴The LORD has made everything for his own purposes, even the wicked for a day of disaster.

⁵The LORD detests the proud; they will surely be punished. ⁶Unfailing love and faithfulness make atonement for sin. By fearing the LORD, people avoid evil. ⁷When people's lives please the LORD, even their enemies are at peace with them.

⁹We can make our plans, but the LORD determines our steps.

¹⁶How much better to get wisdom than gold, and good judgment than silver!

²⁰Those who listen to instruction will prosper; those who trust the LORD will be joyful.

²⁴Kind words are like honey—sweet to the soul and healthy for the body.

~ Proverbs 16:1-7, 9, 16, 20, 24

Words to Learn From

Silver and gold are purified in fire, but God tests people's hearts. Grandchildren are like a king's crown to grandparents. Someone who knows a lot, doesn't air his or her knowledge. A cheerful person is good for one's health. A fool talks himself into trouble.

16³¹Gray hair is a crown of glory; it is gained by living a godly life. ³²Better to be patient than powerful; better to have self-control than to conquer a city.

17³Fire tests the purity of silver and gold, but the LORD tests the heart.

⁶Grandchildren are the crowning glory of the aged; parents are the pride of their children.

¹⁷A friend is always loyal, and a brother is born to help in time of need.

²²A cheerful heart is good medicine, but a broken spirit saps a person's strength.

²⁷A truly wise person uses few words; a person with understanding is even-tempered.

18⁶Fools' words get them into constant quarrels; they are asking for a beating. ⁷The mouths of fools are their ruin; they trap themselves with their lips.

⁸Rumors are dainty morsels that sink deep into one's heart. ⁹A lazy person is as bad as someone who destroys things. ¹⁰The name of the LORD is a strong fortress; the godly run to him and are safe.

²¹The tongue can bring death or life; those who love to talk will reap the consequences.

²⁴There are "friends" who destroy each other, but a real friend sticks closer than a brother.

~ Proverbs 16:31-32; 17:3, 6, 17, 22, 27; 18:6-10, 21, 24

The Characteristics of a Noble Woman

A noble woman is more precious than gemstones. Her husband can rely on her and benefits from her work. She has inner strength, speaks with words of wisdom, and gives with love. Beauty is fleeting, but a woman who serves the Lord will always stay beautiful, inside and out.

¹⁰Who can find a virtuous and capable wife? She is more precious than rubies. ¹¹Her husband can trust her, and she will greatly enrich his life. ¹²She brings him good, not harm, all the days of her life.

¹³She finds wool and flax and busily spins it. ¹⁴She is like a merchant's ship, bringing her food from afar. ¹⁵She gets up before dawn to prepare breakfast for her household and plan the day's work for her servant girls.

¹⁶She goes to inspect a field and buys it; with her earnings she plants a vineyard. ¹⁷She is energetic and strong, a hard worker. ¹⁸She makes sure her dealings are profitable; her lamp burns late into the night.

¹⁹Her hands are busy spinning thread, her fingers twisting fiber. ²⁰She extends a helping hand to the poor and opens her arms to the needy.

²⁶When she speaks, her words are wise, and she gives instructions with kindness. ²⁷She carefully watches everything in her household and suffers nothing from laziness.

²⁸Her children stand and bless her. Her husband praises her: ²⁹"There are many virtuous and capable women in the world, but you surpass them all!"

³⁰Charm is deceptive, and beauty does not last; but a woman who fears the Lord will be greatly praised.

~ Proverbs 31:10-20, 26-30

God's Gift of Life

Sometimes we agree with the author of Ecclesiastes that life is without purpose, because it seems that our hard work leads to nothing. But it is a gift from God to enjoy the good things in life despite suffering. Without God, nothing in life can be truly enjoyed.

[17]So I came to hate life because everything done here under the sun is so troubling. Everything is meaningless—like chasing the wind.

[18]I came to hate all my hard work here on earth, for I must leave to others everything I have earned. [19]And who can tell whether my successors will be wise or foolish? Yet they will control everything I have gained by my skill and hard work under the sun. How meaningless! [20]So I gave up in despair, questioning the value of all my hard work in this world.

[21]Some people work wisely with knowledge and skill, then must leave the fruit of their efforts to someone who hasn't worked for it. This, too, is meaningless, a great tragedy. [22]So what do people get in this life for all their hard work and anxiety? [23]Their days of labor are filled with pain and grief; even at night their minds cannot rest. It is all meaningless.

[24]So I decided there is nothing better than to enjoy food and drink and to find satisfaction in work. Then I realized that these pleasures are from the hand of God. [25]For who can eat or enjoy anything apart from him? [26]God gives wisdom, knowledge, and joy to those who please him. But if a sinner becomes wealthy, God takes the wealth away and gives it to those who please him. This, too, is meaningless—like chasing the wind.

~ Ecclesiastes 2:17-26

A Vision of Eternity

The author of Ecclesiastes observed that there is a set time for everything under the sun. God created the world perfectly and exquisitely, and gave us a vision of eternity so that we can honor Him.

[1]For everything there is a season, a time for every activity under heaven. [2]A time to be born and a time to die. A time to plant and a time to harvest. [3]A time to kill and a time to heal. A time to tear down and a time to build up.

[8]A time to love and a time to hate. A time for war and a time for peace.

[9]What do people really get for all their hard work? [10]I have seen the burden God has placed on us all. [11]Yet God has made everything beautiful for its own time. He has planted eternity in the human heart, but even so, people cannot see the whole scope of God's work from beginning to end.

[12]So I concluded there is nothing better than to be happy and enjoy ourselves as long as we can. [13]And people should eat and drink and enjoy the fruits of their labor, for these are gifts from God.

[14]And I know that whatever God does is final. Nothing can be added to it or taken from it. God's purpose is that people should fear him. [15]What is happening now has happened before, and what will happen in the future has happened before, because God makes the same things happen over and over again.

~ Ecclesiastes 3:1-3, 8-15

Do What You Have Promised

Many women speak too quickly and easily. In the process we make promises to people – and also to God – that we can't keep. God asks you to do what you have promised.

4⁹Two people are better off than one, for they can help each other succeed. ¹⁰If one person falls, the other can reach out and help. But someone who falls alone is in real trouble.

¹¹Likewise, two people lying close together can keep each other warm. But how can one be warm alone? ¹²A person standing alone can be attacked and defeated, but two can stand back-to-back and conquer. Three are even better, for a triple-braided cord is not easily broken.

5¹As you enter the house of God, keep your ears open and your mouth shut. It is evil to make mindless offerings to God. ²Don't make rash promises, and don't be hasty in bringing matters before God. After all, God is in heaven, and you are here on earth. So let your words be few.

³Too much activity gives you restless dreams; too many words make you a fool. ⁴When you make a promise to God, don't delay in following through, for God takes no pleasure in fools. Keep all the promises you make to him.

⁶Don't let your mouth make you sin. And don't defend yourself by telling the Temple messenger that the promise you made was a mistake. That would make God angry, and he might wipe out everything you have achieved.

~ Ecclesiastes 4:9-12; 5:1-4, 6

Live Happily!

Everything on earth is fleeting. Therefore, God's children should focus on living joyfully. Be happy with your share of life, and enjoy it with your spouse. Be devoted to everything you do, for as long as you can.

[1]This, too, I carefully explored: Even though the actions of godly and wise people are in God's hands, no one knows whether God will show them favor.

[3]It seems so tragic that everyone under the sun suffers the same fate. That is why people are not more careful to be good. Instead, they choose their own mad course, for they have no hope. There is nothing ahead but death anyway.

[4]There is hope only for the living. As they say, "It's better to be a live dog than a dead lion!" [5]The living at least know they will die, but the dead know nothing. They have no further reward, nor are they remembered.

[6]Whatever they did in their lifetime—loving, hating, envying—is all long gone. They no longer play a part in anything here on earth. [7]So go ahead. Eat your food with joy, and drink your wine with a happy heart, for God approves of this! [8]Wear fine clothes, with a splash of cologne!

[9]Live happily with the woman you love through all the meaningless days of life that God has given you under the sun. The wife God gives you is your reward for all your earthly toil.

[10]Whatever you do, do well. For when you go to the grave, there will be no work or planning or knowledge or wisdom.

~ Ecclesiastes 9:1, 3-10

God's Work Is Incomprehensible

God's children often experience incomprehensible things. God is so great that we will never be able to understand His works. But, because He loves us, we can have confidence in Him and enjoy the life that He has given us.

[1]Send your grain across the seas, and in time, profits will flow back to you. [2]But divide your investments among many places, for you do not know what risks might lie ahead.

[3]When clouds are heavy, the rains come down. Whether a tree falls north or south, it stays where it falls.

[4]Farmers who wait for perfect weather never plant. If they watch every cloud, they never harvest.

[5]Just as you cannot understand the path of the wind or the mystery of a tiny baby growing in its mother's womb, so you cannot understand the activity of God, who does all things.

[7]Light is sweet; how pleasant to see a new day dawning. [8]When people live to be very old, let them rejoice in every day of life. But let them also remember there will be many dark days. Everything still to come is meaningless.

[9]Young people, it's wonderful to be young! Enjoy every minute of it. Do everything you want to do; take it all in. But remember that you must give an account to God for everything you do.

[10]So refuse to worry, and keep your body healthy. But remember that youth, with a whole life before you, is meaningless.

~ Ecclesiastes 11:1-5, 7-10

The End of Everything

The author of Ecclesiastes endeavored to faithfully record God's truth. He came to the conclusion that the most important thing of all is to serve God and to obey His commands.

¹Don't let the excitement of youth cause you to forget your Creator. Honor him in your youth before you grow old and say, "Life is not pleasant anymore." ²Remember him before the light of the sun, moon, and stars is dim to your old eyes, and rain clouds continually darken your sky. ³Remember him before your legs—the guards of your house—start to tremble; and before your shoulders—the strong men—stoop. Remember him before your teeth—your few remaining servants—stop grinding; and before your eyes—the women looking through the windows—see dimly.

⁴Remember him before the door to life's opportunities is closed and the sound of work fades. ⁵Remember him before you become fearful of falling and worry about danger in the streets; before your hair turns white like an almond tree in bloom, and you drag along without energy like a dying grasshopper, and the caperberry no longer inspires sexual desire. Remember him before you near the grave, your everlasting home, when the mourners will weep at your funeral. ⁶Remember your Creator now before the silver cord of life snaps and the golden bowl is broken. Don't wait until the water jar is smashed at the spring and the pulley is broken at the well. ⁷For then the dust will return to the earth, and the spirit will return to God who gave it.

⁸"Everything is meaningless," says the Teacher, "completely meaningless." ¹³That's the whole story. Here now is my final conclusion: Fear God and obey his commands, for this is everyone's duty. ¹⁴God will judge us for everything we do, including every secret thing, whether good or bad.

~ Ecclesiastes 12:1-8, 13-14

A Flame of God

Love between a man and a woman is a flame of God. It is as strong as death, with the power of an all-consuming fire. True love can never be extinguished and is never for sale. When you have found love, cherish it with all your heart.

7[10]I am my lover's, and he claims me as his own. [11]Come, my love, let us go out to the fields and spend the night among the wildflowers.

[12]Let us get up early and go to the vineyards to see if the grapevines have budded, if the blossoms have opened, and if the pomegranates have bloomed. There I will give you my love.

[13]There the mandrakes give off their fragrance, and the finest fruits are at our door, new delights as well as old, which I have saved for you, my lover.

8[3]Your left arm would be under my head, and your right arm would embrace me.

[4]Promise me, O women of Jerusalem, not to awaken love until the time is right.

[6]Place me like a seal over your heart, like a seal on your arm. For love is as strong as death, its jealousy as enduring as the grave. Love flashes like fire, the brightest kind of flame.

[7]Many waters cannot quench love, nor can rivers drown it. If a man tried to buy love with all his wealth, his offer would be utterly scorned.

~ Song of Songs 7:10-13; 8:3-4, 6-7

God Removes the Stains of Sin

Although God's people deserted Him, He still offered them His grace. If they returned to Him, He would make their scarlet-red sins as white as snow. Through Christ, God has already paid the price for our sins. You should just have faith, confess your sins, and obey God with gratitude.

²Listen, O heavens! Pay attention, earth! This is what the LORD says: "The children I raised and cared for have rebelled against me. ³Even an ox knows its owner, and a donkey recognizes its master's care—but Israel doesn't know its master. My people don't recognize my care for them.

¹⁵"When you lift up your hands in prayer, I will not look. Though you offer many prayers, I will not listen, for your hands are covered with the blood of innocent victims. ¹⁶Wash yourselves and be clean! Get your sins out of my sight. Give up your evil ways. ¹⁷Learn to do good. Seek justice. Help the oppressed. Defend the cause of orphans. Fight for the rights of widows".

¹⁸"Come now, let's settle this," says the LORD. "Though your sins are like scarlet, I will make them as white as snow. Though they are red like crimson, I will make them as white as wool.

¹⁹"If you will only obey me, you will have plenty to eat. ²⁰But if you turn away and refuse to listen, you will be devoured by the sword of your enemies. I, the LORD, have spoken!"

~ Isaiah 1:2-3, 15-20

Messenger Wanted

Isaiah had a vision of God. In God's presence, Isaiah realized his own sinfulness once again. But when God wanted a messenger, Isaiah immediately offered to go. What about you? Are you willing to proclaim God's message – even if it is only where you live and work?

¹It was in the year King Uzziah died that I saw the Lord. He was sitting on a lofty throne, and the train of his robe filled the Temple. ²Attending him were mighty seraphim, each having six wings. With two wings they covered their faces, with two they covered their feet, and with two they flew. ³They were calling out to each other, "Holy, holy, holy is the LORD of Heaven's Armies! The whole earth is filled with his glory!"

⁴Their voices shook the Temple to its foundations, and the entire building was filled with smoke. ⁵Then I said, "It's all over! I am doomed, for I am a sinful man. I have filthy lips, and I live among a people with filthy lips. Yet I have seen the King, the LORD of Heaven's Armies." ⁶Then one of the seraphim flew to me with a burning coal he had taken from the altar with a pair of tongs. ⁷He touched my lips with it and said, "See, this coal has touched your lips. Now your guilt is removed, and your sins are forgiven." ⁸Then I heard the Lord asking, "Whom should I send as a messenger to this people? Who will go for us?" I said, "Here I am. Send me." ⁹And he said, "Yes, go, and say to this people, 'Listen carefully, but do not understand. Watch closely, but learn nothing.'

¹³"If even a tenth—a remnant—survive, it will be invaded again and burned. But as a terebinth or oak tree leaves a stump when it is cut down, so Israel's stump will be a holy seed."

~ Isaiah 6:1-9, 13

To Us a Child Is Born!

People who lived in the darkness of sin saw a great light. To them a Child was born – a Wonderful Counselor, a Mighty God, an Everlasting Father, Prince of Peace. That Child was also born in order for you to become a child of God.

¹Nevertheless, that time of darkness and despair will not go on forever. The land of Zebulun and Naphtali will be humbled, but there will be a time in the future when Galilee of the Gentiles, which lies along the road that runs between the Jordan and the sea, will be filled with glory.

²The people who walk in darkness will see a great light. For those who live in a land of deep darkness, a light will shine.

³You will enlarge the nation of Israel, and its people will rejoice. They will rejoice before you as people rejoice at the harvest and like warriors dividing the plunder.

⁴For you will break the yoke of their slavery and lift the heavy burden from their shoulders. You will break the oppressor's rod, just as you did when you destroyed the army of Midian. ⁵The boots of the warrior and the uniforms bloodstained by war will all be burned. They will be fuel for the fire.

⁶For a child is born to us, a son is given to us. The government will rest on his shoulders. And he will be called: Wonderful Counselor, Mighty God, Everlasting Father, Prince of Peace.

~ Isaiah 9:1-6

God Prepares a Feast

God promised to bring His people back to their country. He prepared a feast for them so that they would realize that He saved them. God also promises you a feast – He is already busy preparing it in heaven.

[1]O Lord, I will honor and praise your name, for you are my God. You do such wonderful things! You planned them long ago, and now you have accomplished them.

[2]You turn mighty cities into heaps of ruins. Cities with strong walls are turned to rubble. Beautiful palaces in distant lands disappear and will never be rebuilt. [3]Therefore, strong nations will declare your glory; ruthless nations will fear you.

[4]But you are a tower of refuge to the poor, O Lord, a tower of refuge to the needy in distress. You are a refuge from the storm and a shelter from the heat. For the oppressive acts of ruthless people are like a storm beating against a wall, [5]or like the relentless heat of the desert. But you silence the roar of foreign nations. As the shade of a cloud cools relentless heat, so the boastful songs of ruthless people are stilled.

[6]In Jerusalem, the Lord of Heaven's Armies will spread a wonderful feast for all the people of the world. It will be a delicious banquet with clear, well-aged wine and choice meat.

[8]He will swallow up death forever! The Sovereign Lord will wipe away all tears. He will remove forever all insults and mockery against his land and people. The Lord has spoken!

[9]In that day the people will proclaim, "This is our God! We trusted in him, and he saved us! This is the Lord, in whom we trusted. Let us rejoice in the salvation he brings!"

~ Isaiah 25:1-6, 8-9

Be Still and Know

God advised His stubborn people to trust and become quiet before Him. He was eagerly awaiting their return so that He could show them His grace. God's immeasurable grace is always available to you – don't ever doubt that.

[8]Write down these words. Write them in a book. They will stand until the end of time as a witness [9]that these people are stubborn rebels who refuse to pay attention to the Lord's instructions.

[15]The Sovereign Lord, the Holy One of Israel, says: "Only in returning to me and resting in me will you be saved. In quietness and confidence is your strength. But you would have none of it. [16]You said, 'No, we will get our help from Egypt. They will give us swift horses for riding into battle.' But the only swiftness you are going to see is the swiftness of your enemies chasing you! [17]One of them will chase a thousand of you. Five of them will make all of you flee. You will be left like a lonely flagpole on a hill or a tattered banner on a distant mountaintop."

[18]So the Lord must wait for you to come to him so he can show you his love and compassion. For the Lord is a faithful God. Blessed are those who wait for his help. [19]O people of Zion, who live in Jerusalem, you will weep no more. He will be gracious if you ask for help. He will surely respond to the sound of your cries. [20]Though the Lord gave you adversity for food and suffering for drink, he will still be with you to teach you. You will see your teacher with your own eyes. [21]Your own ears will hear him. Right behind you a voice will say, "This is the way you should go," whether to the right or to the left.

[26]The moon will be as bright as the sun, and the sun will be seven times brighter—like the light of seven days in one! So it will be when the Lord begins to heal his people and cure the wounds he gave them.

~ Isaiah 30:8-9, 15-21, 26

Hezekiah Is Healed

When Hezekiah pleaded with God to heal him, God granted his wish. As soon as Hezekiah recovered he noticed – to his amazement – that this hardship did him good. God sometimes sends hardship your way to make you grow more in Him.

¹About that time Hezekiah became deathly ill, and the prophet Isaiah son of Amoz went to visit him. He gave the king this message: "This is what the LORD says: 'Set your affairs in order, for you are going to die. You will not recover from this illness.'"

²When Hezekiah heard this, he turned his face to the wall and prayed to the LORD, ³"Remember, O LORD, how I have always been faithful to you and have served you single-mindedly, always doing what pleases you." Then he broke down and wept bitterly.

⁴Then this message came to Isaiah from the LORD: ⁵"Go back to Hezekiah and tell him, 'This is what the LORD, the God of your ancestor David, says: I have heard your prayer and seen your tears. I will add fifteen years to your life, ⁶and I will rescue you and this city from the king of Assyria. Yes, I will defend this city.

⁷"And this is the sign from the LORD to prove that he will do as he promised: ⁸I will cause the sun's shadow to move ten steps backward on the sundial of Ahaz!'" So the shadow on the sundial moved backward ten steps.

~ Isaiah 38:1-8

Like a Shepherd

God cares for His people like a shepherd cares for his sheep. Although people are as transient as grass, God's Word is solid and He accepts responsibility for His children. He also wants to be a Shepherd to you, and fulfill all your needs.

¹"Comfort, comfort my people," says your God. ²"Speak tenderly to Jerusalem. Tell her that her sad days are gone and her sins are pardoned. Yes, the LORD has punished her twice over for all her sins."

³Listen! It's the voice of someone shouting, "Clear the way through the wilderness for the LORD! Make a straight highway through the wasteland for our God! ⁴Fill in the valleys, and level the mountains and hills. Straighten the curves, and smooth out the rough places. ⁵Then the glory of the LORD will be revealed, and all people will see it together. The LORD has spoken!"

⁶A voice said, "Shout!" I asked, "What should I shout?"

"Shout that people are like the grass. Their beauty fades as quickly as the flowers in a field. ⁷The grass withers and the flowers fade beneath the breath of the LORD. And so it is with people. ⁸The grass withers and the flowers fade, but the word of our God stands forever."

⁹O Zion, messenger of good news, shout from the mountaintops! Shout it louder, O Jerusalem. Shout, and do not be afraid. Tell the towns of Judah, "Your God is coming!" ¹⁰Yes, the Sovereign LORD is coming in power. He will rule with a powerful arm. See, he brings his reward with him as he comes.

¹¹He will feed his flock like a shepherd. He will carry the lambs in his arms, holding them close to his heart. He will gently lead the mother sheep with their young.

~ Isaiah 40:1-11

Nothing Compares to God

God is so great that He can't be compared to anything or anyone. He created the world and formed the universe, and yet He knows you intimately. He promises to renew your strength every day when you grow tired.

[12]Who else has held the oceans in his hand? Who has measured off the heavens with his fingers? Who else knows the weight of the earth or has weighed the mountains and hills on a scale? [13]Who is able to advise the Spirit of the LORD? Who knows enough to give him advice or teach him? [14]Has the LORD ever needed anyone's advice? Does he need instruction about what is good? Did someone teach him what is right or show him the path of justice?

[25]"To whom will you compare me? Who is my equal?" asks the Holy One. [26]Look up into the heavens. Who created all the stars? He brings them out like an army, one after another, calling each by its name. Because of his great power and incomparable strength, not a single one is missing. [27]How can you say the LORD does not see your troubles? How can you say God ignores your rights?

[28]Have you never heard? Have you never understood? The LORD is the everlasting God, the Creator of all the earth. He never grows weak or weary. No one can measure the depths of his understanding. [29]He gives power to the weak and strength to the powerless. [30]Even youths will become weak and tired, and young men will fall in exhaustion. [31]But those who trust in the LORD will find new strength. They will soar high on wings like eagles. They will run and not grow weary. They will walk and not faint.

~ Isaiah 40:12-14, 25-31

God Takes You by the Hand

You don't have to be afraid or worried about any-thing, because God has especially chosen you to be His child. He gives you strength and He helps you. He holds on to you and takes your hand. He hears each one of your prayers.

[8]"But as for you, Israel my servant, Jacob my chosen one, de-scended from Abraham my friend, [9]I have called you back from the ends of the earth, saying, 'You are my servant.' For I have chosen you and will not throw you away. [10]Don't be afraid, for I am with you. Don't be discouraged, for I am your God. I will strengthen you and help you. I will hold you up with my victo-rious right hand.

[11]"See, all your angry enemies lie there, confused and humi-liated. Anyone who opposes you will die and come to nothing. [12]You will look in vain for those who tried to conquer you. Those who attack you will come to nothing. [13]For I hold you by your right hand—I, the LORD your God. And I say to you, 'Don't be afraid. I am here to help you. [14]Though you are a lowly worm, O Jacob, don't be afraid, people of Israel, for I will help you. I am the LORD, your Redeemer. I am the Holy One of Israel.'

[15]"You will be a new threshing instrument with many sharp teeth. You will tear your enemies apart, making chaff of moun-tains.

[16]"You will toss them into the air, and the wind will blow them all away; a whirlwind will scatter them. Then you will rejoice in the LORD. You will glory in the Holy One of Israel.

[17]"When the poor and needy search for water and there is none, and their tongues are parched from thirst, then I, the LORD, will answer them. I, the God of Israel, will never abandon them."

~ Isaiah 41:8-17

Darkness Turns into Light

You worship a wonderful God! This God called you personally, holds on to you, protects you from danger, and confirms His covenant with you. He turns your darkness into light and finds pleasure in being faithful to you.

¹"Look at my servant, whom I strengthen. He is my chosen one, who pleases me. I have put my Spirit upon him. He will bring justice to the nations.

²"He will not shout or raise his voice in public. ³He will not crush the weakest reed or put out a flickering candle. He will bring justice to all who have been wronged. ⁴He will not falter or lose heart until justice prevails throughout the earth. Even distant lands beyond the sea will wait for his instruction."

⁵God, the LORD, created the heavens and stretched them out. He created the earth and everything in it. He gives breath to everyone, life to everyone who walks the earth. And it is he who says, ⁶"I, the LORD, have called you to demonstrate my righteousness. I will take you by the hand and guard you, and I will give you to my people, Israel, as a symbol of my covenant with them. And you will be a light to guide the nations. ⁷You will open the eyes of the blind. You will free the captives from prison, releasing those who sit in dark dungeons.

⁸"I am the LORD; that is my name! I will not give my glory to anyone else, nor share my praise with carved idols. ⁹Everything I prophesied has come true, and now I will prophesy again. I will tell you the future before it happens."

¹⁰Sing a new song to the LORD! Sing his praises from the ends of the earth! Sing, all you who sail the seas, all you who live in distant coastlands.

~ Isaiah 42:1-10

God Knows Your Name

Although God is great, almighty and worshiped by many people, He knows your name – you belong to Him. When you go through crises, He promises to be with you. He makes you His own, because you are precious to Him.

¹But now, O Jacob, listen to the Lord who created you. O Israel, the one who formed you says, "Do not be afraid, for I have ransomed you. I have called you by name; you are mine. ²When you go through deep waters, I will be with you. When you go through rivers of difficulty, you will not drown. When you walk through the fire of oppression, you will not be burned up; the flames will not consume you. ³For I am the Lord, your God, the Holy One of Israel, your Savior. I gave Egypt as a ransom for your freedom; I gave Ethiopia and Seba in your place. ⁴Others were given in exchange for you. I traded their lives for yours because you are precious to me. You are honored, and I love you.

⁵"Do not be afraid, for I am with you. I will gather you and your children from east and west. ⁶I will say to the north and south, 'Bring my sons and daughters back to Israel from the distant corners of the earth. ⁷Bring all who claim me as their God, for I have made them for my glory. It was I who created them.'"

¹⁹"For I am about to do something new. See, I have already begun! Do you not see it? I will make a pathway through the wilderness. I will create rivers in the dry wasteland. ²⁰The wild animals in the fields will thank me, the jackals and owls, too, for giving them water in the desert. Yes, I will make rivers in the dry wasteland so my chosen people can be refreshed. ²¹I have made Israel for myself, and they will someday honor me before the whole world."

~ Isaiah 43:1-7, 19-21

You Are Chosen by God

God wants to bless you abundantly. He has chosen you, and formed you in your mother's womb. He is still there to help you. Everyone who worships idols will be disappointed, but God promises to help you and forgive all your sins.

[1]"But now, listen to me, Jacob my servant, Israel my chosen one. [2]The LORD who made you and helps you says: Do not be afraid, O Jacob, my servant, O dear Israel, my chosen one. [3]For I will pour out water to quench your thirst and to irrigate your parched fields. And I will pour out my Spirit on your descendants, and my blessing on your children. [4]They will thrive like watered grass, like willows on a riverbank. [5]Some will proudly claim, 'I belong to the LORD.' Others will say, 'I am a descendant of Jacob.' Some will write the LORD's name on their hands and will take the name of Israel as their own."

[6]This is what the LORD says—Israel's King and Redeemer, the LORD of Heaven's Armies: "I am the First and the Last; there is no other God."

[9]How foolish are those who manufacture idols. These prized objects are really worthless. The people who worship idols don't know this, so they are all put to shame. [10]Who but a fool would make his own god—an idol that cannot help him one bit? [11]All who worship idols will be disgraced along with all these craftsmen—mere humans—who claim they can make a god. They may all stand together, but they will stand in terror and shame.

[21]"Pay attention, O Jacob, for you are my servant, O Israel. I, the LORD, made you, and I will not forget you. [22]I have swept away your sins like a cloud. I have scattered your offenses like the morning mist. Oh, return to me, for I have paid the price to set you free."

~ Isaiah 44:1-6, 9-11, 21-22

Salvation Only Comes from God

God summoned His people – and you too – to come to Him for salvation. He promised to go ahead of them and to remove the obstacles from their path. Salvation and strength comes only from God. Accept His invitation!

²This is what the Lord says: "I will go before you, Cyrus, and level the mountains. I will smash down gates of bronze and cut through bars of iron. ³And I will give you treasures hidden in the darkness—secret riches. I will do this so you may know that I am the Lord, the God of Israel, the one who calls you by name.

⁴"And why have I called you for this work? Why did I call you by name when you did not know me? It is for the sake of Jacob my servant, Israel my chosen one.

⁵"I am the Lord; there is no other God. I have equipped you for battle, though you don't even know me, ⁶so all the world from east to west will know there is no other God. I am the Lord, and there is no other.

⁷"I create the light and make the darkness. I send good times and bad times. I, the Lord, am the one who does these things.

¹²"I am the one who made the earth and created people to live on it. With my hands I stretched out the heavens. All the stars are at my command."

¹⁸For the Lord is God, and he created the heavens and earth and put everything in place. He made the world to be lived in, not to be a place of empty chaos. "I am the Lord," he says, "and there is no other."

²²"Let all the world look to me for salvation! For I am God; there is no other."

~ Isaiah 45:2-7, 12, 18, 22

June

God Will Save You and Carry You

God promises to be your God throughout your whole life. He cares for you from childhood, and will carry you until you are old. He made you and He will be with you. He will support you in everything and rescue you from every danger.

³"Listen to me, descendants of Jacob, all you who remain in Israel. I have cared for you since you were born. Yes, I carried you before you were born. ⁴I will be your God throughout your lifetime—until your hair is white with age. I made you, and I will care for you. I will carry you along and save you.

⁵"To whom will you compare me? Who is my equal? ⁶Some people pour out their silver and gold and hire a craftsman to make a god from it. Then they bow down and worship it! ⁷They carry it around on their shoulders, and when they set it down, it stays there. It can't even move! And when someone prays to it, there is no answer. It can't rescue anyone from trouble.

⁸"Do not forget this! Keep it in mind! Remember this, you guilty ones. ⁹Remember the things I have done in the past. For I alone am God! I am God, and there is none like me.

¹⁰"Only I can tell you the future before it even happens. Everything I plan will come to pass, for I do whatever I wish. ¹¹I will call a swift bird of prey from the east—a leader from a distant land to come and do my bidding. I have said what I would do, and I will do it.

¹³"For I am ready to set things right, not in the distant future, but right now! I am ready to save Jerusalem and show my glory to Israel."

~ Isaiah 46:3-11, 13

Being Refined Is Good

God sometimes refines His children by letting them go through hardship. But He always saves them. He wants to teach you what is right and guide you on the right path. Listen to His commands and obey Him.

¹"Listen to me, O family of Jacob, you who are called by the name of Israel and born into the family of Judah. Listen, you who take oaths in the name of the LORD and call on the God of Israel. You don't keep your promises, ²even though you call yourself the holy city and talk about depending on the God of Israel, whose name is the LORD of Heaven's Armies.

¹⁰I have refined you, but not as silver is refined. Rather, I have refined you in the furnace of suffering. ¹¹I will rescue you for my sake—yes, for my own sake! I will not let my reputation be tarnished, and I will not share my glory with idols!

¹²"Listen to me, O family of Jacob, Israel my chosen one! I alone am God, the First and the Last. ¹³It was my hand that laid the foundations of the earth, my right hand that spread out the heavens above. When I call out the stars, they all appear in order."

¹⁷This is what the LORD says—your Redeemer, the Holy One of Israel: "I am the LORD your God, who teaches you what is good for you and leads you along the paths you should follow.

¹⁸"Oh, that you had listened to my commands! Then you would have had peace flowing like a gentle river and righteousness rolling over you like waves in the sea. ¹⁹Your descendants would have been like the sands along the seashore—too many to count! There would have been no need for your destruction, or for cutting off your family name."

~ Isaiah 48:1-2, 10-13, 17-19

God Cannot Forget You!

God calls each of His children to witness for Him and proclaim the Good News to the ends of the earth. Even if a mother can forget her child, it is impossible for God to forget you.

[1]Listen to me, all you in distant lands! Pay attention, you who are far away! The LORD called me before my birth; from within the womb he called me by name. [2]He made my words of judgment as sharp as a sword. He has hidden me in the shadow of his hand. I am like a sharp arrow in his quiver.

[3]He said to me, "You are my servant, Israel, and you will bring me glory."

[5]And now the LORD speaks—the one who formed me in my mother's womb to be his servant, who commissioned me to bring Israel back to him. The LORD has honored me, and my God has given me strength. [6]He says, "You will do more than restore the people of Israel to me. I will make you a light to the Gentiles, and you will bring my salvation to the ends of the earth."

[15]"Never! Can a mother forget her nursing child? Can she feel no love for the child she has borne? But even if that were possible, I would not forget you! [16]See, I have written your name on the palms of my hands. Always in my mind is a picture of Jerusalem's walls in ruins.

[17]Soon your descendants will come back, and all who are trying to destroy you will go away. [18]Look around you and see, for all your children will come back to you. As surely as I live," says the LORD, "they will be like jewels or bridal ornaments for you to display."

~ Isaiah 49:1-3, 5-6, 15-18

You Belong to God

When God redeems you from sin, you can't help being overjoyed. He protects you in the shadows of His wings and confirms that you are His – just like Israel belonged to Him. No one can ever snatch you out of His hand.

[1]"Listen to me, all who hope for deliverance—all who seek the LORD! Consider the rock from which you were cut, the quarry from which you were mined.

[4]"Listen to me, my people. Hear me, Israel, for my law will be proclaimed, and my justice will become a light to the nations. [5]My mercy and justice are coming soon. My salvation is on the way. My strong arm will bring justice to the nations. All distant lands will look to me and wait in hope for my powerful arm.

[6]"Look up to the skies above, and gaze down on the earth below. For the skies will disappear like smoke, and the earth will wear out like a piece of clothing. The people of the earth will die like flies, but my salvation lasts forever. My righteous rule will never end!

[7]"Listen to me, you who know right from wrong, you who cherish my law in your hearts. Do not be afraid of people's scorn, nor fear their insults."

[11]Those who have been ransomed by the LORD will return. They will enter Jerusalem singing, crowned with everlasting joy. Sorrow and mourning will disappear, and they will be filled with joy and gladness.

[16]"And I have put my words in your mouth and hidden you safely in my hand. I stretched out the sky like a canopy and laid the foundations of the earth. I am the one who says to Israel, 'You are my people!'"

~ Isaiah 51:1, 4-7, 11, 16

Jesus Suffered for You

Jesus is God's Servant who came to earth to suffer for us. He endured your pain in His body on the cross, He was punished for your sins, and He carried all your guilt so that God can forgive your sins.

[1]Who has believed our message? To whom has the LORD revealed his powerful arm? [2]My servant grew up in the LORD's presence like a tender green shoot, like a root in dry ground. There was nothing beautiful or majestic about his appearance, nothing to attract us to him. [3]He was despised and rejected—a man of sorrows, acquainted with deepest grief. We turned our backs on him and looked the other way. He was despised, and we did not care.

[4]Yet it was our weaknesses he carried; it was our sorrows that weighed him down. And we thought his troubles were a punishment from God, a punishment for his own sins! [5]But he was pierced for our rebellion, crushed for our sins. He was beaten so we could be whole. He was whipped so we could be healed.

[6]All of us, like sheep, have strayed away. We have left God's paths to follow our own. Yet the LORD laid on him the sins of us all.

[11]When he sees all that is accomplished by his anguish, he will be satisfied. And because of his experience, my righteous servant will make it possible for many to be counted righteous, for he will bear all their sins.

[12]I will give him the honors of a victorious soldier, because he exposed himself to death. He was counted among the rebels. He bore the sins of many and interceded for rebels.

~ Isaiah 53:1-6, 11-12

An Open Invitation

God invites you to come to Him and to enjoy free food and drink. But you shouldn't wait until it's too late. God's thoughts are not your thoughts, and His Word always reaches the special purpose it was intended for.

[1]"Is anyone thirsty? Come and drink—even if you have no money! Come, take your choice of wine or milk—it's all free! [2]Why spend your money on food that does not give you strength? Why pay for food that does you no good? Listen to me, and you will eat what is good. You will enjoy the finest food.

[3]"Come to me with your ears wide open. Listen, and you will find life. I will make an everlasting covenant with you. I will give you all the unfailing love I promised to David.

[8]"My thoughts are nothing like your thoughts," says the LORD. "And my ways are far beyond anything you could imagine. [9]For just as the heavens are higher than the earth, so my ways are higher than your ways and my thoughts higher than your thoughts.

[10]"The rain and snow come down from the heavens and stay on the ground to water the earth. They cause the grain to grow, producing seed for the farmer and bread for the hungry. [11]It is the same with my word. I send it out, and it always produces fruit. It will accomplish all I want it to, and it will prosper everywhere I send it. [12]You will live in joy and peace. The mountains and hills will burst into song, and the trees of the field will clap their hands!

[13]"Where once there were thorns, cypress trees will grow. Where nettles grew, myrtles will sprout up. These events will bring great honor to the LORD's name; they will be an everlasting sign of his power and love."

~ Isaiah 55:1-3, 8-13

Reach Out to Others

Here the Lord shows us the difference between artificial faith and real faith. Israel thought that their rituals would get God's approval, but instead God wanted hearts that loved Him and deeds that confirmed it. He expects the same from you.

⁶"No, this is the kind of fasting I want: Free those who are wrongly imprisoned; lighten the burden of those who work for you. Let the oppressed go free, and remove the chains that bind people. ⁷Share your food with the hungry, and give shelter to the homeless. Give clothes to those who need them, and do not hide from relatives who need your help.

⁸"Then your salvation will come like the dawn, and your wounds will quickly heal. Your godliness will lead you forward, and the glory of the LORD will protect you from behind.

⁹"Then when you call, the LORD will answer. 'Yes, I am here,' he will quickly reply. "Remove the heavy yoke of oppression. Stop pointing your finger and spreading vicious rumors! ¹⁰Feed the hungry, and help those in trouble. Then your light will shine out from the darkness, and the darkness around you will be as bright as noon. ¹¹The LORD will guide you continually, giving you water when you are dry and restoring your strength. You will be like a well-watered garden, like an ever-flowing spring.

¹³"Keep the Sabbath day holy. Don't pursue your own interests on that day, but enjoy the Sabbath and speak of it with delight as the LORD's holy day. Honor the Sabbath in everything you do on that day, and don't follow your own desires or talk idly. ¹⁴Then the LORD will be your delight. I will give you great honor and satisfy you with the inheritance I promised to your ancestor Jacob. I, the LORD, have spoken!"

~ Isaiah 58:6-11, 13-14

Comfort to the Mourning

Isaiah brought a message of redemption to a discouraged, humiliated, and sad nation. Since this message is fulfilled in the New Testament through Christ, you can rejoice and be glad because God clothed you with salvation.

¹The Spirit of the Sovereign Lord is upon me, for the Lord has anointed me to bring good news to the poor. He has sent me to comfort the brokenhearted and to proclaim that captives will be released and prisoners will be freed. ²He has sent me to tell those who mourn that the time of the Lord's favor has come, and with it, the day of God's anger against their enemies. ³To all who mourn in Israel, he will give a crown of beauty for ashes, a joyous blessing instead of mourning, festive praise instead of despair. In their righteousness, they will be like great oaks that the Lord has planted for his own glory.

⁶You will be called priests of the Lord, ministers of our God. You will feed on the treasures of the nations and boast in their riches. ⁷Instead of shame and dishonor, you will enjoy a double share of honor. You will possess a double portion of prosperity in your land, and everlasting joy will be yours.

⁸"For I, the Lord, love justice. I hate robbery and wrongdoing. I will faithfully reward my people for their suffering and make an everlasting covenant with them. ⁹Their descendants will be recognized and honored among the nations. Everyone will realize that they are a people the Lord has blessed."

¹⁰I am overwhelmed with joy in the Lord my God! For he has dressed me with the clothing of salvation and draped me in a robe of righteousness. I am like a bridegroom in his wedding suit or a bride with her jewels.

~ Isaiah 61:1-3, 6-10

A Prayer for Forgiveness

In the same way that sin came between God and His people, our sins can also stand between God and us. Then your best deeds are like dirty clothes before Him. But in His wonderful grace He frees you from your offences through Jesus' atoning death. You must just believe in Jesus and confess your sins.

³When you came down long ago, you did awesome deeds beyond our highest expectations. And oh, how the mountains quaked! ⁴For since the world began, no ear has heard and no eye has seen a God like you, who works for those who wait for him! ⁵You welcome those who gladly do good, who follow godly ways. But you have been very angry with us, for we are not godly. We are constant sinners; how can people like us be saved?

⁶We are all infected and impure with sin. When we display our righteous deeds, they are nothing but filthy rags. Like autumn leaves, we wither and fall, and our sins sweep us away like the wind. ⁷Yet no one calls on your name or pleads with you for mercy. Therefore, you have turned away from us and turned us over to our sins.

⁸And yet, O Lord, you are our Father. We are the clay, and you are the potter. We all are formed by your hand. ⁹Don't be so angry with us, Lord. Please don't remember our sins forever. Look at us, we pray, and see that we are all your people.

¹⁰Your holy cities are destroyed. Zion is a wilderness; yes, Jerusalem is a desolate ruin. ¹¹The holy and beautiful Temple where our ancestors praised you has been burned down, and all the things of beauty are destroyed. ¹²After all this, Lord, must you still refuse to help us? Will you continue to be silent and punish us?

~ Isaiah 64:3-12

God Creates a Brand-New World

God doesn't leave His people's sins unpunished, but He does promise them a new world where everyone will be happy; where the hunter will graze with its prey. In Revelation 21 we also read about this promise, and we can be excited about this new heaven and earth too.

¹The LORD says, "I was ready to respond, but no one asked for help. I was ready to be found, but no one was looking for me. I said, 'Here I am, here I am!' to a nation that did not call on my name.

¹⁶"All who invoke a blessing or take an oath will do so by the God of truth. For I will put aside my anger and forget the evil of earlier days.

¹⁷"Look! I am creating new heavens and a new earth, and no one will even think about the old ones anymore. ¹⁸Be glad; rejoice forever in my creation! And look! I will create Jerusalem as a place of happiness. Her people will be a source of joy. ¹⁹I will rejoice over Jerusalem and delight in my people. And the sound of weeping and crying will be heard in it no more.

²³"They will not work in vain, and their children will not be doomed to misfortune. For they are people blessed by the LORD, and their children, too, will be blessed. ²⁴I will answer them before they even call to me. While they are still talking about their needs, I will go ahead and answer their prayers!

²⁵"The wolf and the lamb will feed together. The lion will eat hay like a cow. But the snakes will eat dust. In those days no one will be hurt or destroyed on my holy mountain. I, the LORD, have spoken!"

~ Isaiah 65:1, 16-19, 23-25

God Chooses You as a Witness

God called the prophet Jeremiah to witness about Him to all the heathen nations. But Jeremiah offered many excuses: he was not a good speaker and he was too young. But God promised to strengthen and protect him. He will help you to proclaim His Word too.

⁴The LORD gave me this message: ⁵"I knew you before I formed you in your mother's womb. Before you were born I set you apart and appointed you as my prophet to the nations."

⁶"O Sovereign LORD," I said, "I can't speak for you! I'm too young!"

⁷"The LORD replied, "Don't say, 'I'm too young,' for you must go wherever I send you and say whatever I tell you. ⁸And don't be afraid of the people, for I will be with you and will protect you. I, the LORD, have spoken!"

⁹"Then the LORD reached out and touched my mouth and said, "Look, I have put my words in your mouth! ¹⁰Today I appoint you to stand up against nations and kingdoms. Some you must uproot and tear down, destroy and overthrow. Others you must build up and plant.

¹⁷"Get up and prepare for action. Go out and tell them everything I tell you to say. Do not be afraid of them, or I will make you look foolish in front of them. ¹⁸For see, today I have made you strong like a fortified city that cannot be captured, like an iron pillar or a bronze wall. You will stand against the whole land—the kings, officials, priests, and people of Judah. ¹⁹They will fight you, but they will fail. For I am with you, and I will take care of you. I, the LORD, have spoken!"

~ Jeremiah 1:4-10, 17-19

Honeymoon Love

Israel's initial devotion to God faded quickly. They deserted Him and worshiped idols. Is your love for God still the same sincere devotion as when you were converted? If not, you must return to your honeymoon love for Him.

[1]The LORD gave me another message. He said, [2]"Go and shout this message to Jerusalem. This is what the LORD says: "I remember how eager you were to please me as a young bride long ago, how you loved me and followed me even through the barren wilderness. [3]In those days Israel was holy to the LORD, the first of his children. All who harmed his people were declared guilty, and disaster fell on them. I, the LORD, have spoken!

[13]"For my people have done two evil things: They have abandoned me—the fountain of living water. And they have dug for themselves cracked cisterns that can hold no water at all!

[19]"Your wickedness will bring its own punishment. Your turning from me will shame you. You will see what an evil, bitter thing it is to abandon the LORD your God and not to fear him. I, the Lord, the LORD of Heaven's Armies, have spoken!

[20]"Long ago I broke the yoke that oppressed you and tore away the chains of your slavery, but still you said, 'I will not serve you.' On every hill and under every green tree, you have prostituted yourselves by bowing down to idols.

[21]"But I was the one who planted you, choosing a vine of the purest stock—the very best. How did you grow into this corrupt wild vine? [22]No amount of soap or lye can make you clean. I still see the stain of your guilt. I, the Sovereign LORD, have spoken!"

~ Jeremiah 2:1-3, 13, 19-22

Set Your Priorities Straight

God warned Israel to change their lives and to do what was right to each other. But they didn't listen. Therefore the Lord was going to reject them. This warning is still true for you today!

¹The Lord gave another message to Jeremiah. He said, ²"Go to the entrance of the Lord's Temple, and give this message to the people: 'O Judah, listen to this message from the Lord! Listen to it, all of you who worship here!

³This is what the Lord of Heaven's Armies, the God of Israel, says: 'Even now, if you quit your evil ways, I will let you stay in your own land. ⁴But don't be fooled by those who promise you safety simply because the Lord's Temple is here. They chant, "The Lord's Temple is here! The Lord's Temple is here!"

⁵"But I will be merciful only if you stop your evil thoughts and deeds and start treating each other with justice; ⁶only if you stop exploiting foreigners, orphans, and widows; only if you stop your murdering; and only if you stop harming yourselves by worshiping idols. ⁷Then I will let you stay in this land that I gave to your ancestors to keep forever.

⁸"Don't be fooled into thinking that you will never suffer because the Temple is here. It's a lie! ⁹Do you really think you can steal, murder, commit adultery, lie, and burn incense to Baal and all those other new gods of yours, ¹⁰and then come here and stand before me in my Temple and chant, "We are safe!"—only to go right back to all those evils again? ¹¹Don't you yourselves admit that this Temple, which bears my name, has become a den of thieves? Surely I see all the evil going on there. I, the Lord, have spoken!'"

~ Jeremiah 7:1-11

The Creator of Everything

Whenever we compare God to an idol, we discover who the living God is – the Almighty Creator of everything and everyone. Worship and serve Him only.

¹Hear the word that the LORD speaks to you, O Israel! ²This is what the LORD says: "Do not act like the other nations, who try to read their future in the stars. Do not be afraid of their predictions, even though other nations are terrified by them. ³Their ways are futile and foolish. They cut down a tree, and a craftsman carves an idol. ⁴They decorate it with gold and silver and then fasten it securely with hammer and nails so it won't fall over. ⁵Their gods are like helpless scarecrows in a cucumber field! They cannot speak, and they need to be carried because they cannot walk. Do not be afraid of such gods, for they can neither harm you nor do you any good."

⁶LORD, there is no one like you! For you are great, and your name is full of power. ⁷Who would not fear you, O King of nations? That title belongs to you alone! Among all the wise people of the earth and in all the kingdoms of the world, there is no one like you.

¹⁰But the LORD is the only true God. He is the living God and the everlasting King! The whole earth trembles at his anger. The nations cannot stand up to his wrath.

¹⁴The whole human race is foolish and has no knowledge! The craftsmen are disgraced by the idols they make, for their carefully shaped works are a fraud. These idols have no breath or power. ¹⁵Idols are worthless; they are ridiculous lies! On the day of reckoning they will all be destroyed. ¹⁶But the God of Israel is no idol! He is the Creator of everything that exists, including Israel, his own special possession. The LORD of Heaven's Armies is his name!

~ Jeremiah 10:1-7, 10, 14-16

Put Your Trust in God

People who live without God have no prospect for the future. But someone who trusts in God is like a tree that grows beside a flowing river and bears fruit – even in times of drought. God wants to be your fountain of living water.

5This is what the LORD says: "Cursed are those who put their trust in mere humans, who rely on human strength and turn their hearts away from the LORD. 6They are like stunted shrubs in the desert, with no hope for the future. They will live in the barren wilderness, in an uninhabited salty land.

7"But blessed are those who trust in the LORD and have made the LORD their hope and confidence. 8They are like trees planted along a riverbank, with roots that reach deep into the water. Such trees are not bothered by the heat or worried by long months of drought. Their leaves stay green, and they never stop producing fruit.

9"The human heart is the most deceitful of all things, and desperately wicked. Who really knows how bad it is? 10But I, the LORD, search all hearts and examine secret motives. I give all people their due rewards, according to what their actions deserve."

11Like a partridge that hatches eggs she has not laid, so are those who get their wealth by unjust means. At midlife they will lose their riches; in the end, they will become poor old fools. 12But we worship at your throne—eternal, high, and glorious!

13O LORD, the hope of Israel, all who turn away from you will be disgraced. They will be buried in the dust of the earth, for they have abandoned the LORD, the fountain of living water.

~ Jeremiah 17:5-13

A Word Like Fire and a Hammer

God is almighty and omniscient. He knows everything about you; there is absolutely nothing you can hide from Him. His Word is like a burning fire and like a hammer that breaks a rock into pieces. His Word should be conveyed truthfully.

23"Am I a God who is only close at hand?" says the LORD. "No, I am far away at the same time. 24Can anyone hide from me in a secret place? Am I not everywhere in all the heavens and earth?" says the LORD.

25"I have heard these prophets say, 'Listen to the dream I had from God last night.' And then they proceed to tell lies in my name. 26How long will this go on? If they are prophets, they are prophets of deceit, inventing everything they say. 27By telling these false dreams, they are trying to get my people to forget me, just as their ancestors did by worshiping the idols of Baal.

28"Let these false prophets tell their dreams, but let my true messengers faithfully proclaim my every word. There is a difference between straw and grain! 29Does not my word burn like fire?" says the LORD. "Is it not like a mighty hammer that smashes a rock to pieces?

30"Therefore," says the LORD, "I am against these prophets who steal messages from each other and claim they are from me. 31I am against these smooth-tongued prophets who say, 'This prophecy is from the LORD!'

32"I am against these false prophets. Their imaginary dreams are flagrant lies that lead my people into sin. I did not send or appoint them, and they have no message at all for my people. I, the LORD have spoken!"

~ Jeremiah 23:23-32

God's Perfect Plan for You

God wants His children to prosper, have hope, and a bright future. If you call out to Him, He will listen; if you seek Him, you will find Him. God wants to give you hope for a heavenly future with Him.

⁴This is what the Lᴏʀᴅ of Heaven's Armies, the God of Israel, says to all the captives he has exiled to Babylon from Jerusalem: ⁵"Build homes, and plan to stay. Plant gardens, and eat the food they produce.

⁶"Marry and have children. Then find spouses for them so that you may have many grandchildren. Multiply! Do not dwindle away! ⁷And work for the peace and prosperity of the city where I sent you into exile. Pray to the Lᴏʀᴅ for it, for its welfare will determine your welfare."

⁸This is what the Lᴏʀᴅ of Heaven's Armies, the God of Israel, says: "Do not let your prophets and fortune-tellers who are with you in the land of Babylon trick you. Do not listen to their dreams, ⁹because they are telling you lies in my name. I have not sent them," says the Lᴏʀᴅ.

¹⁰This is what the Lᴏʀᴅ says: "You will be in Babylon for seventy years. But then I will come and do for you all the good things I have promised, and I will bring you home again.

¹¹"For I know the plans I have for you," says the Lᴏʀᴅ. "They are plans for good and not for disaster, to give you a future and a hope. ¹²In those days when you pray, I will listen. ¹³If you look for me wholeheartedly, you will find me. ¹⁴I will be found by you," says the Lᴏʀᴅ. "I will end your captivity and restore your fortunes. I will gather you out of the nations where I sent you and will bring you home again to your own land."

~ Jeremiah 29:4-14

God's Faithful Promises

During Israel's crises, God gave Jeremiah a handful of positive promises: If His children prayed, He would answer them; He would restore the circumstances of His suffering people; and He would heal the sick. His love and faithfulness will last forever – even for you!

¹While Jeremiah was still confined in the courtyard of the guard, the LORD gave him this second message: ²"This is what the LORD says—the LORD who made the earth, who formed and established it, whose name is the LORD: ³Ask me and I will tell you remarkable secrets you do not know about things to come. ⁴For this is what the LORD, the God of Israel, says: You have torn down the houses of this city and even the king's palace to get materials to strengthen the walls against the siege ramps and swords of the enemy.

⁵"You expect to fight the Babylonians, but the men of this city are already as good as dead, for I have determined to destroy them in my terrible anger. I have abandoned them because of all their wickedness.

⁶"Nevertheless, the time will come when I will heal Jerusalem's wounds and give it prosperity and true peace. ⁷I will restore the fortunes of Judah and Israel and rebuild their towns. ⁸I will cleanse them of their sins against me and forgive all their sins of rebellion.

¹⁰"Yet in the empty streets of Jerusalem and Judah's other towns, there will be heard once more ¹¹the sounds of joy and laughter. The joyful voices of bridegrooms and brides will be heard again, along with the joyous songs of people bringing thanksgiving offerings to the LORD. They will sing, 'Give thanks to the LORD of Heaven's Armies, for the LORD is good. His faithful love endures forever!' For I will restore the prosperity of this land to what it was in the past, says the LORD."

~ Jeremiah 33:1-8, 10-11

When Hope Seems Lost

Jeremiah felt that God left him to walk on a path with no light, and that God didn't want to answer his prayers. He felt completely hopeless. In times of hardship we might also feel that God is far away, but He will never leave you on your own.

¹I am the one who has seen the afflictions that come from the rod of the Lord's anger. ²He has led me into darkness, shutting out all light. ³He has turned his hand against me again and again, all day long.

⁴He has made my skin and flesh grow old. He has broken my bones. ⁵He has besieged and surrounded me with anguish and distress. ⁶He has buried me in a dark place, like those long dead.

⁷He has walled me in, and I cannot escape. He has bound me in heavy chains. ⁸And though I cry and shout, he has shut out my prayers. ⁹He has blocked my way with a high stone wall; he has made my road crooked.

¹⁰He has hidden like a bear or a lion, waiting to attack me. ¹¹He has dragged me off the path and torn me in pieces, leaving me helpless and devastated. ¹²He has drawn his bow and made me the target for his arrows.

¹⁸I cry out, "My splendor is gone! Everything I had hoped for from the Lord is lost!"

¹⁹The thought of my suffering and homelessness is bitter beyond words. ²⁰I will never forget this awful time, as I grieve over my loss.

~ Lamentations 3:1-12, 18-20

Hope in God!

Like Jeremiah, you will also discover that God is faithful. He never stops caring about you. In times of hardship you only have to wait patiently and pray for God to save you – He always will. Return to Him so that He can forgive your sins.

[21]Yet I still dare to hope when I remember this:

[22]The faithful love of the LORD never ends! His mercies never cease. [23]Great is his faithfulness; his mercies begin afresh each morning. [24]I say to myself, "The LORD is my inheritance; therefore, I will hope in him!"

[25]The LORD is good to those who depend on him, to those who search for him. [26]So it is good to wait quietly for salvation from the LORD. [27]And it is good for people to submit at an early age to the yoke of his discipline:

[28]Let them sit alone in silence beneath the LORD's demands. [29]Let them lie face down in the dust, for there may be hope at last. [30]Let them turn the other cheek to those who strike them and accept the insults of their enemies.

[31]For no one is abandoned by the Lord forever. [32]Though he brings grief, he also shows compassion because of the greatness of his unfailing love. [33]For he does not enjoy hurting people or causing them sorrow.

[39]Then why should we, mere humans, complain when we are punished for our sins?

[40]Instead, let us test and examine our ways. Let us turn back to the LORD. [41]Let us lift our hearts and hands to God in heaven and say, [42]"We have sinned and rebelled, and you have not forgiven us."

~ Lamentations 3:21-33, 39-42

The Good Shepherd

God promises to look after His sheep, to care for them, and to bring them back to safety. God wants to be your Shepherd too. You are part of God's flock, and He is the Shepherd who will look after you.

¹¹For this is what the Sovereign LORD says: I myself will search and find my sheep. ¹²I will be like a shepherd looking for his scattered flock. I will find my sheep and rescue them from all the places where they were scattered on that dark and cloudy day. ¹³I will bring them back home to their own land of Israel from among the peoples and nations.

¹⁴"Yes, I will give them good pastureland on the high hills of Israel. There they will lie down in pleasant places and feed in the lush pastures of the hills. ¹⁵I myself will tend my sheep and give them a place to lie down in peace, says the Sovereign LORD. ¹⁶I will search for my lost ones who strayed away, and I will bring them safely home again. I will bandage the injured and strengthen the weak.

²⁵"I will make a covenant of peace with my people and drive away the dangerous animals from the land. Then they will be able to camp safely in the wildest places and sleep in the woods without fear. ²⁶I will bless my people and their homes around my holy hill. And in the proper season I will send the showers they need. There will be showers of blessing. ²⁷The orchards and fields of my people will yield bumper crops, and everyone will live in safety. When I have broken their chains of slavery and rescued them from those who enslaved them, then they will know that I am the LORD.

³⁰"In this way, they will know that I, the LORD their God, am with them. ³¹You are my flock, the sheep of my pasture. You are my people, and I am your God."

~ Ezekiel 34:11-16, 25-27, 30-31

Prayer of Confession

Daniel confessed Israel's guilt and pleaded with God to forgive their sins and notice their distress. God wants you to confess your sins so that He can forgive you too. Don't postpone this any longer!

[4]I prayed to the LORD my God and confessed: "O Lord, you are a great and awesome God! You always fulfill your covenant and keep your promises of unfailing love to those who love you and obey your commands. [5]But we have sinned and done wrong. We have rebelled against you and scorned your commands and regulations. [6]We have refused to listen to your servants the prophets, who spoke on your authority.

[7]"Lord, you are in the right; but as you see, our faces are covered with shame. This is true of all of us, including the people of Judah and Jerusalem and all Israel, scattered near and far, wherever you have driven us because of our disloyalty to you.

[15]"O Lord our God, you brought lasting honor to your name by rescuing your people from Egypt in a great display of power. But we have sinned and are full of wickedness. [16]In view of all your faithful mercies, Lord, please turn your furious anger away from your city Jerusalem, your holy mountain. All the neighboring nations mock Jerusalem and your people because of our sins and the sins of our ancestors.

[17]"O our God, hear your servant's prayer! Listen as I plead. For your own sake, Lord, smile again on your desolate sanctuary. [18]O my God, lean down and listen to me. Open your eyes and see our despair. See how your city—the city that bears your name—lies in ruins. We make this plea, not because we deserve help, but because of your mercy. [19]O Lord, hear. O Lord, forgive. O Lord, listen and act! For your own sake, do not delay, O my God, for your people and your city bear your name."

~ Daniel 9:4-7, 15-19

A Message from God

In answer to Daniel's prayer of confession, God sent the angel Gabriel to Daniel with the message that his prayer had already been answered. He also assured Daniel that he could stop worrying and be strong, because God loved him. When you pray sincerely, God listens and answers your prayers.

9²¹As I was praying, Gabriel, whom I had seen in the earlier vision, came swiftly to me at the time of the evening sacrifice. ²²He explained to me, "Daniel, I have come here to give you insight and understanding."

10¹²Then he said, "Don't be afraid, Daniel. Since the first day you began to pray for understanding and to humble yourself before your God, your request has been heard in heaven. I have come in answer to your prayer.

¹³"But for twenty-one days the spirit prince of the kingdom of Persia blocked my way. Then Michael, one of the archangels, came to help me, and I left him there with the spirit prince of the kingdom of Persia. ¹⁴Now I am here to explain what will happen to your people in the future, for this vision concerns a time yet to come."

¹⁸Then the one who looked like a man touched me again, and I felt my strength returning. ¹⁹"Don't be afraid," he said, "for you are very precious to God. Peace! Be encouraged! Be strong!" As he spoke these words to me, I suddenly felt stronger and said to him, "Please speak to me, my lord, for you have strengthened me."

~ Daniel 9:21-22; 10:12-14, 18-19

God Wants to Bring You Home

God's children often wander away from Him, but He loves us too much to give up on us. He promises that if you are willing to return to Him, He will forgive your sins and take you back as His child.

10[12]"I said, 'Plant the good seeds of righteousness, and you will harvest a crop of love. Plow up the hard ground of your hearts, for now is the time to seek the LORD, that he may come and shower righteousness upon you.'

11[1]"When Israel was a child, I loved him, and I called my son out of Egypt. [2]But the more I called to him, the farther he moved from me, offering sacrifices to the images of Baal and burning incense to idols.

[3]"I myself taught Israel how to walk, leading him along by the hand. But he doesn't know or even care that it was I who took care of him. [4]I led Israel along with my ropes of kindness and love. I lifted the yoke from his neck, and I myself stooped to feed him.

[5]"But since my people refuse to return to me, they will return to Egypt and will be forced to serve Assyria. [6]War will swirl through their cities; their enemies will crash through their gates. They will destroy them, trapping them in their own evil plans.

[8]"Oh, how can I give you up, Israel? How can I let you go? My heart is torn within me, and my compassion overflows. [9]No, I will not unleash my fierce anger. I will not completely destroy Israel, for I am God and not a mere mortal. I am the Holy One living among you, and I will not come to destroy."

~ Hosea 10:12; 11:1-6, 8-9

Return to the Lord!

Sin always separates us from God. Confess your sins, ask God to forgive each one of them, and turn back to Him. He will then pour His grace onto you so that you can bring Him a praise offering.

¹Return, O Israel, to the LORD your God, for your sins have brought you down. ²Bring your confessions, and return to the LORD. Say to him, "Forgive all our sins and graciously receive us, so that we may offer you our praises. ³Assyria cannot save us, nor can our warhorses. Never again will we say to the idols we have made, 'You are our gods.' No, in you alone do the orphans find mercy."

⁴The LORD says, "Then I will heal you of your faithlessness; my love will know no bounds, for my anger will be gone forever. ⁵I will be to Israel like a refreshing dew from heaven. Israel will blossom like the lily; it will send roots deep into the soil like the cedars in Lebanon.

⁶"Its branches will spread out like beautiful olive trees, as fragrant as the cedars of Lebanon. ⁷My people will again live under my shade. They will flourish like grain and blossom like grapevines. They will be as fragrant as the wines of Lebanon.

⁸"O Israel, stay away from idols! I am the one who answers your prayers and cares for you. I am like a tree that is always green; all your fruit comes from me."

⁹Let those who are wise understand these things. Let those with discernment listen carefully. The paths of the LORD are true and right, and righteous people live by walking in them. But in those paths sinners stumble and fall.

~ Hosea 14:1-9

A Promise of Restoration

God promised to restore His people. He didn't only send them rain so there would be food in the land, but He also poured His Spirit out on all His people so that everyone who prayed to Him would be saved.

¹⁸Then the LORD will pity his people and jealously guard the honor of his land. ¹⁹The LORD will reply, "Look! I am sending you grain and new wine and olive oil, enough to satisfy your needs. You will no longer be an object of mockery among the surrounding nations. ²⁰I will drive away these armies from the north. I will send them into the parched wastelands. The stench of their rotting bodies will rise over the land." Surely the LORD has done great things!

²¹Don't be afraid, my people. Be glad now and rejoice, for the LORD has done great things. ²²Don't be afraid, you animals of the field, for the wilderness pastures will soon be green. The trees will again be filled with fruit; fig trees and grapevines will be loaded down once more.

²³Rejoice, you people of Jerusalem! Rejoice in the LORD your God! For the rain he sends demonstrates his faithfulness. Once more the autumn rains will come, as well as the rains of spring. ²⁴The threshing floors will again be piled high with grain, and the presses will overflow with new wine and olive oil.

²⁷"Then you will know that I am among my people Israel, that I am the LORD your God, and there is no other. Never again will my people be disgraced.

²⁸"Then, after doing all those things, I will pour out my Spirit upon all people. Your sons and daughters will prophesy. Your old men will dream dreams, and your young men will see visions. ²⁹In those days I will pour out my Spirit even on servants—men and women alike."

~ Joel 2:18-24, 27-29

God Chose You

God chose Israel as His people, but because they abandoned Him, He punished them. He refined them until only the pure were left. God chose you to be His child – but He expects you to serve Him with a sincere heart.

²"From among all the families on the earth, I have been intimate with you alone. That is why I must punish you for all your sins."

³Can two people walk together without agreeing on the direction? ⁴Does a lion ever roar in a thicket without first finding a victim? Does a young lion growl in its den without first catching its prey?

⁵Does a bird ever get caught in a trap that has no bait? Does a trap spring shut when there's nothing to catch? ⁶When the ram's horn blows a warning, shouldn't the people be alarmed? Does disaster come to a city unless the LORD has planned it?

⁷Indeed, the Sovereign LORD never does anything until he reveals his plans to his servants the prophets. ⁸The lion has roared—so who isn't frightened?

¹³"Now listen to this, and announce it throughout all Israel," says the Lord, the LORD God of Heaven's Armies.

¹⁴"On the very day I punish Israel for its sins, I will destroy the pagan altars at Bethel. The horns of the altar will be cut off and fall to the ground.

¹⁵"And I will destroy the beautiful homes of the wealthy— their winter mansions and their summer houses, too—all their palaces filled with ivory," says the LORD. The Sovereign LORD has spoken—so who can refuse to proclaim his message?

~ Amos 3:2-8, 13-15

God Grants Prosperity Again

God punished His sinful people, but promised that He would not destroy them completely. He would restore them in future, grant them prosperity, and re-establish them in their own country. Despite Israel's unfaithfulness, God is faithful to His promises.

[8]"I, the Sovereign LORD, am watching this sinful nation of Israel. I will destroy it from the face of the earth. But I will never completely destroy the family of Israel," says the LORD.

[9]"For I will give the command and will shake Israel along with the other nations as grain is shaken in a sieve, yet not one true kernel will be lost. [10]But all the sinners will die by the sword—all those who say, 'Nothing bad will happen to us.'

[11]"In that day I will restore the fallen house of David. I will repair its damaged walls. From the ruins I will rebuild it and restore its former glory. [12]And Israel will possess what is left of Edom and all the nations I have called to be mine." The LORD has spoken, and he will do these things.

[13]"The time will come," says the LORD, "when the grain and grapes will grow faster than they can be harvested. Then the terraced vineyards on the hills of Israel will drip with sweet wine!

[14]"I will bring my exiled people of Israel back from distant lands, and they will rebuild their ruined cities and live in them again. They will plant vineyards and gardens; they will eat their crops and drink their wine. [15]I will firmly plant them there in their own land. They will never again be uprooted from the land I have given them," says the LORD your God.

~ Amos 9:8-15

God Is the Hearer of Prayer

Jonah was only willing to obey God when there was no other way out. He called on God. God heard his prayer and rescued him. Sometimes we also wait for emergency situations before we call on God. God often gives us second chances like He did for Jonah.

¹Then Jonah prayed to the Lord his God from inside the fish. ²He said, "I cried out to the Lord in my great trouble, and he answered me. I called to you from the land of the dead, and Lord, you heard me! ³You threw me into the ocean depths, and I sank down to the heart of the sea. The mighty waters engulfed me; I was buried beneath your wild and stormy waves. ⁴Then I said, 'O Lord, you have driven me from your presence. Yet I will look once more toward your holy Temple.'

⁵"I sank beneath the waves, and the waters closed over me. Seaweed wrapped itself around my head. ⁶I sank down to the very roots of the mountains. I was imprisoned in the earth, whose gates lock shut forever. But you, O Lord my God, snatched me from the jaws of death! ⁷As my life was slipping away, I remembered the Lord. And my earnest prayer went out to you in your holy Temple. ⁸Those who worship false gods turn their backs on all God's mercies. ⁹But I will offer sacrifices to you with songs of praise, and I will fulfill all my vows. For my salvation comes from the Lord alone."

¹⁰Then the Lord ordered the fish to spit Jonah out onto the beach.

~ Jonah 2

God Rules!

God wanted to teach His people how to live so that they would obey Him in their lives. He wanted to be their King and rule over them forever. God wants to be the King of your life too, as long as you trust and serve Him alone.

¹In the last days, the mountain of the LORD's house will be the highest of all—the most important place on earth. It will be raised above the other hills, and people from all over the world will stream there to worship.

²People from many nations will come and say, "Come, let us go up to the mountain of the LORD, to the house of Jacob's God. There he will teach us his ways, and we will walk in his paths." For the LORD's teaching will go out from Zion; his word will go out from Jerusalem.

³The LORD will mediate between peoples and will settle disputes between strong nations far away. They will hammer their swords into plowshares and their spears into pruning hooks. Nation will no longer fight against nation, nor train for war anymore. ⁴Everyone will live in peace and prosperity, enjoying their own grapevines and fig trees, for there will be nothing to fear. The LORD of Heaven's Armies has made this promise! ⁵Though the nations around us follow their idols, we will follow the LORD our God forever and ever.

⁶"In that coming day," says the LORD, "I will gather together those who are lame, those who have been exiles, and those whom I have filled with grief. ⁷Those who are weak will survive as a remnant; those who were exiles will become a strong nation. Then I, the LORD, will rule from Jerusalem as their king forever."

~ Micah 4:1-7

July

What God Asks from You

God doesn't expect physical offerings from His children anymore. But He still requires you to love and serve Him, to live a righteous life, to prove your love and faithfulness to Him, and to live humbly before Him. Strive for this with your whole heart.

[6]What can we bring to the Lord? What kind of offerings should we give him? Should we bow before God with offerings of yearling calves? [7]Should we sacrifice our firstborn children to pay for our sins? [8]No, O people, the Lord has told you what is good, and this is what he requires of you: to do what is right, to love mercy, and to walk humbly with your God.

[9]Fear the Lord if you are wise! His voice calls to everyone in Jerusalem: "The armies of destruction are coming; the Lord is sending them. [10]What shall I say about the homes of the wicked filled with treasures gained by cheating? [11]How can I tolerate your merchants who use dishonest scales and weights? [12]The rich among you have become wealthy through extortion and violence. Your citizens are so used to lying that their tongues can no longer tell the truth.

[13]"Therefore, I will wound you! I will bring you to ruin for all your sins. [14]You will eat but never have enough. Your hunger pangs and emptiness will remain. And though you try to save your money, it will come to nothing in the end. You will save a little, but I will give it to those who conquer you.

[15]"You will plant crops but not harvest them. You will press your olives but not get enough oil to anoint yourselves. You will trample the grapes but get no juice to make your wine. [16]You keep only the laws of evil King Omri; you follow only the example of wicked King Ahab! Therefore, I will make an example of you, bringing you to complete ruin. You will be treated with contempt, mocked by all who see you."

~ Micah 6:6-16

God Forgives Sins

Other nations were surprised to know what God did for His own people. He was willing to forgive them their sins and restore His relationship with them. This same merciful God also forgives your sins, through Jesus Christ.

[8]Do not gloat over me, my enemies! For though I fall, I will rise again. Though I sit in darkness, the LORD will be my light. [9]I will be patient as the LORD punishes me, for I have sinned against him. But after that, he will take up my case and give me justice for all I have suffered from my enemies. The LORD will bring me into the light, and I will see his righteousness.

[10]Then my enemies will see that the LORD is on my side. They will be ashamed that they taunted me, saying, "So where is the LORD—that God of yours?" With my own eyes I will see their downfall; they will be trampled like mud in the streets.

[11]In that day, Israel, your cities will be rebuilt, and your borders will be extended. [14]O LORD, protect your people with your shepherd's staff; lead your flock, your special possession. Though they live alone in a thicket on the heights of Mount Carmel, let them graze in the fertile pastures of Bashan and Gilead as they did long ago.

[15]"Yes," says the LORD, "I will do mighty miracles for you, like those I did when I rescued you from slavery in Egypt."

[18]Where is another God like you, who pardons the guilt of the remnant, overlooking the sins of his special people? You will not stay angry with your people forever, because you delight in showing unfailing love. [19]Once again you will have compassion on us. You will trample our sins under your feet and throw them into the depths of the ocean! [20]You will show us your faithfulness and unfailing love as you promised to our ancestors Abraham and Jacob long ago.

~ Micah 7:8-11, 14-15, 18-20

God is Your Safe Shelter

In biblical times God promised to free His people from their enemies. Today, He is still good to His children – in times of need He still wants to be your safe shelter. He knows everyone who trusts in Him.

³The LORD is slow to get angry, but his power is great, and he never lets the guilty go unpunished. He displays his power in the whirlwind and the storm. The billowing clouds are the dust beneath his feet.

⁴At his command the oceans dry up, and the rivers disappear. ⁵In his presence the mountains quake, and the hills melt away; the earth trembles, and its people are destroyed. ⁶Who can survive his burning fury? His rage blazes forth like fire, and the mountains crumble to dust in his presence.

⁷The LORD is good, a strong refuge when trouble comes. He is close to those who trust in him. ⁸But he will sweep away his enemies in an overwhelming flood. He will pursue his foes into the darkness of night.

⁹Why are you scheming against the LORD? He will destroy you with one blow; he won't need to strike twice! ¹⁰His enemies, tangled like thornbushes and staggering like drunks, will be burned up like dry stubble in a field.

¹²The LORD says: "Though the Assyrians have many allies, they will be destroyed and disappear. O my people, I have punished you before, but I will not punish you again. ¹³Now I will break the yoke of bondage from your neck and tear off the chains of Assyrian oppression."

¹⁵Look! A messenger is coming over the mountains with good news! He is bringing a message of peace. Celebrate your festivals, O people of Judah, and fulfill all your vows, for your wicked enemies will never invade your land again. They will be completely destroyed!

~ Nahum 1:3-10, 12-13, 15

When God Doesn't Seem to Listen ...

Like the prophet Habakkuk, we also sometimes feel that we call on God in vain. It seems as if He doesn't want to listen to us. In times like these you just have to wait patiently. God answers in His own time and way.

1 [2]How long, O LORD, must I call for help? But you do not listen! "Violence is everywhere!" I cry, but you do not come to save. [3]Must I forever see these evil deeds? Why must I watch all this misery? Wherever I look, I see destruction and violence. I am surrounded by people who love to argue and fight. [4]The law has become paralyzed, and there is no justice in the courts. The wicked far outnumber the righteous, so that justice has become perverted.

[5]The LORD replied, "Look around at the nations; look and be amazed! For I am doing something in your own day, something you wouldn't believe even if someone told you about it."

2 [1]I will climb up to my watchtower and stand at my guard-post. There I will wait to see what the LORD says and how he will answer my complaint.

[2]Then the LORD said to me, "Write my answer plainly on tablets, so that a runner can carry the correct message to others. [3]This vision is for a future time. It describes the end, and it will be fulfilled. If it seems slow in coming, wait patiently, for it will surely take place. It will not be delayed."

[14]"For as the waters fill the sea, the earth will be filled with an awareness of the glory of the LORD. [20]But the LORD is in his holy Temple. Let all the earth be silent before him."

~ Habakkuk 1:2-5; 2:1-3, 14, 20

Even If ... But Still

Habakkuk was amazed at everything that God had achieved in the past. He promised to praise God, even if things didn't go his way. Are you willing to praise God even if He doesn't give you everything you ask for; and in spite of your circumstances?

²I have heard all about you, LORD. I am filled with awe by your amazing works. In this time of our deep need, help us again as you did in years gone by. And in your anger, remember your mercy.

³I see God moving across the deserts from Edom, the Holy One coming from Mount Paran. His brilliant splendor fills the heavens, and the earth is filled with his praise.

¹²You marched across the land in anger and trampled the nations in your fury. ¹³You went out to rescue your chosen people, to save your anointed ones. You crushed the heads of the wicked and stripped their bones from head to toe. ¹⁴With his own weapons, you destroyed the chief of those who rushed out like a whirlwind, thinking Israel would be easy prey.

¹⁵You trampled the sea with your horses, and the mighty waters piled high. ¹⁶I trembled inside when I heard this; my lips quivered with fear. My legs gave way beneath me, and I shook in terror. I will wait quietly for the coming day when disaster will strike the people who invade us.

¹⁷Even though the fig trees have no blossoms, and there are no grapes on the vines; even though the olive crop fails, and the fields lie empty and barren; even though the flocks die in the fields, and the cattle barns are empty, ¹⁸yet I will rejoice in the LORD! I will be joyful in the God of my salvation! ¹⁹The Sovereign LORD is my strength! He makes me as surefooted as a deer, able to tread upon the heights.

~ Habakkuk 3:2-3, 12-19

Seek the Lord and Be Humble

The prophet Zephaniah said that the Day of the Lord – when unfaithful people will be destroyed – will surely come. The only way to avoid this day is to seek God, to do what He asks from you, and to live a humble life.

1 ¹⁴"That terrible day of the LORD is near. Swiftly it comes—a day of bitter tears, a day when even strong men will cry out.

¹⁵"It will be a day when the LORD's anger is poured out—a day of terrible distress and anguish, a day of ruin and desolation, a day of darkness and gloom, a day of clouds and blackness, ¹⁶a day of trumpet calls and battle cries. Down go the walled cities and the strongest battlements!

¹⁷"Because you have sinned against the LORD, I will make you grope around like the blind. Your blood will be poured into the dust, and your bodies will lie rotting on the ground.

¹⁸"Your silver and gold will not save you on that day of the LORD's anger. For the whole land will be devoured by the fire of his jealousy. He will make a terrifying end of all the people on earth."

2 ¹Gather together—yes, gather together, you shameless nation. ²Gather before judgment begins, before your time to repent is blown away like chaff. Act now, before the fierce fury of the LORD falls and the terrible day of the LORD's anger begins.

³Seek the LORD, all who are humble, and follow his commands. Seek to do what is right and to live humbly. Perhaps even yet the LORD will protect you—protect you from his anger on that day of destruction.

~ Zephaniah 1:14-2:3

Become Quiet in God's Love

God's punishment does not last forever. He promised to bring back and restore the honor of His remaining righteous people. Therefore, don't be afraid because God saves everyone who humbly comes to Him. He delights in you and His love will calm you.

⁸"Therefore, be patient," says the LORD. "Soon I will stand and accuse these evil nations. For I have decided to gather the kingdoms of the earth and pour out my fiercest anger and fury on them. All the earth will be devoured by the fire of my jealousy.

¹¹"On that day you will no longer need to be ashamed, for you will no longer be rebels against me. I will remove all proud and arrogant people from among you. There will be no more haughtiness on my holy mountain. ¹²Those who are left will be the lowly and humble, for it is they who trust in the name of the LORD. ¹³The remnant of Israel will do no wrong; they will never tell lies or deceive one another. They will eat and sleep in safety, and no one will make them afraid."

¹⁵For the LORD will remove his hand of judgment and will disperse the armies of your enemy. And the LORD himself, the King of Israel, will live among you! At last your troubles will be over, and you will never again fear disaster. ¹⁶On that day the announcement to Jerusalem will be, "Cheer up, Zion! Don't be afraid! ¹⁷For the LORD your God is living among you. He is a mighty savior. He will take delight in you with gladness. With his love, he will calm all your fears. He will rejoice over you with joyful songs."

¹⁹"And I will deal severely with all who have oppressed you. I will save the weak and helpless ones; I will bring together those who were chased away. I will give glory and fame to my former exiles, wherever they have been mocked and shamed."

~ Zephaniah 3:8, 11-13, 15-17, 19

With God by Your Side

Haggai assured the people that God was with them and that they could take heart and rebuild the temple without being afraid – God's Spirit would be with them to give them peace. You, too, can do your work with the assurance that God is with you.

1 [13]Then Haggai, the LORD's messenger, gave the people this message from the LORD: "I am with you, says the LORD!" [14]So the LORD sparked the enthusiasm of the whole remnant of God's people. They began to work on the house of their God, the LORD of Heaven's Armies, [15]on September 21 of the second year of King Darius's reign.

2 [1]Then on October 17 of that same year, the LORD sent another message through the prophet Haggai. [2]"Say this to Zerubbabel son of Shealtiel, governor of Judah, and to Jeshua son of Jehozadak, the high priest, and to the remnant of God's people there in the land: [3]'Does anyone remember this house—this Temple—in its former splendor? How, in comparison, does it look to you now? It must seem like nothing at all! [4]But now the LORD says: Be strong, all you people still left in the land. And now get to work, for I am with you, says the LORD of Heaven's Armies. [5]My Spirit remains among you, just as I promised when you came out of Egypt. So do not be afraid.' [6]For this is what the LORD of Heaven's Armies says: In just a little while I will again shake the heavens and the earth, the oceans and the dry land. [7]I will shake all the nations, and the treasures of all the nations will be brought to this Temple. I will fill this place with glory.

[19]"I am giving you a promise now while the seed is still in the barn. You have not yet harvested your grain, and your grapevines, fig trees, pomegranates, and olive trees have not yet produced their crops. But from this day onward I will bless you."

~ Haggai 1:13-15; 2:1-7, 19

Promised Blessings

God promised to restore His covenant with Israel, to destroy His people's enemies, and to bring them back to their land. When you belong to God you may apply these promised blessings to your life.

9⁹Look, your king is coming to you. He is righteous and victorious, yet he is humble, riding on a donkey—riding on a donkey's colt. ¹⁰I will remove the battle chariots from Israel and the warhorses from Jerusalem. I will destroy all the weapons used in battle, and your king will bring peace to the nations. His realm will stretch from sea to sea and from the Euphrates River to the ends of the earth.

10⁶"I will strengthen Judah and save Israel; I will restore them because of my compassion. It will be as though I had never rejected them, for I am the LORD their God, who will hear their cries. ⁷The people of Israel will become like mighty warriors, and their hearts will be made happy as if by wine. Their children, too, will see it and be glad; their hearts will rejoice in the LORD. ⁸When I whistle to them, they will come running, for I have redeemed them. From the few who are left, they will grow as numerous as they were before.

⁹"Though I have scattered them like seeds among the nations, they will still remember me in distant lands. They and their children will survive and return again to Israel. ¹⁰I will bring them back from Egypt and gather them from Assyria. I will resettle them in Gilead and Lebanon until there is no more room for them all. ¹¹They will pass safely through the sea of distress, for the waves of the sea will be held back, and the waters of the Nile will dry up. The pride of Assyria will be crushed, and the rule of Egypt will end. ¹²By my power I will make my people strong, and by my authority they will go wherever they wish. I, the LORD, have spoken!"

~ Zechariah 9:9-10; 10:6-12

Bring Your Whole Tithe!

God commanded His people to bring their tithes to the temple so that there would be enough food in His house. If they obeyed Him, they would prosper. This promise is still true today. Give to God His due, and you will receive His blessing.

[6]"I am the LORD, and I do not change. That is why you descendants of Jacob are not already destroyed. [7]Ever since the days of your ancestors, you have scorned my decrees and failed to obey them. Now return to me, and I will return to you," says the LORD of Heaven's Armies. "But you ask, 'How can we return when we have never gone away?'

[8]"Should people cheat God? Yet you have cheated me! But you ask, 'What do you mean? When did we ever cheat you?' You have cheated me of the tithes and offerings due to me.

[9]"You are under a curse, for your whole nation has been cheating me. [10]Bring all the tithes into the storehouse so there will be enough food in my Temple. If you do," says the LORD of Heaven's Armies, "I will open the windows of heaven for you. I will pour out a blessing so great you won't have enough room to take it in! Try it! Put me to the test!

[11]"Your crops will be abundant, for I will guard them from insects and disease. Your grapes will not fall from the vine before they are ripe," says the LORD of Heaven's Armies. [12]"Then all nations will call you blessed, for your land will be such a delight," says the LORD of Heaven's Armies.

~ Malachi 3:6-12

The Sun of Righteousness

Although God's Judgment Day cannot be avoided, there will be justice and healing for those who honor and respect Him. Make sure that your life is in line with God's will before this day comes.

3 ¹⁶Then those who feared the LORD spoke with each other, and the LORD listened to what they said. In his presence, a scroll of remembrance was written to record the names of those who feared him and always thought about the honor of his name. ¹⁷"They will be my people," says the LORD of Heaven's Armies. "On the day when I act in judgment, they will be my own special treasure. I will spare them as a father spares an obedient child. ¹⁸Then you will again see the difference between the righteous and the wicked, between those who serve God and those who do not."

4 ¹The LORD of Heaven's Armies says, "The day of judgment is coming, burning like a furnace. On that day the arrogant and the wicked will be burned up like straw. They will be consumed— roots, branches, and all. ²"But for you who fear my name, the Sun of Righteousness will rise with healing in his wings. And you will go free, leaping with joy like calves let out to pasture.

³"On the day when I act, you will tread upon the wicked as if they were dust under your feet," says the LORD of Heaven's Armies. ⁴"Remember to obey the Law of Moses, my servant—all the decrees and regulations that I gave him on Mount Sinai for all Israel.

⁵"Look, I am sending you the prophet Elijah before the great and dreadful day of the LORD arrives. ⁶His preaching will turn the hearts of fathers to their children, and the hearts of children to their fathers. Otherwise I will come and strike the land with a curse."

~ Malachi 3:16-4:6

God with Us

When Mary became pregnant before their wedding, Joseph planned to break off their engagement. But in a dream an angel told him that the Holy Spirit had impregnated Mary with the child she was expecting. His name would be Immanuel – God with us. Jesus is still the God that is with you.

[18]This is how Jesus the Messiah was born. His mother, Mary, was engaged to be married to Joseph. But before the marriage took place, while she was still a virgin, she became pregnant through the power of the Holy Spirit.

[19]Joseph, her fiancé, was a good man and did not want to disgrace her publicly, so he decided to break the engagement quietly. [20]As he considered this, an angel of the Lord appeared to him in a dream. "Joseph, son of David," the angel said, "do not be afraid to take Mary as your wife. For the child within her was conceived by the Holy Spirit.

[21]"And she will have a son, and you are to name him Jesus, for he will save his people from their sins." [22]All of this occurred to fulfill the Lord's message through his prophet:

[23]"Look! The virgin will conceive a child! She will give birth to a son, and they will call him Immanuel, which means 'God is with us.'"

[24]When Joseph woke up, he did as the angel of the Lord commanded and took Mary as his wife. [25]But he did not have sexual relations with her until her son was born. And Joseph named him Jesus.

~ Matthew 1:18-25

Wise Men Worship Jesus

Wise men from the east visited Jerusalem in search of the King that had been born. There they heard that Israel's Leader was to be born in Bethlehem. When they found Jesus in Bethlehem, they worshiped Him and gave Him precious gifts.

¹Jesus was born in Bethlehem in Judea, during the reign of King Herod. About that time some wise men from eastern lands arrived in Jerusalem, asking, ²"Where is the newborn king of the Jews? We saw his star as it rose, and we have come to worship him."

³King Herod was deeply disturbed when he heard this, as was everyone in Jerusalem. ⁴He called a meeting of the leading priests and teachers of religious law and asked, "Where is the Messiah supposed to be born?"

⁵"In Bethlehem in Judea," they said, "for this is what the prophet wrote: ⁶'And you, O Bethlehem in the land of Judah, are not least among the ruling cities of Judah, for a ruler will come from you who will be the shepherd for my people Israel.'"

⁷Then Herod called for a private meeting with the wise men, and he learned from them the time when the star first appeared. ⁹After this interview the wise men went their way. And the star they had seen in the east guided them to Bethlehem. It went ahead of them and stopped over the place where the child was.

¹⁰When they saw the star, they were filled with joy! ¹¹They entered the house and saw the child with his mother, Mary, and they bowed down and worshiped him. Then they opened their treasure chests and gave him gifts of gold, frankincense, and myrrh. ¹²When it was time to leave, they returned to their own country by another route, for God had warned them in a dream not to return to Herod.

~ Matthew 2:1-7, 9-12

Jesus Is Baptized

Jesus went to the Jordan River to be baptized by John. When Jesus got out of the water, the Holy Spirit descended on Him like a dove and a voice from heaven confirmed that He is God's beloved Son.

[7]But when he saw many Pharisees and Sadducees coming to watch him baptize, he denounced them. "You brood of snakes!" he exclaimed. "Who warned you to flee God's coming wrath? [8]Prove by the way you live that you have repented of your sins and turned to God.

[11]"I baptize with water those who repent of their sins and turn to God. But someone is coming soon who is greater than I am—so much greater that I'm not worthy even to be his slave and carry his sandals. He will baptize you with the Holy Spirit and with fire."

[13]Then Jesus went from Galilee to the Jordan River to be baptized by John. [14]But John tried to talk him out of it. "I am the one who needs to be baptized by you," he said, "so why are you coming to me?"

[15]But Jesus said, "It should be done, for we must carry out all that God requires." So John agreed to baptize him.

[16]After his baptism, as Jesus came up out of the water, the heavens were opened and he saw the Spirit of God descending like a dove and settling on him. [17]And a voice from heaven said, "This is my dearly loved Son, who brings me great joy."

~ Matthew 3:7-8, 11, 13-17

Jesus Is Tempted by the Devil

The Devil tempted Jesus three times in the desert, but Jesus resisted each time. After the Devil had left Jesus, angels attended to Him. You can also resist the temptations on the road of life through the power of Jesus Christ.

¹Then Jesus was led by the Spirit into the wilderness to be tempted there by the devil. ²For forty days and forty nights he fasted and became very hungry.

³During that time the devil came and said to him, "If you are the Son of God, tell these stones to become loaves of bread." ⁴But Jesus told him, "No! The Scriptures say, 'People do not live by bread alone, but by every word that comes from the mouth of God.'"

⁵Then the devil took him to the holy city, Jerusalem, to the highest point of the Temple, ⁶and said, "If you are the Son of God, jump off! For the Scriptures say, 'He will order his angels to protect you. And they will hold you up with their hands so you won't even hurt your foot on a stone.'"

⁷Jesus responded, "The Scriptures also say, 'You must not test the LORD your God.'" ⁸Next the devil took him to the peak of a very high mountain and showed him all the kingdoms of the world and their glory. ⁹"I will give it all to you," he said, "if you will kneel down and worship me."

¹⁰"Get out of here, Satan," Jesus told him. "For the Scriptures say, 'You must worship the LORD your God and serve only him.'"

¹¹Then the devil went away, and angels came and took care of Jesus.

~ Matthew 4:1-11

Jesus Calls His Disciples

Jesus chose twelve disciples to help Him in His earthly ministry. All of them were willing to follow Him immediately. He also calls you to follow Him. Are you prepared to follow Him unconditionally and expand His Kingdom on earth?

¹⁸One day as Jesus was walking along the shore of the Sea of Galilee, he saw two brothers—Simon, also called Peter, and Andrew—throwing a net into the water, for they fished for a living.

¹⁹Jesus called out to them, "Come, follow me, and I will show you how to fish for people!" ²⁰And they left their nets at once and followed him.

²¹A little farther up the shore he saw two other brothers, James and John, sitting in a boat with their father, Zebedee, repairing their nets. And he called them to come, too. ²²They immediately followed him, leaving the boat and their father behind.

²³Jesus traveled throughout the region of Galilee, teaching in the synagogues and announcing the Good News about the Kingdom. And he healed every kind of disease and illness.

²⁴News about him spread as far as Syria, and people soon began bringing to him all who were sick. And whatever their sickness or disease, or if they were demon possessed or epileptic or paralyzed—he healed them all.

²⁵Large crowds followed him wherever he went—people from Galilee, the Ten Towns, Jerusalem, from all over Judea, and from east of the Jordan River.

~ Matthew 4:18-25

The Citizens of God's Kingdom

God often chooses people to represent His Kingdom that we don't think are fit for the job. People such as mourners, the hungry, peacemakers, and even people who are being persecuted. If you are suffering because you're doing what is right, God will reward you in the end.

¹One day as he saw the crowds gathering, Jesus went up on the mountainside and sat down. His disciples gathered around him, ²and he began to teach them.

³"God blesses those who are poor and realize their need for him, for the Kingdom of Heaven is theirs.

⁴"God blesses those who mourn, for they will be comforted.

⁵"God blesses those who are humble, for they will inherit the whole earth.

⁶"God blesses those who hunger and thirst for justice, for they will be satisfied.

⁷"God blesses those who are merciful, for they will be shown mercy.

⁸"God blesses those whose hearts are pure, for they will see God.

⁹"God blesses those who work for peace, for they will be called the children of God.

¹⁰"God blesses those who are persecuted for doing right, for the Kingdom of Heaven is theirs.

¹¹"God blesses you when people mock you and persecute you and lie about you and say all sorts of evil things against you because you are my followers.

¹²"Be happy about it! Be very glad! For a great reward awaits you in heaven. And remember, the ancient prophets were persecuted in the same way."

~ Matthew 5:1-12

Salt and Light

Jesus asks that His children should be the salt and the light of the world – salt to make the earth a better place, and light to illuminate the world. He wants your life to radiate so much light that people will praise God for your presence in their lives.

[13]"You are the salt of the earth. But what good is salt if it has lost its flavor? Can you make it salty again? It will be thrown out and trampled underfoot as worthless.

[14]"You are the light of the world—like a city on a hilltop that cannot be hidden.

[15]"No one lights a lamp and then puts it under a basket. Instead, a lamp is placed on a stand, where it gives light to everyone in the house.

[16]"In the same way, let your good deeds shine out for all to see, so that everyone will praise your heavenly Father."

~ Matthew 5:13-16

Love without Boundaries

The type of love that God expects from you includes love for your enemies and those who persecute you. He wants you to love others without boundaries, just like He loves all people completely. You will only be able to do this if the Holy Spirit makes it possible for you.

38"You have heard the law that says the punishment must match the injury: 'An eye for an eye, and a tooth for a tooth.' 39But I say, do not resist an evil person! If someone slaps you on the right cheek, offer the other cheek also.

40"If you are sued in court and your shirt is taken from you, give your coat, too. 41If a soldier demands that you carry his gear for a mile, carry it two miles. 42Give to those who ask, and don't turn away from those who want to borrow.

43"You have heard the law that says, 'Love your neighbor' and hate your enemy. 44But I say, love your enemies! Pray for those who persecute you! 45In that way, you will be acting as true children of your Father in heaven. For he gives his sunlight to both the evil and the good, and he sends rain on the just and the unjust alike.

46"If you love only those who love you, what reward is there for that? Even corrupt tax collectors do that much. 47If you are kind only to your friends, how are you different from anyone else? Even pagans do that. 48But you are to be perfect, even as your Father in heaven is perfect."

~ Matthew 5:38-48

A Blueprint for Prayer

Jesus taught His disciples how to pray by giving them the Lord's Prayer. Build your own prayers on this and don't worry about using the right words, because God already knows exactly what you need. Forgive those who sin against you so that God can also forgive you.

[5]"When you pray, don't be like the hypocrites who love to pray publicly on street corners and in the synagogues where everyone can see them. I tell you the truth, that is all the reward they will ever get.

[6]"But when you pray, go away by yourself, shut the door behind you, and pray to your Father in private. Then your Father, who sees everything, will reward you.

[7]"When you pray, don't babble on and on as people of other religions do. They think their prayers are answered merely by repeating their words again and again. [8]Don't be like them, for your Father knows exactly what you need even before you ask him! [9]Pray like this: Our Father in heaven, may your name be kept holy. [10]May your Kingdom come soon. May your will be done on earth, as it is in heaven. [11]Give us today the food we need, [12]and forgive us our sins, as we have forgiven those who sin against us. [13]And don't let us yield to temptation, but rescue us from the evil one.

[14]"If you forgive those who sin against you, your heavenly Father will forgive you. [15]But if you refuse to forgive others, your Father will not forgive your sins."

~ Matthew 6:5-15

Treasures in Heaven

People are obsessed with earthly treasures that don't last. Having treasures in heaven are much better, because your heart is where your treasures are. God will take even better care of you than He takes care of the birds and the flowers.

¹⁹"Don't store up treasures here on earth, where moths eat them and rust destroys them, and where thieves break in and steal. ²⁰Store your treasures in heaven, where moths and rust cannot destroy, and thieves do not break in and steal. ²¹Wherever your treasure is, there the desires of your heart will also be.

²⁵"That is why I tell you not to worry about everyday life—whether you have enough food and drink, or enough clothes to wear. Isn't life more than food, and your body more than clothing?

²⁶"Look at the birds. They don't plant or harvest or store food in barns, for your heavenly Father feeds them. And aren't you far more valuable to him than they are? ²⁷Can all your worries add a single moment to your life?

²⁸"And why worry about your clothing? Look at the lilies of the field and how they grow. They don't work or make their clothing, ²⁹yet Solomon in all his glory was not dressed as beautifully as they are.

³⁰"And if God cares so wonderfully for wildflowers that are here today and thrown into the fire tomorrow, he will certainly care for you. Why do you have so little faith?"

~ Matthew 6:19-21, 25-30

The Cost of Discipleship

If you want to be Jesus' disciple, you have to be willing to give up everything and follow Him to the end. He is the One whom even the wind and the waters obey. If you firmly believe that Christ's redemption is also for you, then you are truly saved.

18When Jesus saw the crowd around him, he instructed his disciples to cross to the other side of the lake. 19Then one of the teachers of religious law said to him, "Teacher, I will follow you wherever you go."

20But Jesus replied, "Foxes have dens to live in, and birds have nests, but the Son of Man has no place even to lay his head." 21Another of his disciples said, "Lord, first let me return home and bury my father." 22But Jesus told him, "Follow me now. Let the spiritually dead bury their own dead."

23Then Jesus got into the boat and started across the lake with his disciples. 24Suddenly, a fierce storm struck the lake, with waves breaking into the boat. But Jesus was sleeping.

25The disciples went and woke him up, shouting, "Lord, save us! We're going to drown!" 26Jesus responded, "Why are you afraid? You have so little faith!" Then he got up and rebuked the wind and waves, and suddenly there was a great calm.

27The disciples were amazed. "Who is this man?" they asked. "Even the winds and waves obey him!"

~ Matthew 8:18-27

Jesus Performs Miracles

Jesus went with Jairus to heal his sick daughter. Along the way Jesus paused for a woman with an incurable condition, and healed her. In the meantime the little girl died, but Jesus raised her from the dead. It is never too late for God to do wonders, even if you feel that it's too late in your life today.

[18] As Jesus was saying this, the leader of a synagogue came and knelt before him. "My daughter has just died," he said, "but you can bring her back to life again if you just come and lay your hand on her."

[19] So Jesus and his disciples got up and went with him. [20] Just then a woman who had suffered for twelve years with constant bleeding came up behind him. She touched the fringe of his robe, [21] for she thought, "If I can just touch his robe, I will be healed."

[22] Jesus turned around, and when he saw her he said, "Daughter, be encouraged! Your faith has made you well." And the woman was healed at that moment.

[23] When Jesus arrived at the official's home, he saw the noisy crowd and heard the funeral music. [24] "Get out!" he told them. "The girl isn't dead; she's only asleep." But the crowd laughed at him.

[25] After the crowd was put outside, however, Jesus went in and took the girl by the hand, and she stood up! [26] The report of this miracle swept through the entire countryside.

~ Matthew 9:18-26

According to Your Faith

When two blind men asked Jesus to have mercy on them and heal them, He said that it would be done according to their faith. Jesus' words are still true for you. If you don't believe in Him, He can't do anything for you.

^{27}After Jesus left the girl's home, two blind men followed along behind him, shouting, "Son of David, have mercy on us!"

^{28}They went right into the house where he was staying, and Jesus asked them, "Do you believe I can make you see?" "Yes, Lord," they told him, "we do." ^{29}Then he touched their eyes and said, "Because of your faith, it will happen."

^{30}Then their eyes were opened, and they could see! Jesus sternly warned them, "Don't tell anyone about this." ^{31}But instead, they went out and spread his fame all over the region.

^{32}When they left, a demon-possessed man who couldn't speak was brought to Jesus. ^{33}So Jesus cast out the demon, and then the man began to speak. The crowds were amazed. "Nothing like this has ever happened in Israel!" they exclaimed. ^{34}But the Pharisees said, "He can cast out demons because he is empowered by the prince of demons."

^{35}Jesus traveled through all the towns and villages of that area, teaching in the synagogues and announcing the Good News about the Kingdom. And he healed every kind of disease and illness.

~ Matthew 9:27-35

More than Sparrows

God's children don't have to fear anything. Not even
a sparrow falls to the ground without God knowing
about it. And where it concerns you – you are worth
more than a whole flock of sparrows. God has even
numbered every hair on your head!

²⁸"Don't be afraid of those who want to kill your body; they
cannot touch your soul. Fear only God, who can destroy both
soul and body in hell. ²⁹What is the price of two sparrows—one
copper coin? But not a single sparrow can fall to the ground
without your Father knowing it.

³⁰"And the very hairs on your head are all numbered. ³¹So
don't be afraid; you are more valuable to God than a whole flock
of sparrows.

³²"Everyone who acknowledges me publicly here on earth, I
will also acknowledge before my Father in heaven. ³³But everyone who denies me here on earth, I will also deny before my
Father in heaven.

³⁴"Don't imagine that I came to bring peace to the earth! I
came not to bring peace, but a sword. ³⁵'I have come to set a
man against his father, a daughter against her mother, and a
daughter-in-law against her mother-in-law. ³⁶Your enemies will
be right in your own household!'

³⁷"If you love your father or mother more than you love me,
you are not worthy of being mine; or if you love your son or
daughter more than me, you are not worthy of being mine.

³⁸"If you refuse to take up your cross and follow me, you are
not worthy of being mine. ³⁹If you cling to your life, you will lose
it; but if you give up your life for me, you will find it."

~ Matthew 10:28-39

When You Are Tired ...

When you are tired and you feel like you can't carry on by yourself anymore, Jesus invites you to come to Him so that He can renew your life. His yoke is soft, and His burden is light. Feel free to exchange your heavy burden for God's lighter one.

[25]At that time Jesus prayed this prayer: "O Father, Lord of heaven and earth, thank you for hiding these things from those who think themselves wise and clever, and for revealing them to the childlike. [26]Yes, Father, it pleased you to do it this way!

[27]"My Father has entrusted everything to me. No one truly knows the Son except the Father, and no one truly knows the Father except the Son and those to whom the Son chooses to reveal him."

[28]Then Jesus said, "Come to me, all of you who are weary and carry heavy burdens, and I will give you rest. [29]Take my yoke upon you. Let me teach you, because I am humble and gentle at heart, and you will find rest for your souls. [30]For my yoke is easy to bear, and the burden I give you is light."

~ Matthew 11:25-30

God's Precious Kingdom

God's Kingdom is so precious that you need to give up everything to share in it. Make sure that nothing else in your life is more important than God's Kingdom.

[31]Here is another illustration Jesus used: "The Kingdom of Heaven is like a mustard seed planted in a field. [32]It is the smallest of all seeds, but it becomes the largest of garden plants; it grows into a tree, and birds come and make nests in its branches."

[33]Jesus also used this illustration: "The Kingdom of Heaven is like the yeast a woman used in making bread. Even though she put only a little yeast in three measures of flour, it permeated every part of the dough."

[34]Jesus always used stories and illustrations like these when speaking to the crowds. In fact, he never spoke to them without using such parables. [35]This fulfilled what God had spoken through the prophet: "I will speak to you in parables. I will explain things hidden since the creation of the world."

[44]"The Kingdom of Heaven is like a treasure that a man discovered hidden in a field. In his excitement, he hid it again and sold everything he owned to get enough money to buy the field.

[45]"Again, the Kingdom of Heaven is like a merchant on the lookout for choice pearls. [46]When he discovered a pearl of great value, he sold everything he owned and bought it!"

~ Matthew 13:31-35, 44-46

Jesus Feeds More than Five Thousand People

When Jesus saw that His followers did not have any food to eat, He asked His disciples to bring Him the food they had. After He thanked God for it, He divided the food and fed more than five thousand people with it. God can and will fulfill your needs too.

[13]As soon as Jesus heard the news, he left in a boat to a remote area to be alone. But the crowds heard where he was headed and followed on foot from many towns.

[14]Jesus saw the huge crowd as he stepped from the boat, and he had compassion on them and healed their sick. [15]That evening the disciples came to him and said, "This is a remote place, and it's already getting late. Send the crowds away so they can go to the villages and buy food for themselves."

[16]But Jesus said, "That isn't necessary—you feed them."
[17]"But we have only five loaves of bread and two fish!" they answered. [18]"Bring them here," he said.

[19]Then he told the people to sit down on the grass. Jesus took the five loaves and two fish, looked up toward heaven, and blessed them. Then, breaking the loaves into pieces, he gave the bread to the disciples, who distributed it to the people.

[20]They all ate as much as they wanted, and afterward, the disciples picked up twelve baskets of leftovers. [21]About 5,000 men were fed that day, in addition to all the women and children!

~ Matthew 14:13-21

Faith that Doubts

Peter was courageous enough to get out of the boat and walk on the water toward Jesus. But when he saw how big the waves were, he got scared and started to sink. Fortunately, Jesus was there to grab hold of his hand and save him.

[22]Immediately after this, Jesus insisted that his disciples get back into the boat and cross to the other side of the lake, while he sent the people home.

[23]After sending them home, he went up into the hills by himself to pray. Night fell while he was there alone. [24]Meanwhile, the disciples were in trouble far away from land, for a strong wind had risen, and they were fighting heavy waves.

[25]About three o'clock in the morning Jesus came toward them, walking on the water. [26]When the disciples saw him walking on the water, they were terrified. In their fear, they cried out, "It's a ghost!" [27]But Jesus spoke to them at once. "Don't be afraid," he said. "Take courage. I am here!"

[28]Then Peter called to him, "Lord, if it's really you, tell me to come to you, walking on the water."

[29]"Yes, come," Jesus said. So Peter went over the side of the boat and walked on the water toward Jesus.

[30]But when he saw the strong wind and the waves, he was terrified and began to sink. "Save me, Lord!" he shouted. [31]Jesus immediately reached out and grabbed him. "You have so little faith," Jesus said. "Why did you doubt me?" [32]When they climbed back into the boat, the wind stopped. [33]Then the disciples worshiped him. "You really are the Son of God!" they exclaimed.

~ Matthew 14:22-33

A Heathen Woman's Faith

A heathen woman came to Jesus and asked Him to heal her sick daughter, but Jesus ignored her. However, the woman refused to give up. She kept on asking, and because of her faith, Jesus granted her request.

²¹Then Jesus left Galilee and went north to the region of Tyre and Sidon. ²²A Gentile woman who lived there came to him, pleading, "Have mercy on me, O Lord, Son of David! For my daughter is possessed by a demon that torments her severely."

²³But Jesus gave her no reply, not even a word. Then his disciples urged him to send her away. "Tell her to go away," they said. "She is bothering us with all her begging."

²⁴Then Jesus said to the woman, "I was sent only to help God's lost sheep—the people of Israel." ²⁵But she came and worshiped him, pleading again, "Lord, help me!" ²⁶Jesus responded, "It isn't right to take food from the children and throw it to the dogs."

²⁷She replied, "That's true, Lord, but even dogs are allowed to eat the scraps that fall beneath their masters' table."

²⁸"Dear woman," Jesus said to her, "your faith is great. Your request is granted." And her daughter was instantly healed.

~ Matthew 15:21-28

Are You Willing to Follow Jesus?

To be a follower of Jesus is not easy. It asks from you to take up your cross and follow Him, to be willing to deny your own selfish ambitions and perhaps even to lay down your life for Him.

21From then on Jesus began to tell his disciples plainly that it was necessary for him to go to Jerusalem, and that he would suffer many terrible things at the hands of the elders, the leading priests, and the teachers of religious law. He would be killed, but on the third day he would be raised from the dead.

22But Peter took him aside and began to reprimand him for saying such things. "Heaven forbid, Lord," he said. "This will never happen to you!" 23Jesus turned to Peter and said, "Get away from me, Satan! You are a dangerous trap to me. You are seeing things merely from a human point of view, not from God's."

24Then Jesus said to his disciples, "If any of you wants to be my follower, you must turn from your selfish ways, take up your cross, and follow me. 25If you try to hang on to your life, you will lose it. But if you give up your life for my sake, you will save it.

26"And what do you benefit if you gain the whole world but lose your own soul? Is anything worth more than your soul? 27For the Son of Man will come with his angels in the glory of his Father and will judge all people according to their deeds.

28"And I tell you the truth, some standing here right now will not die before they see the Son of Man coming in his Kingdom."

~ Matthew 16:21-28

August

On the Mount of Transfiguration

Jesus took three of His disciples with Him to a high mountain. There His appearance was transfigured, He had a conversation with Moses and Elijah, and God confirmed that Jesus is His Son. For the first time the disciples experienced His glory first hand.

[1]Six days later Jesus took Peter and the two brothers, James and John, and led them up a high mountain to be alone. [2]As the men watched, Jesus' appearance was transformed so that his face shone like the sun, and his clothes became as white as light.

[3]Suddenly, Moses and Elijah appeared and began talking with Jesus. [4]Peter exclaimed, "Lord, it's wonderful for us to be here! If you want, I'll make three shelters as memorials—one for you, one for Moses, and one for Elijah."

[5]But even as he spoke, a bright cloud overshadowed them, and a voice from the cloud said, "This is my dearly loved Son, who brings me great joy. Listen to him." [6]The disciples were terrified and fell face down on the ground. [7]Then Jesus came over and touched them. "Get up," he said. "Don't be afraid." [8]And when they looked up, Moses and Elijah were gone, and they saw only Jesus.

[9]As they went back down the mountain, Jesus commanded them, "Don't tell anyone what you have seen until the Son of Man has been raised from the dead." [10]Then his disciples asked him, "Why do the teachers of religious law insist that Elijah must return before the Messiah comes?"

[11]Jesus replied, "Elijah is indeed coming first to get everything ready. [12]But I tell you, Elijah has already come, but he wasn't recognized, and they chose to abuse him. And in the same way they will also make the Son of Man suffer."

~ Matthew 17:1-12

Faith As a Mustard Seed

When the disciples were unable to heal a demon-possessed boy because of their little faith, Jesus told them that a person only needs faith as small as a mustard seed to perform wonders. How big is your faith?

¹⁴At the foot of the mountain, a large crowd was waiting for them. A man came and knelt before Jesus and said, ¹⁵"Lord, have mercy on my son. He has seizures and suffers terribly. He often falls into the fire or into the water.

¹⁶"So I brought him to your disciples, but they couldn't heal him." ¹⁷Jesus said, "You faithless and corrupt people! How long must I be with you? How long must I put up with you? Bring the boy here to me." ¹⁸Then Jesus rebuked the demon in the boy, and it left him. From that moment the boy was well.

¹⁹Afterward the disciples asked Jesus privately, "Why couldn't we cast out that demon?" ²⁰"You don't have enough faith," Jesus told them. "I tell you the truth, if you had faith even as small as a mustard seed, you could say to this mountain, 'Move from here to there,' and it would move. Nothing would be impossible."

²²After they gathered again in Galilee, Jesus told them, "The Son of Man is going to be betrayed into the hands of his enemies. ²³He will be killed, but on the third day he will be raised from the dead." And the disciples were filled with grief.

~ Matthew 17:14-20, 22-23

The Greatest in the Kingdom of Heaven

When the disciples asked Jesus which one of them were going to be the greatest in God's kingdom, Jesus called a child. He explained that whoever humbles themselves like children, is the greatest in the Kingdom. And anyone who welcomes a child in His name, also welcomes Him.

18 ¹About that time the disciples came to Jesus and asked, "Who is greatest in the Kingdom of Heaven?" ²Jesus called a little child to him and put the child among them. ³Then he said, "I tell you the truth, unless you turn from your sins and become like little children, you will never get into the Kingdom of Heaven.

⁴"So anyone who becomes as humble as this little child is the greatest in the Kingdom of Heaven. ⁵And anyone who welcomes a little child like this on my behalf is welcoming me.

⁶"But if you cause one of these little ones who trusts in me to fall into sin, it would be better for you to have a large millstone tied around your neck and be drowned in the depths of the sea.

¹⁰"Beware that you don't look down on any of these little ones. For I tell you that in heaven their angels are always in the presence of my heavenly Father."

19 ¹³One day some parents brought their children to Jesus so he could lay his hands on them and pray for them. But the disciples scolded the parents for bothering him. ¹⁴But Jesus said, "Let the children come to me. Don't stop them! For the Kingdom of Heaven belongs to those who are like these children."

~ Matthew 18:1-6, 10; 19:13-14

Forgive from Your Heart

Peter asked Jesus if it would be enough to forgive someone who has sinned against you seven times. But Jesus replied that we should not forgive seven times, but seventy-seven times. God expects unlimited forgiveness from you, in the same way we can rely on His unlimited forgiveness.

21Then Peter came to him and asked, "Lord, how often should I forgive someone who sins against me? Seven times?"

22"No, not seven times," Jesus replied, "but seventy times seven! 23Therefore, the Kingdom of Heaven can be compared to a king who decided to bring his accounts up to date with servants who had borrowed money from him. 24In the process, one of his debtors was brought in who owed him millions of dollars.

26"But the man fell down before his master and begged him, 'Please, be patient with me, and I will pay it all.' 27Then his master was filled with pity for him, and he released him and forgave his debt. 28But when the man left the king, he went to a fellow servant who owed him a few thousand dollars. He grabbed him by the throat and demanded instant payment. 29"His fellow servant fell down before him and begged for a little more time. 'Be patient with me, and I will pay it,' he pleaded. 30But his creditor wouldn't wait. He had the man arrested and put in prison until the debt could be paid in full.

32"Then the king called in the man he had forgiven and said, 'You evil servant! I forgave you that tremendous debt because you pleaded with me. 33Shouldn't you have mercy on your fellow servant, just as I had mercy on you?' 34Then the angry king sent the man to prison to be tortured until he had paid his entire debt. 35That's what my heavenly Father will do to you if you refuse to forgive your brothers and sisters from your heart."

~ Matthew 18:21-24, 26-30, 32-35

Marriage Is Holy

Your marriage is holy and established by God. People may not separate what He has joined together. These days almost half of all marriages end in divorce. How holy is your marriage? Are you doing enough to protect it?

[3]Some Pharisees came and tried to trap him with this question: "Should a man be allowed to divorce his wife for just any reason?"

[4]"Haven't you read the Scriptures?" Jesus replied. "They record that from the beginning 'God made them male and female.'

[5]"And he said, 'This explains why a man leaves his father and mother and is joined to his wife, and the two are united into one.' [6]Since they are no longer two but one, let no one split apart what God has joined together."

[7]"Then why did Moses say in the law that a man could give his wife a written notice of divorce and send her away?" they asked. [8]Jesus replied, "Moses permitted divorce only as a concession to your hard hearts, but it was not what God had originally intended.

[9]"And I tell you this, whoever divorces his wife and marries someone else commits adultery—unless his wife has been unfaithful." [10]Jesus' disciples then said to him, "If this is the case, it is better not to marry!"

[11]"Not everyone can accept this statement," Jesus said. "Only those whom God helps. [12]Some are born as eunuchs, some have been made eunuchs by others, and some choose not to marry for the sake of the Kingdom of Heaven. Let anyone accept this who can."

~ Matthew 19:3-12

Wealth and the Kingdom

A wealthy young man did everything God wanted, but he was not willing to give up his possessions. The richer you are, the more difficult it becomes to follow Jesus unconditionally. Be careful that your possessions don't stand between you and going to heaven.

[16]Someone came to Jesus with this question: "Teacher, what good deed must I do to have eternal life?"

[17]"Why ask me about what is good?" Jesus replied. "There is only One who is good. But to answer your question—if you want to receive eternal life, keep the commandments."

[18]"Which ones?" the man asked. And Jesus replied: "'You must not murder. You must not commit adultery. You must not steal. You must not testify falsely. [19]Honor your father and mother. Love your neighbor as yourself.'"

[20]"I've obeyed all these commandments," the young man replied. "What else must I do?" [21]Jesus told him, "If you want to be perfect, go and sell all your possessions and give the money to the poor, and you will have treasure in heaven. Then come, follow me." [22]But when the young man heard this, he went away sad, for he had many possessions. [23]Then Jesus said to his disciples, "I tell you the truth, it is very hard for a rich person to enter the Kingdom of Heaven.

[24]"I'll say it again—it is easier for a camel to go through the eye of a needle than for a rich person to enter the Kingdom of God!" [25]The disciples were astounded. "Then who in the world can be saved?" they asked. [26]Jesus looked at them intently and said, "Humanly speaking, it is impossible. But with God everything is possible."

~ Matthew 19:16-26

The Greatest Commandment

When Jesus was asked which is the greatest commandment in God's Law, He was ready with an answer: Love God with your entire being and love your neighbor as yourself. This commandment is still valid today. Do your deeds show that you love God and your neighbors?

³⁴But when the Pharisees heard that he had silenced the Sadducees with his reply, they met together to question him again.

³⁵One of them, an expert in religious law, tried to trap him with this question: ³⁶"Teacher, which is the most important commandment in the law of Moses?"

³⁷Jesus replied, "'You must love the LORD your God with all your heart, all your soul, and all your mind.' ³⁸This is the first and greatest commandment. ³⁹A second is equally important: 'Love your neighbor as yourself.' ⁴⁰The entire law and all the demands of the prophets are based on these two commandments."

~ Matthew 22:34-40

When Jesus Returns

Jesus told His disciples that everyone will see Him return on the clouds with power and glory. Nobody except God knows exactly when this will happen. We must be ready for it every day, because Jesus will come unexpectedly.

[27]"For as the lightning flashes in the east and shines to the west, so it will be when the Son of Man comes.

[29]"Immediately after the anguish of those days, the sun will be darkened, the moon will give no light, the stars will fall from the sky, and the powers in the heavens will be shaken.

[30]"And then at last, the sign that the Son of Man is coming will appear in the heavens, and there will be deep mourning among all the peoples of the earth. And they will see the Son of Man coming on the clouds of heaven with power and great glory.

[31]"And he will send out his angels with the mighty blast of a trumpet, and they will gather his chosen ones from all over the world—from the farthest ends of the earth and heaven. [32]Now learn a lesson from the fig tree. When its branches bud and its leaves begin to sprout, you know that summer is near. [33]In the same way, when you see all these things, you can know his return is very near, right at the door.

[34]"I tell you the truth, this generation will not pass from the scene until all these things take place. [35]Heaven and earth will disappear, but my words will never disappear.

[36]"However, no one knows the day or hour when these things will happen, not even the angels in heaven or the Son himself. Only the Father knows."

~ Matthew 24:27, 29-36

Make the Most of Your Gifts

God gave unique talents and gifts to each of His children. If you don't use your God-given talents to serve God and others, they have no value. But when you use your talents to further God's kingdom on earth, you will receive even more in future.

24"Then the servant with the one bag of silver came and said, 'Master, I knew you were a harsh man, harvesting crops you didn't plant and gathering crops you didn't cultivate. 25I was afraid I would lose your money, so I hid it in the earth. Look, here is your money back.'

26"But the master replied, 'You wicked and lazy servant! If you knew I harvested crops I didn't plant and gathered crops I didn't cultivate, 27why didn't you deposit my money in the bank? At least I could have gotten some interest on it.'

28"Then he ordered, 'Take the money from this servant, and give it to the one with the ten bags of silver. 29To those who use well what they are given, even more will be given, and they will have an abundance. But from those who do nothing, even what little they have will be taken away. 30Now throw this useless servant into outer darkness, where there will be weeping and gnashing of teeth.'"

~ Matthew 25:24-30

Care About Others

It is God's will that you truly care about other people and help them. Everything you do for others, you also do for God. When Jesus comes again, you will be judged according to the help you gave to the less fortunate.

[31]"But when the Son of Man comes in his glory, and all the angels with him, then he will sit upon his glorious throne. [32]All the nations will be gathered in his presence, and he will separate the people as a shepherd separates the sheep from the goats. [33]He will place the sheep at his right hand and the goats at his left.

[34]"Then the King will say to those on his right, 'Come, you who are blessed by my Father, inherit the Kingdom prepared for you from the creation of the world. [35]For I was hungry, and you fed me. I was thirsty, and you gave me a drink. I was a stranger, and you invited me into your home. [36]I was naked, and you gave me clothing. I was sick, and you cared for me. I was in prison, and you visited me.'

[37]"Then these righteous ones will reply, 'Lord, when did we ever see you hungry and feed you? Or thirsty and give you something to drink? [38]Or a stranger and show you hospitality? Or naked and give you clothing? [39]When did we ever see you sick or in prison and visit you?'

[40]"And the King will say, 'I tell you the truth, when you did it to one of the least of these my brothers and sisters, you were doing it to me!'"

~ Matthew 25:31-40

A Woman's Intuition

A woman anointed Jesus with very expensive perfume and His disciples were very unhappy because they could have sold the perfume and given the money to the poor. But Jesus knew that by doing this, the woman showed her love for Him and was preparing His body for burial.

[6]Meanwhile, Jesus was in Bethany at the home of Simon, a man who had previously had leprosy. [7]While he was eating, a woman came in with a beautiful alabaster jar of expensive perfume and poured it over his head.

[8]The disciples were indignant when they saw this. "What a waste!" they said. [9]"It could have been sold for a high price and the money given to the poor."

[10]But Jesus, aware of this, replied, "Why criticize this woman for doing such a good thing to me? [11]You will always have the poor among you, but you will not always have me. [12]She has poured this perfume on me to prepare my body for burial.

[13]"I tell you the truth, wherever the Good News is preached throughout the world, this woman's deed will be remembered and discussed."

~ Matthew 26:6-13

Jesus Institutes Holy Communion

Jesus instituted Holy Communion by saying that the communion bread is His body, and the communion wine is His blood. When you partake in Holy Communion, think about Jesus' body that was broken and His blood that was shed to redeem you.

20When it was evening, Jesus sat down at the table with the twelve disciples. 21While they were eating, he said, "I tell you the truth, one of you will betray me."

22Greatly distressed, each one asked in turn, "Am I the one, Lord?" 23He replied, "One of you who has just eaten from this bowl with me will betray me. 24For the Son of Man must die, as the Scriptures declared long ago. But how terrible it will be for the one who betrays him. It would be far better for that man if he had never been born!"

25Judas, the one who would betray him, also asked, "Rabbi, am I the one?" And Jesus told him, "You have said it."

26As they were eating, Jesus took some bread and blessed it. Then he broke it in pieces and gave it to the disciples, saying, "Take this and eat it, for this is my body." 27And he took a cup of wine and gave thanks to God for it. He gave it to them and said, "Each of you drink from it, 28for this is my blood, which confirms the covenant between God and his people. It is poured out as a sacrifice to forgive the sins of many.

29"Mark my words—I will not drink wine again until the day I drink it new with you in my Father's Kingdom." 30Then they sang a hymn and went out to the Mount of Olives.

~ Matthew 26:20-30

Put God's Will First

Jesus prayed earnestly in Gethsemane that God spare Him the suffering that lay ahead; yet He still put God's will first. You may ask God for things as long as you are willing to abide in His will.

³⁶Jesus went with them to the olive grove called Gethsemane, and he said, "Sit here while I go over there to pray." ³⁷He took Peter and Zebedee's two sons, James and John, and he became anguished and distressed.

³⁸He told them, "My soul is crushed with grief to the point of death. Stay here and keep watch with me." ³⁹He went on a little farther and bowed with his face to the ground, praying, "My Father! If it is possible, let this cup of suffering be taken away from me. Yet I want your will to be done, not mine."

⁴⁰Then he returned to the disciples and found them asleep. He said to Peter, "Couldn't you watch with me even one hour? ⁴¹Keep watch and pray, so that you will not give in to temptation. For the spirit is willing, but the body is weak!"

⁴²Then Jesus left them a second time and prayed, "My Father! If this cup cannot be taken away unless I drink it, your will be done." ⁴³When he returned to them again, he found them sleeping, for they couldn't keep their eyes open. ⁴⁴So he went to pray a third time, saying the same things again.

⁴⁵Then he came to the disciples and said, "Go ahead and sleep. Have your rest. But look—the time has come. The Son of Man is betrayed into the hands of sinners. ⁴⁶Up, let's be going. Look, my betrayer is here!"

~ Matthew 26:36-46

Peter Denies Jesus

Peter said that he would never deny Jesus, but then he did exactly that – three times in a row. Before you judge Peter, think carefully if you don't sometimes deny Jesus with your words or deeds.

³¹On the way, Jesus told them, "Tonight all of you will desert me. For the Scriptures say, 'God will strike the Shepherd, and the sheep of the flock will be scattered.'

³²"But after I have been raised from the dead, I will go ahead of you to Galilee and meet you there." ³³Peter declared, "Even if everyone else deserts you, I will never desert you." ³⁴Jesus replied, "I tell you the truth, Peter—this very night, before the rooster crows, you will deny three times that you even know me."

³⁵"No!" Peter insisted. "Even if I have to die with you, I will never deny you!" And all the other disciples vowed the same.

⁶⁹Meanwhile, Peter was sitting outside in the courtyard. A servant girl came over and said to him, "You were one of those with Jesus the Galilean." ⁷⁰But Peter denied it in front of everyone. "I don't know what you're talking about," he said.

⁷¹Later, out by the gate, another servant girl noticed him and said to those standing around, "This man was with Jesus of Nazareth." ⁷²Again Peter denied it, this time with an oath. "I don't even know the man," he said. ⁷³A little later some of the other bystanders came over to Peter and said, "You must be one of them; we can tell by your Galilean accent."

⁷⁴Peter swore, "A curse on me if I'm lying—I don't know the man!" And immediately the rooster crowed. ⁷⁵Suddenly, Jesus' words flashed through Peter's mind: "Before the rooster crows, you will deny three times that you even know me." And he went away, weeping bitterly.

~ Matthew 26:31-35, 69-75

Jesus Is Crucified

Jesus was sentenced to death as an innocent Man, tortured, and then crucified while the people that He came to earth for ridiculed Him. Never forget how much He had to suffer so that God can forgive your sins.

³²Along the way, they came across a man named Simon, who was from Cyrene, and the soldiers forced him to carry Jesus' cross. ³³And they went out to a place called Golgotha (which means "Place of the Skull").

³⁴The soldiers gave him wine mixed with bitter gall, but when he had tasted it, he refused to drink it. ³⁵After they had nailed him to the cross, the soldiers gambled for his clothes by throwing dice. ³⁶Then they sat around and kept guard as he hung there.

³⁷A sign was fastened above Jesus' head, announcing the charge against him. It read: "This is Jesus, the King of the Jews." ³⁸Two revolutionaries were crucified with him, one on his right and one on his left.

³⁹The people passing by shouted abuse, shaking their heads in mockery. ⁴⁰"Look at you now!" they yelled at him. "You said you were going to destroy the Temple and rebuild it in three days. Well then, if you are the Son of God, save yourself and come down from the cross!"

⁴¹The leading priests, the teachers of religious law, and the elders also mocked Jesus. ⁴²"He saved others," they scoffed, "but he can't save himself! So he is the King of Israel, is he? Let him come down from the cross right now, and we will believe in him! ⁴³He trusted God, so let God rescue him now if he wants him! For he said, 'I am the Son of God.'"

~ Matthew 27:32-43

Abandoned by God

While hanging on the cross Jesus experienced that even His Father, on whose support He could always count, abandoned Him. Before He died He called out, "My God, My God, why have You forsaken Me?" Jesus suffered and died so that you would never have to be without God again.

⁴⁵At noon, darkness fell across the whole land until three o'clock. ⁴⁶At about three o'clock, Jesus called out with a loud voice, *"Eli, Eli, lema sabachthani?"* which means "My God, my God, why have you abandoned me?" ⁴⁷Some of the bystanders misunderstood and thought he was calling for the prophet Elijah.

⁴⁸One of them ran and filled a sponge with sour wine, holding it up to him on a reed stick so he could drink. ⁴⁹But the rest said, "Wait! Let's see whether Elijah comes to save him." ⁵⁰Then Jesus shouted out again, and he released his spirit.

⁵¹At that moment the curtain in the sanctuary of the Temple was torn in two, from top to bottom. The earth shook, rocks split apart, ⁵²and tombs opened. The bodies of many godly men and women who had died were raised from the dead. ⁵³They left the cemetery after Jesus' resurrection, went into the holy city of Jerusalem, and appeared to many people. ⁵⁴The Roman officer and the other soldiers at the crucifixion were terrified by the earthquake and all that had happened. They said, "This man truly was the Son of God!"

⁵⁵And many women who had come from Galilee with Jesus to care for him were watching from a distance. ⁵⁶Among them were Mary Magdalene, Mary (the mother of James and Joseph), and the mother of James and John, the sons of Zebedee.

~ Matthew 27:45-56

The Great Commission

After Jesus' resurrection He appeared to His disciples. He asked them to make disciples of all the nations; to baptize them in the name of the Father, the Son, and the Holy Spirit. He also promised to be with them forever. This commission and promise is yours too.

¹⁶Then the eleven disciples left for Galilee, going to the mountain where Jesus had told them to go.

¹⁷When they saw him, they worshiped him—but some of them doubted! ¹⁸Jesus came and told his disciples, "I have been given all authority in heaven and on earth.

¹⁹"Therefore, go and make disciples of all the nations, baptizing them in the name of the Father and the Son and the Holy Spirit.

²⁰"Teach these new disciples to obey all the commands I have given you. And be sure of this: I am with you always, even to the end of the age."

~ Matthew 28:16-20

Follow Jesus!

Jesus calls on people to follow Him and to help Him make fishers of men. The first disciples were ready to leave everything and follow Jesus unconditionally. Do you understand what it means to be a fisher of men?

[14]Later on, after John was arrested, Jesus went into Galilee, where he preached God's Good News. [15]"The time promised by God has come at last!" he announced. "The Kingdom of God is near! Repent of your sins and believe the Good News!"

[16]One day as Jesus was walking along the shore of the Sea of Galilee, he saw Simon and his brother Andrew throwing a net into the water, for they fished for a living.

[17]Jesus called out to them, "Come, follow me, and I will show you how to fish for people!" [18]And they left their nets at once and followed him.

[19]A little farther up the shore Jesus saw Zebedee's sons, James and John, in a boat repairing their nets. [20]He called them at once, and they also followed him, leaving their father, Zebedee, in the boat with the hired men.

~ Mark 1:14-20

Inner Healing

Four men brought their paralyzed friend to Jesus to be healed. They impressed Jesus with their faith. Jesus did not only heal him, but also forgave his sins. When Jesus touches your life, you are healed, inside and outside.

¹When Jesus returned to Capernaum several days later, the news spread quickly that he was back home. ²Soon the house where he was staying was so packed with visitors that there was no more room, even outside the door. While he was preaching God's word to them, ³four men arrived carrying a paralyzed man on a mat.

⁴They couldn't bring him to Jesus because of the crowd, so they dug a hole through the roof above his head. Then they lowered the man on his mat, right down in front of Jesus.

⁵Seeing their faith, Jesus said to the paralyzed man, "My child, your sins are forgiven." ⁶But some of the teachers of religious law who were sitting there thought to themselves, ⁷"What is he saying? This is blasphemy! Only God can forgive sins!"

⁸Jesus knew immediately what they were thinking, so he asked them, "Why do you question this in your hearts? ⁹Is it easier to say to the paralyzed man 'Your sins are forgiven,' or 'Stand up, pick up your mat, and walk'? ¹⁰So I will prove to you that the Son of Man has the authority on earth to forgive sins." Then Jesus turned to the paralyzed man and said, ¹¹"Stand up, pick up your mat, and go home!"

¹²And the man jumped up, grabbed his mat, and walked out through the stunned onlookers. They were all amazed and praised God, exclaiming, "We've never seen anything like this before!"

~ Mark 2:1-12

Everything Is Possible if You Believe

Although the father of a demon-possessed child did believe, he still asked Jesus to take away his doubt. Jesus answered him that if a person believes, anything is possible. Sometimes we do believe, but still doubt a little. Jesus wants to turn your doubt into faith.

²⁰So they brought the boy. But when the evil spirit saw Jesus, it threw the child into a violent convulsion, and he fell to the ground, writhing and foaming at the mouth. ²¹"How long has this been happening?" Jesus asked the boy's father. He replied, "Since he was a little boy. ²²The spirit often throws him into the fire or into water, trying to kill him. Have mercy on us and help us, if you can."

²³"What do you mean, 'If I can'?" Jesus asked. "Anything is possible if a person believes." ²⁴The father instantly cried out, "I do believe, but help me overcome my unbelief!"

²⁵When Jesus saw that the crowd of onlookers was growing, he rebuked the evil spirit. Listen, you spirit that makes this boy unable to hear and speak," he said. "I command you to come out of this child and never enter him again!"

²⁶Then the spirit screamed and threw the boy into another violent convulsion and left him. The boy appeared to be dead. A murmur ran through the crowd as people said, "He's dead." ²⁷But Jesus took him by the hand and helped him to his feet, and he stood up.

²⁸Afterward, when Jesus was alone in the house with his disciples, they asked him, "Why couldn't we cast out that evil spirit?" ²⁹Jesus replied, "This kind can be cast out only by prayer."

~ Mark 9:20-29

Are You Willing to Serve Jesus?

We all like visiting the best places, and it feels good to be served. But it doesn't work this way in God's kingdom. If you want to be important there, you must be last in line and willing to serve others.

³⁵He sat down, called the twelve disciples over to him, and said, "Whoever wants to be first must take last place and be the servant of everyone else."

³⁶Then he put a little child among them. Taking the child in his arms, he said to them, ³⁷"Anyone who welcomes a little child like this on my behalf welcomes me, and anyone who welcomes me welcomes not only me but also my Father who sent me."

³⁸John said to Jesus, "Teacher, we saw someone using your name to cast out demons, but we told him to stop because he wasn't in our group."

³⁹"Don't stop him!" Jesus said. "No one who performs a miracle in my name will soon be able to speak evil of me. ⁴⁰Anyone who is not against us is for us.

⁴¹"If anyone gives you even a cup of water because you belong to the Messiah, I tell you the truth, that person will surely be rewarded.

⁴²"But if you cause one of these little ones who trusts in me to fall into sin, it would be better for you to be thrown into the sea with a large millstone hung around your neck."

~ Mark 9:35-42

Leaders Must Be Servants

James and John asked Jesus for a place of honor in His kingdom. But Jesus replied that anyone who wants to be great, must first be a servant. Jesus Himself did not come to the world to be served, but to be a servant and to offer His life as a ransom for many.

[35]Then James and John, the sons of Zebedee, came over and spoke to him. "Teacher," they said, "we want you to do us a favor." [36]"What is your request?" he asked. [37]They replied, "When you sit on your glorious throne, we want to sit in places of honor next to you, one on your right and the other on your left."

[38]But Jesus said to them, "You don't know what you are asking! Are you able to drink from the bitter cup of suffering I am about to drink? Are you able to be baptized with the baptism of suffering I must be baptized with?"

[39]"Oh yes," they replied, "we are able!" Then Jesus told them, "You will indeed drink from my bitter cup and be baptized with my baptism of suffering. [40]But I have no right to say who will sit on my right or my left. God has prepared those places for the ones he has chosen."

[42]So Jesus called them together and said, "You know that the rulers in this world lord it over their people, and officials flaunt their authority over those under them. [43]But among you it will be different. Whoever wants to be a leader among you must be your servant, [44]and whoever wants to be first among you must be the slave of everyone else. [45]For even the Son of Man came not to be served but to serve others and to give his life as a ransom for many."

~ Mark 10:35-40, 42-45

Keep on Praying

The blind Bartimaeus called out to Jesus until Jesus heard and healed him. If your prayers are not answered immediately, keep on praying until Jesus answers you – even if His final answer differs from what you expected.

46Then they reached Jericho, and as Jesus and his disciples left town, a large crowd followed him. A blind beggar named Bartimaeus (son of Timaeus) was sitting beside the road.

47When Bartimaeus heard that Jesus of Nazareth was nearby, he began to shout, "Jesus, Son of David, have mercy on me!"

48"Be quiet!" many of the people yelled at him. But he only shouted louder, "Son of David, have mercy on me!"

49When Jesus heard him, he stopped and said, "Tell him to come here." So they called the blind man. "Cheer up," they said. "Come on, he's calling you!"

50Bartimaeus threw aside his coat, jumped up, and came to Jesus. 51"What do you want me to do for you?" Jesus asked. "My rabbi," the blind man said, "I want to see!"

52And Jesus said to him, "Go, for your faith has healed you." Instantly the man could see, and he followed Jesus down the road.

~ Mark 10:46-52

Jesus Clears the Temple

When traders dishonored His Father's house by buying and selling there, Jesus chased them out of the temple. He was strict because He was protecting His Father's honor. Are you willing to do the same?

[15]When they arrived back in Jerusalem, Jesus entered the Temple and began to drive out the people buying and selling animals for sacrifices. He knocked over the tables of the money changers and the chairs of those selling doves, [16]and he stopped everyone from using the Temple as a marketplace.

[17]He said to them, "The Scriptures declare, 'My Temple will be called a house of prayer for all nations,' but you have turned it into a den of thieves." [18]When the leading priests and teachers of religious law heard what Jesus had done, they began planning how to kill him. But they were afraid of him because the people were so amazed at his teaching.

[19]That evening Jesus and the disciples left the city. [20]The next morning as they passed by the fig tree he had cursed, the disciples noticed it had withered from the roots up. [21]Peter remembered what Jesus had said to the tree on the previous day and exclaimed, "Look, Rabbi! The fig tree you cursed has withered and died!"

[22]Then Jesus said to the disciples, "Have faith in God. [23]I tell you the truth, you can say to this mountain, 'May you be lifted up and thrown into the sea,' and it will happen. But you must really believe it will happen and have no doubt in your heart. [24]I tell you, you can pray for anything, and if you believe that you've received it, it will be yours. [25]But when you are praying, first forgive anyone you are holding a grudge against, so that your Father in heaven will forgive your sins, too."

~ Mark 11:15-25

Pay Your Taxes!

Many Jews were unsure whether to pay taxes to the Romans or not. When they asked Jesus, He said that they must give to Caesar what is Caesar's, but also give God His due. Are you honest in paying your taxes and tithing?

[13]Later the leaders sent some Pharisees and supporters of Herod to trap Jesus into saying something for which he could be arrested.

[14]"Teacher," they said, "we know how honest you are. You are impartial and don't play favorites. You teach the way of God truthfully. Now tell us—is it right to pay taxes to Caesar or not?"

[15]"Should we pay them, or shouldn't we?" Jesus saw through their hypocrisy and said, "Why are you trying to trap me? Show me a Roman coin, and I'll tell you."

[16]When they handed it to him, he asked, "Whose picture and title are stamped on it?" "Caesar's," they replied.

[17]"Well, then," Jesus said, "give to Caesar what belongs to Caesar, and give to God what belongs to God." His reply completely amazed them.

~ Mark 12:13-17

Mary Accepts God's Challenge

Mary was young and unmarried when an angel told her that she was going to have a Son – the long-awaited Messiah. Mary was willing to say yes to God without worrying about what this decision may cost her. Are you willing to trust God unconditionally?

²⁶In the sixth month of Elizabeth's pregnancy, God sent the angel Gabriel to Nazareth, a village in Galilee, ²⁷to a virgin named Mary. She was engaged to be married to a man named Joseph, a descendant of King David.

²⁸Gabriel appeared to her and said, "Greetings, favored woman! The Lord is with you!" ²⁹Confused and disturbed, Mary tried to think what the angel could mean. ³⁰"Don't be afraid, Mary," the angel told her, "for you have found favor with God! ³¹You will conceive and give birth to a son, and you will name him Jesus. ³²He will be very great and will be called the Son of the Most High. The Lord God will give him the throne of his ancestor David. ³³And he will reign over Israel forever; his Kingdom will never end!"

³⁴Mary asked the angel, "But how can this happen? I am a virgin." ³⁵The angel replied, "The Holy Spirit will come upon you, and the power of the Most High will overshadow you. So the baby to be born will be holy, and he will be called the Son of God.

³⁶"What's more, your relative Elizabeth has become pregnant in her old age! People used to say she was barren, but she has conceived a son and is now in her sixth month. ³⁷For nothing is impossible with God."

³⁸Mary responded, "I am the Lord's servant. May everything you have said about me come true." And then the angel left her.

~ Luke 1:26-38

The Coming of the Light

John's father, Zechariah, prophesied about the birth of Christ by announcing that the Child will bring light to those living in darkness, and that He will lead His people to peace. Jesus wants to be the light in your life and lead you to peace too.

⁶⁷Then his father, Zechariah, was filled with the Holy Spirit and gave this prophecy:

⁶⁸"Praise the Lord, the God of Israel, because he has visited and redeemed his people. ⁶⁹He has sent us a mighty Savior from the royal line of his servant David, ⁷⁰just as he promised through his holy prophets long ago. ⁷¹Now we will be saved from our enemies and from all who hate us.

⁷²"He has been merciful to our ancestors by remembering his sacred covenant—⁷³the covenant he swore with an oath to our ancestor Abraham. ⁷⁴We have been rescued from our enemies so we can serve God without fear, ⁷⁵in holiness and righteousness for as long as we live.

⁷⁶"And you, my little son, will be called the prophet of the Most High, because you will prepare the way for the Lord. ⁷⁷You will tell his people how to find salvation through forgiveness of their sins.

⁷⁸"Because of God's tender mercy, the morning light from heaven is about to break upon us, ⁷⁹to give light to those who sit in darkness and in the shadow of death, and to guide us to the path of peace."

~ Luke 1:67-79

The Birth of Jesus

Joseph and Mary had to travel to Bethlehem to register for the census. While there, Mary gave birth to her Son. She wrapped Him in cloths and placed Him in a manger, because there was no room for them in the inn.

[1]At that time the Roman emperor, Augustus, decreed that a census should be taken throughout the Roman Empire. [2](This was the first census taken when Quirinius was governor of Syria.)

[3]All returned to their own ancestral towns to register for this census. [4]And because Joseph was a descendant of King David, he had to go to Bethlehem in Judea, David's ancient home. He traveled there from the village of Nazareth in Galilee.

[5]He took with him Mary, his fiancée, who was now obviously pregnant. [6]And while they were there, the time came for her baby to be born.

[7]She gave birth to her first child, a son. She wrapped him snugly in strips of cloth and laid him in a manger, because there was no lodging available for them.

~ Luke 2:1-7

A Joyous Angelic Message

An angelic host appeared to a group of shepherds and announced that the Savior had been born in Bethlehem that night. They praised God singing, "Glory to God in the highest, and on earth peace to men on whom His favor rests."

[8]That night there were shepherds staying in the fields nearby, guarding their flocks of sheep. [9]Suddenly, an angel of the Lord appeared among them, and the radiance of the Lord's glory surrounded them. They were terrified, [10]but the angel reassured them. "Don't be afraid!" he said. "I bring you good news that will bring great joy to all people.

[11]"The Savior—yes, the Messiah, the Lord—has been born today in Bethlehem, the city of David! [12]And you will recognize him by this sign: You will find a baby wrapped snugly in strips of cloth, lying in a manger." [13]Suddenly, the angel was joined by a vast host of others—the armies of heaven—praising God and saying, [14]"Glory to God in highest heaven, and peace on earth to those with whom God is pleased." [15]When the angels had returned to heaven, the shepherds said to each other, "Let's go to Bethlehem! Let's see this thing that has happened, which the Lord has told us about." [16]They hurried to the village and found Mary and Joseph. And there was the baby, lying in the manger. [17]After seeing him, the shepherds told everyone what had happened and what the angel had said to them about this child.

[18]All who heard the shepherds' story were astonished, [19]but Mary kept all these things in her heart and thought about them often. [20]The shepherds went back to their flocks, glorifying and praising God for all they had heard and seen. It was just as the angel had told them.

~ Luke 2:8-20

Love Your Enemy!

Jesus expects more from you than to only love God, family and friends. Even sinners do that. It is His will that you must also love your enemies, and do good to those who mistreat you. Only then will you be rewarded in heaven.

27"But to you who are willing to listen, I say, love your enemies! Do good to those who hate you. 28Bless those who curse you. Pray for those who hurt you.

29"If someone slaps you on one cheek, offer the other cheek also. If someone demands your coat, offer your shirt also. 30Give to anyone who asks; and when things are taken away from you, don't try to get them back. 31Do to others as you would like them to do to you.

32"If you love only those who love you, why should you get credit for that? Even sinners love those who love them!

33"And if you do good only to those who do good to you, why should you get credit? Even sinners do that much! 34And if you lend money only to those who can repay you, why should you get credit? Even sinners will lend to other sinners for a full return.

35"Love your enemies! Do good to them. Lend to them without expecting to be repaid. Then your reward from heaven will be very great, and you will truly be acting as children of the Most High, for he is kind to those who are unthankful and wicked.

36"You must be compassionate, just as your Father is compassionate".

~ Luke 6:27-36

Whose Neighbor Are You?

Jesus told the parable of a man who was attacked by robbers. A Jewish priest and a Levite passed him by. But a Samaritan, who the Jews looked down on, helped the man. Being a neighbor means you should do the same.

[30]Jesus replied with a story: "A Jewish man was traveling from Jerusalem down to Jericho, and he was attacked by bandits. They stripped him of his clothes, beat him up, and left him half dead beside the road.

[31]"By chance a priest came along. But when he saw the man lying there, he crossed to the other side of the road and passed him by. [32]A Temple assistant walked over and looked at him lying there, but he also passed by on the other side.

[33]"Then a despised Samaritan came along, and when he saw the man, he felt compassion for him. [34]Going over to him, the Samaritan soothed his wounds with olive oil and wine and bandaged them. Then he put the man on his own donkey and took him to an inn, where he took care of him.

[35]"The next day he handed the innkeeper two silver coins, telling him, 'Take care of this man. If his bill runs higher than this, I'll pay you the next time I'm here.'

[36]"Now which of these three would you say was a neighbor to the man who was attacked by bandits?" Jesus asked. [37]The man replied, "The one who showed him mercy." Then Jesus said, "Yes, now go and do the same."

~ Luke 10:30-37

September

Set Your Priorities Straight

Martha was indignant at Mary who just sat at Jesus' feet and listened to Him while she had to do all the work. Martha asked Jesus to intervene in the situation. But Jesus said that Mary did the right thing; she chose the *one* thing that was really important: Him. Make sure you choose what is most important.

³⁸As Jesus and the disciples continued on their way to Jerusalem, they came to a certain village where a woman named Martha welcomed him into her home.

³⁹Her sister, Mary, sat at the Lord's feet, listening to what he taught. ⁴⁰But Martha was distracted by the big dinner she was preparing. She came to Jesus and said, "Lord, doesn't it seem unfair to you that my sister just sits here while I do all the work? Tell her to come and help me."

⁴¹But the Lord said to her, "My dear Martha, you are worried and upset over all these details! ⁴²There is only one thing worth being concerned about. Mary has discovered it, and it will not be taken away from her."

~ Luke 10:38-42

True Riches

People are often more concerned about their wealth and earthly riches than they are about eternal life. But in truth, money is not important. You can't take your earthly possessions with you to heaven – rather make sure that you have a personal relationship with God.

[13]Then someone called from the crowd, "Teacher, please tell my brother to divide our father's estate with me." [14]Jesus replied, "Friend, who made me a judge over you to decide such things as that?"

[15]Then he said, "Beware! Guard against every kind of greed. Life is not measured by how much you own." [16]Then he told them a story: "A rich man had a fertile farm that produced fine crops.

[17]"He said to himself, 'What should I do? I don't have room for all my crops.' [18]Then he said, 'I know! I'll tear down my barns and build bigger ones. Then I'll have room enough to store all my wheat and other goods. [19]And I'll sit back and say to myself, "My friend, you have enough stored away for years to come. Now take it easy! Eat, drink, and be merry!"'

[20]"But God said to him, 'You fool! You will die this very night. Then who will get everything you worked for?' [21]Yes, a person is a fool to store up earthly wealth but not have a rich relationship with God."

~ Luke 12:13-21

The Father Waits

Jesus told a parable of a son who demanded his inheritance and squandered everything in a far-off land. Jesus wants to assure us that God never abandons His children. He always welcomes us back with open arms when we return to Him. If you have ever wandered away from God, know that your heavenly Father is waiting expectantly for your return.

[17]"When he finally came to his senses, he said to himself, 'At home even the hired servants have food enough to spare, and here I am dying of hunger! [18]I will go home to my father and say, "Father, I have sinned against both heaven and you, [19]and I am no longer worthy of being called your son. Please take me on as a hired servant."'

[20]"So he returned home to his father. And while he was still a long way off, his father saw him coming. Filled with love and compassion, he ran to his son, embraced him, and kissed him. [21]His son said to him, 'Father, I have sinned against both heaven and you, and I am no longer worthy of being called your son.'

[22]"But his father said to the servants, 'Quick! Bring the finest robe in the house and put it on him. Get a ring for his finger and sandals for his feet. [23]And kill the calf we have been fattening. We must celebrate with a feast, [24]for this son of mine was dead and has now returned to life. He was lost, but now he is found.' So the party began."

~ Luke 15:17-24

Be Thankful!

When Jesus healed ten lepers, only one came back to thank Him. "Were not all ten cleansed? Where are the other nine?" Jesus asked. Does your life reflect your gratitude to God for His salvation?

¹¹As Jesus continued on toward Jerusalem, he reached the border between Galilee and Samaria. ¹²As he entered a village there, ten lepers stood at a distance, ¹³crying out, "Jesus, Master, have mercy on us!"

¹⁴He looked at them and said, "Go show yourselves to the priests." And as they went, they were cleansed of their leprosy. ¹⁵One of them, when he saw that he was healed, came back to Jesus, shouting, "Praise God!"

¹⁶He fell to the ground at Jesus' feet, thanking him for what he had done. This man was a Samaritan. ¹⁷Jesus asked, "Didn't I heal ten men? Where are the other nine? ¹⁸Has no one returned to give glory to God except this foreigner?" ¹⁹And Jesus said to the man, "Stand up and go. Your faith has healed you."

~ Luke 17:11-19

Jesus Notices You

Zacchaeus was sitting in a fig tree so that he could see Jesus better. Jesus saw him and told him to come down because He was going to eat at Zacchaeus's house. Jesus showed that He accepted Zacchaeus even though he was a tax collector who was hated by many. Jesus also notices you when you are searching for Him.

[1]Jesus entered Jericho and made his way through the town. [2]There was a man there named Zacchaeus. He was the chief tax collector in the region, and he had become very rich.

[3]He tried to get a look at Jesus, but he was too short to see over the crowd. [4]So he ran ahead and climbed a sycamore-fig tree beside the road, for Jesus was going to pass that way.

[5]When Jesus came by, he looked up at Zacchaeus and called him by name. "Zacchaeus!" he said. "Quick, come down! I must be a guest in your home today." [6]Zacchaeus quickly climbed down and took Jesus to his house in great excitement and joy.

[7]The people were displeased. "He has gone to be the guest of a notorious sinner," they grumbled. [8]Meanwhile, Zacchaeus stood before the Lord and said, "I will give half my wealth to the poor, Lord, and if I have cheated people on their taxes, I will give them back four times as much!"

[9]Jesus responded, "Salvation has come to this home today, for this man has shown himself to be a true son of Abraham. [10]For the Son of Man came to seek and save those who are lost."

~ Luke 19:1-10

Together in Paradise

When Jesus was crucified, two criminals hung on either side of Him. One of them asked Jesus to have mercy on him, and Jesus promised him that they would be together in paradise. It is never too late to surrender your life to Jesus.

³²Two others, both criminals, were led out to be executed with him. ³³When they came to a place called The Skull, they nailed him to the cross. And the criminals were also crucified—one on his right and one on his left.

³⁴Jesus said, "Father, forgive them, for they don't know what they are doing." And the soldiers gambled for his clothes by throwing dice. ³⁵The crowd watched and the leaders scoffed. "He saved others," they said, "let him save himself if he is really God's Messiah, the Chosen One."

³⁶The soldiers mocked him, too, by offering him a drink of sour wine. ³⁷They called out to him, "If you are the King of the Jews, save yourself!" ³⁸A sign was fastened above him with these words: "This is the King of the Jews." ³⁹One of the criminals hanging beside him scoffed, "So you're the Messiah, are you? Prove it by saving yourself—and us, too, while you're at it!"

⁴⁰But the other criminal protested, "Don't you fear God even when you have been sentenced to die? ⁴¹We deserve to die for our crimes, but this man hasn't done anything wrong." ⁴²Then he said, "Jesus, remember me when you come into your Kingdom." ⁴³And Jesus replied, "I assure you, today you will be with me in paradise."

~ Luke 23:32-43

Jesus Has Risen!

The Sunday morning after the crucifixion the women went to Jesus' grave to anoint His body, but the grave was empty. There were two angels who told them that Jesus had risen. Jesus had conquered death. You will also rise from the grave one day.

[1]But very early on Sunday morning the women went to the tomb, taking the spices they had prepared. [2]They found that the stone had been rolled away from the entrance. [3]So they went in, but they didn't find the body of the Lord Jesus.

[4]As they stood there puzzled, two men suddenly appeared to them, clothed in dazzling robes. [5]The women were terrified and bowed with their faces to the ground. Then the men asked, "Why are you looking among the dead for someone who is alive? [6]He isn't here! He is risen from the dead! Remember what he told you back in Galilee, [7]that the Son of Man must be betrayed into the hands of sinful men and be crucified, and that he would rise again on the third day."

[8]Then they remembered that he had said this. [9]So they rushed back from the tomb to tell his eleven disciples—and everyone else—what had happened. [10]It was Mary Magdalene, Joanna, Mary the mother of James, and several other women who told the apostles what had happened.

[11]But the story sounded like nonsense to the men, so they didn't believe it. [12]However, Peter jumped up and ran to the tomb to look. Stooping, he peered in and saw the empty linen wrappings; then he went home again, wondering what had happened.

~ Luke 24:1-12

The Word Became Flesh

Jesus came to earth to make God known to us, but His own people didn't accept Him. Yet in spite of this for everyone who believes in Him, He grants the right to become a child of God. He is the Word who became flesh and made His home among us.

[1]In the beginning the Word already existed. The Word was with God, and the Word was God. [2]He existed in the beginning with God.

[3]God created everything through him, and nothing was created except through him. [4]The Word gave life to everything that was created, and his life brought light to everyone. [5]The light shines in the darkness, and the darkness can never extinguish it.

[9]The one who is the true light, who gives light to everyone, was coming into the world. [10]He came into the very world he created, but the world didn't recognize him. [11]He came to his own people, and even they rejected him. [12]But to all who believed him and accepted him, he gave the right to become children of God.

[13]They are reborn—not with a physical birth resulting from human passion or plan, but a birth that comes from God. [14]So the Word became human and made his home among us. He was full of unfailing love and faithfulness. And we have seen his glory, the glory of the Father's one and only Son.

[15]John testified about him when he shouted to the crowds, "This is the one I was talking about when I said, 'Someone is coming after me who is far greater than I am, for he existed long before me.'" [16]From his abundance we have all received one gracious blessing after another.

~ John 1:1-5, 9-16

Jesus Loves You This Much

When Nicodemus came to Jesus one night, Jesus told him how much God loves His children. God loves us so much that He sent His one and only Son so that everyone who believes in Him will not perish, but live with Him forever. God gave His Son to die on a cross so that you can be His child.

¹There was a man named Nicodemus, a Jewish religious leader who was a Pharisee. ²After dark one evening, he came to speak with Jesus. "Rabbi," he said, "we all know that God has sent you to teach us. Your miraculous signs are evidence that God is with you."

³Jesus replied, "I tell you the truth, unless you are born again, you cannot see the Kingdom of God."

⁴"What do you mean?" exclaimed Nicodemus. "How can an old man go back into his mother's womb and be born again?"

⁵Jesus replied, "I assure you, no one can enter the Kingdom of God without being born of water and the Spirit. ⁶Humans can reproduce only human life, but the Holy Spirit gives birth to spiritual life. ⁷So don't be surprised when I say, 'You must be born again.'

⁸"The wind blows wherever it wants. Just as you can hear the wind but can't tell where it comes from or where it is going, so you can't explain how people are born of the Spirit.

¹⁶"For God loved the world so much that he gave his one and only Son, so that everyone who believes in him will not perish but have eternal life."

~ John 3:1-8, 16

Living Water

Jesus told a Samaritan woman that whoever drinks of the water He gives would never thirst. When the woman asked Jesus to give her some of this water, her whole life as well as the lives of the people in her small town were changed.

⁷Soon a Samaritan woman came to draw water, and Jesus said to her, "Please give me a drink." ⁸He was alone at the time because his disciples had gone into the village to buy some food.

⁹The woman was surprised, for Jews refuse to have anything to do with Samaritans. She said to Jesus, "You are a Jew, and I am a Samaritan woman. Why are you asking me for a drink?" ¹⁰Jesus replied, "If you only knew the gift God has for you and who you are speaking to, you would ask me, and I would give you living water."

¹¹"But sir, you don't have a rope or a bucket," she said, "and this well is very deep. Where would you get this living water? ¹²And besides, do you think you're greater than our ancestor Jacob, who gave us this well? How can you offer better water than he and his sons and his animals enjoyed?"

¹³Jesus replied, "Anyone who drinks this water will soon become thirsty again. ¹⁴But those who drink the water I give will never be thirsty again. It becomes a fresh, bubbling spring within them, giving them eternal life."

¹⁵"Please, sir," the woman said, "give me this water! Then I'll never be thirsty again, and I won't have to come here to get water."

³⁹Many Samaritans from the village believed in Jesus because the woman had said, "He told me everything I ever did!"

~ John 4:7-15, 39

Don't Throw Stones

The Pharisees brought a woman to Jesus caught in the act of adultery. He said that if anyone was without sin, let him throw the first stone. When the people heard this, they left one by one. Jesus told her that He didn't condemn her, but asked her to leave her life of sin.

[1]Jesus returned to the Mount of Olives, [2]but early the next morning he was back again at the Temple. A crowd soon gathered, and he sat down and taught them.

[3]As he was speaking, the teachers of religious law and the Pharisees brought a woman who had been caught in the act of adultery. They put her in front of the crowd.

[4]"Teacher," they said to Jesus, "this woman was caught in the act of adultery. [5]The law of Moses says to stone her. What do you say?" [6]They were trying to trap him into saying something they could use against him, but Jesus stooped down and wrote in the dust with his finger.

[7]They kept demanding an answer, so he stood up again and said, "All right, but let the one who has never sinned throw the first stone!" [8]Then he stooped down again and wrote in the dust.

[9]When the accusers heard this, they slipped away one by one, beginning with the oldest, until only Jesus was left in the middle of the crowd with the woman.

[10]Then Jesus stood up again and said to the woman, "Where are your accusers? Didn't even one of them condemn you?"

[11]"No, Lord," she said. And Jesus said, "Neither do I. Go and sin no more."

~ John 8:1-11

A Slave to Sin

Although we are born into sin, Jesus can save us from a life of sin. Through His death on the cross He made it possible for you to be a child of God; a child who is forever free from the burden of sin.

[23]Jesus continued, "You are from below; I am from above. You belong to this world; I do not. [24]That is why I said that you will die in your sins; for unless you believe that I Am who I claim to be, you will die in your sins."

[28]So Jesus said, "When you have lifted up the Son of Man on the cross, then you will understand that I Am he. I do nothing on my own but say only what the Father taught me. [29]And the one who sent me is with me—he has not deserted me. For I always do what pleases him." [30]Then many who heard him say these things believed in him.

[31]Jesus said to the people who believed in him, "You are truly my disciples if you remain faithful to my teachings. [32]And you will know the truth, and the truth will set you free."

[33]"But we are descendants of Abraham," they said. "We have never been slaves to anyone. What do you mean, 'You will be set free'?"

[34]Jesus replied, "I tell you the truth, everyone who sins is a slave of sin. [35]A slave is not a permanent member of the family, but a son is part of the family forever. [36]So if the Son sets you free, you are truly free."

~ John 8:23-24, 28-36

Jesus, Your Shepherd

Jesus is the Good Shepherd who sacrifices His life for His sheep. He knows His sheep and they know His voice and follow Him. Jesus wants to be your Shepherd. He has already sacrificed His life for you. Do you follow Him with your whole heart?

¹"I tell you the truth, anyone who sneaks over the wall of a sheepfold, rather than going through the gate, must surely be a thief and a robber! ²But the one who enters through the gate is the shepherd of the sheep.

³"The gatekeeper opens the gate for him, and the sheep recognize his voice and come to him. He calls his own sheep by name and leads them out. ⁴After he has gathered his own flock, he walks ahead of them, and they follow him because they know his voice. ⁵They won't follow a stranger; they will run from him because they don't know his voice."

⁶Those who heard Jesus use this illustration didn't understand what he meant, ⁷so he explained it to them: "I tell you the truth, I am the gate for the sheep. ⁸All who came before me were thieves and robbers. But the true sheep did not listen to them. ⁹Yes, I am the gate. Those who come in through me will be saved. They will come and go freely and will find good pastures.

¹⁴"I am the good shepherd; I know my own sheep, and they know me, ¹⁵just as my Father knows me and I know the Father. So I sacrifice my life for the sheep. ¹⁶I have other sheep, too, that are not in this sheepfold. I must bring them also. They will listen to my voice, and there will be one flock with one shepherd."

~ John 10:1-9, 14-16

The Resurrection and the Life

Jesus told Martha, who was very sad about the death of her brother, that He is the Resurrection and the Life. Anyone who believes in Him will live even though they die. If you believe in Jesus the promise of eternal life is yours too!

²⁰When Martha got word that Jesus was coming, she went to meet him. But Mary stayed in the house. ²¹Martha said to Jesus, "Lord, if only you had been here, my brother would not have died. ²²But even now I know that God will give you whatever you ask." ²³Jesus told her, "Your brother will rise again."

²⁴"Yes," Martha said, "he will rise when everyone else rises, at the last day."

²⁵Jesus told her, "I am the resurrection and the life. Anyone who believes in me will live, even after dying. ²⁶Everyone who lives in me and believes in me will never ever die. Do you believe this, Martha?"

²⁷"Yes, Lord," she told him. "I have always believed you are the Messiah, the Son of God, the one who has come into the world from God." ²⁸Then she returned to Mary. She called Mary aside from the mourners and told her, "The Teacher is here and wants to see you." ²⁹So Mary immediately went to him.

³⁰Jesus had stayed outside the village, at the place where Martha met him. ³¹When the people who were at the house consoling Mary saw her leave so hastily, they assumed she was going to Lazarus's grave to weep. So they followed her there. ³²When Mary arrived and saw Jesus, she fell at his feet and said, "Lord, if only you had been here, my brother would not have died."

~ John 11:20-32

From Death to Life

Jesus was so sad about the death of Lazarus that He cried. After that He went to Lazarus's grave and raised him from the dead, after he had been dead for four days. Jesus fulfilled His promise to Martha.

33When Jesus saw her weeping and saw the other people wailing with her, a deep anger welled up within him, and he was deeply troubled. 34"Where have you put him?" he asked them. They told him, "Lord, come and see."

35Then Jesus wept. 36The people who were standing nearby said, "See how much he loved him!" 37But some said, "This man healed a blind man. Couldn't he have kept Lazarus from dying?" 38Jesus was still angry as he arrived at the tomb, a cave with a stone rolled across its entrance.

39"Roll the stone aside," Jesus told them. But Martha, the dead man's sister, protested, "Lord, he has been dead for four days. The smell will be terrible."

40Jesus responded, "Didn't I tell you that you would see God's glory if you believe?" 41So they rolled the stone aside. Then Jesus looked up to heaven and said, "Father, thank you for hearing me. 42You always hear me, but I said it out loud for the sake of all these people standing here, so that they will believe you sent me."

43Then Jesus shouted, "Lazarus, come out!" 44And the dead man came out, his hands and feet bound in graveclothes, his face wrapped in a headcloth. Jesus told them, "Unwrap him and let him go!"

~ John 11:33-44

Only One Way to Heaven

There is no other way to know God except through faith in Jesus. And if you believe in Jesus you have the assurance that He has prepared a place for you in heaven. He will return and take you to be with Him forever.

[1]"Don't let your hearts be troubled. Trust in God, and trust also in me. [2]There is more than enough room in my Father's home. If this were not so, would I have told you that I am going to prepare a place for you?

[3]"When everything is ready, I will come and get you, so that you will always be with me where I am. [4]And you know the way to where I am going."

[5]"No, we don't know, Lord," Thomas said. "We have no idea where you are going, so how can we know the way?"

[6]Jesus told him, "I am the way, the truth, and the life. No one can come to the Father except through me. [7]If you had really known me, you would know who my Father is. From now on, you do know him and have seen him!" [8]Philip said, "Lord, show us the Father, and we will be satisfied."

[9]Jesus replied, "Have I been with you all this time, Philip, and yet you still don't know who I am? Anyone who has seen me has seen the Father! So why are you asking me to show him to you? [10]Don't you believe that I am in the Father and the Father is in me? The words I speak are not my own, but my Father who lives in me does his work through me. [11]Just believe that I am in the Father and the Father is in me. Or at least believe because of the work you have seen me do."

~ John 14:1-11

Does God Grant Your Every Request?

You already know the answer to this question, right? We don't always receive everything we ask of God. Sometimes God says no. However, there is one thing you can be sure of: God always gives what's best for you.

[12]"I tell you the truth, anyone who believes in me will do the same works I have done, and even greater works, because I am going to be with the Father. [13]You can ask for anything in my name, and I will do it, so that the Son can bring glory to the Father. [14]Yes, ask me for anything in my name, and I will do it!

[15]"If you love me, obey my commandments. [16]And I will ask the Father, and he will give you another Advocate, who will never leave you. [17]He is the Holy Spirit, who leads into all truth. The world cannot receive him, because it isn't looking for him and doesn't recognize him. But you know him, because he lives with you now and later will be in you.

[18]"No, I will not abandon you as orphans—I will come to you. [19]Soon the world will no longer see me, but you will see me. Since I live, you also will live. [20]When I am raised to life again, you will know that I am in my Father, and you are in me, and I am in you.

[21]"Those who accept my commandments and obey them are the ones who love me. And because they love me, my Father will love them. And I will love them and reveal myself to each of them."

~ John 14:12-21

A Counselor to Be with You

Jesus promised to send another Counselor, the Holy Spirit, to earth when He returned to His Father. The Holy Spirit is still with you today to teach and guide you, and to remind you of everything that Jesus said while here on earth.

¹⁵"If you love me, obey my commandments. ¹⁶And I will ask the Father, and he will give you another Advocate, who will never leave you. ¹⁷He is the Holy Spirit, who leads into all truth. The world cannot receive him, because it isn't looking for him and doesn't recognize him. But you know him, because he lives with you now and later will be in you.

¹⁸"No, I will not abandon you as orphans—I will come to you. ¹⁹Soon the world will no longer see me, but you will see me. Since I live, you also will live. ²⁰When I am raised to life again, you will know that I am in my Father, and you are in me, and I am in you. ²¹Those who accept my commandments and obey them are the ones who love me. And because they love me, my Father will love them. And I will love them and reveal myself to each of them."

²³Jesus replied, "All who love me will do what I say. My Father will love them, and we will come and make our home with each of them. ²⁴Anyone who doesn't love me will not obey me. And remember, my words are not my own. What I am telling you is from the Father who sent me. ²⁵I am telling you these things now while I am still with you. ²⁶But when the Father sends the Advocate as my representative—that is, the Holy Spirit—he will teach you everything and will remind you of everything I have told you."

~ John 14:15-21, 23-26

The Secret to
Bearing Much Fruit

There is only one way in which a branch can bear fruit: by staying connected to the vine. Only by abiding in Christ and obeying His commands can we bear fruit. He chose us in Him to bear much fruit.

[1]"I am the true grapevine, and my Father is the gardener. [2]He cuts off every branch of mine that doesn't produce fruit, and he prunes the branches that do bear fruit so they will produce even more. [3]You have already been pruned and purified by the message I have given you. [4]Remain in me, and I will remain in you. For a branch cannot produce fruit if it is severed from the vine, and you cannot be fruitful unless you remain in me.

[5]"Yes, I am the vine; you are the branches. Those who remain in me, and I in them, will produce much fruit. For apart from me you can do nothing. [6]Anyone who does not remain in me is thrown away like a useless branch and withers. Such branches are gathered into a pile to be burned.

[7]"But if you remain in me and my words remain in you, you may ask for anything you want, and it will be granted! [8]When you produce much fruit, you are my true disciples. This brings great glory to my Father.

[9]"I have loved you even as the Father has loved me. Remain in my love. [10]When you obey my commandments, you remain in my love, just as I obey my Father's commandments and remain in his love. [11]I have told you these things so that you will be filled with my joy. Yes, your joy will overflow! [12]This is my commandment: Love each other in the same way I have loved you. [13]There is no greater love than to lay down one's life for one's friends."

~ John 15:1-13

Jesus Prays for His Disciples

Jesus interceded for His disciples with His Father and asked that they would share His joy, and that God would protect them from the Evil One. He asked that they would be one and live in an intimate relationship with Him.

[9]"My prayer is not for the world, but for those you have given me, because they belong to you.

[13]"Now I am coming to you. I told them many things while I was with them in this world so they would be filled with my joy. [14]I have given them your word. And the world hates them because they do not belong to the world, just as I do not belong to the world. [15]I'm not asking you to take them out of the world, but to keep them safe from the Evil One.

[16]"They do not belong to this world any more than I do. [17]Make them holy by your truth; teach them your word, which is truth. [18]Just as you sent me into the world, I am sending them into the world. [19]And I give myself as a holy sacrifice for them so they can be made holy by your truth.

[20]"I am praying not only for these disciples but also for all who will ever believe in me through their message. [21]I pray that they will all be one, just as you and I are one—as you are in me, Father, and I am in you. And may they be in us so that the world will believe you sent me.

[22]"I have given them the glory you gave me, so they may be one as we are one. [23]I am in them and you are in me. May they experience such perfect unity that the world will know that you sent me and that you love them as much as you love me."

~ John 17:9, 13-23

Pilate Condemns Jesus to Death

Even though Pilate knew Jesus was innocent, he yielded to the crowd's request that Jesus be crucified, but only after Jesus said to him that he would have no power over Him if it were not given to him from above.

⁴Pilate went outside again and said to the people, "I am going to bring him out to you now, but understand clearly that I find him not guilty." ⁵Then Jesus came out wearing the crown of thorns and the purple robe. And Pilate said, "Look, here is the man!"

⁶When they saw him, the leading priests and Temple guards began shouting, "Crucify him! Crucify him!"

"Take him yourselves and crucify him," Pilate said. "I find him not guilty." ⁷The Jewish leaders replied, "By our law he ought to die because he called himself the Son of God." ⁸When Pilate heard this, he was more frightened than ever. ⁹He took Jesus back into the headquarters again and asked him, "Where are you from?" But Jesus gave no answer.

¹⁰"Why don't you talk to me?" Pilate demanded. "Don't you realize that I have the power to release you or crucify you?" ¹¹Then Jesus said, "You would have no power over me at all unless it were given to you from above. So the one who handed me over to you has the greater sin." ¹²Then Pilate tried to release him, but the Jewish leaders shouted, "If you release this man, you are no 'friend of Caesar.' Anyone who declares himself a king is a rebel against Caesar."

¹⁵"Away with him," they yelled. "Away with him! Crucify him!"

"What? Crucify your king?" Pilate asked. "We have no king but Caesar," the leading priests shouted back. ¹⁶Then Pilate turned Jesus over to them to be crucified. So they took Jesus away.

~ John 19:4-12, 15-16

Jesus Dies

After brutal suffering on the cross, Jesus died. The soldiers saw that He was dead, and one even pierced Jesus' side with a spear so that water and blood flowed from the wound. Jesus was really dead – of this you can be sure.

[28]Jesus knew that his mission was now finished, and to fulfill Scripture he said, "I am thirsty." [29]A jar of sour wine was sitting there, so they soaked a sponge in it, put it on a hyssop branch, and held it up to his lips.

[30]When Jesus had tasted it, he said, "It is finished!" Then he bowed his head and released his spirit. [31]It was the day of preparation, and the Jewish leaders didn't want the bodies hanging there the next day, which was the Sabbath (and a very special Sabbath, because it was the Passover). So they asked Pilate to hasten their deaths by ordering that their legs be broken. Then their bodies could be taken down.

[32]So the soldiers came and broke the legs of the two men crucified with Jesus. [33]But when they came to Jesus, they saw that he was already dead, so they didn't break his legs. [34]One of the soldiers, however, pierced his side with a spear, and immediately blood and water flowed out.

[35](This report is from an eyewitness giving an accurate account. He speaks the truth so that you also can believe.) [36]These things happened in fulfillment of the Scriptures that say, "Not one of his bones will be broken," [37]and "They will look on the one they pierced."

~ John 19:28-37

An Empty Grave

When Mary Magdalene discovered that Jesus' tomb was empty, she was deeply upset. Peter and John only found strips of linen in the tomb. John stated that they did not yet understand the whole truth behind the Resurrection. Do you realize the significance of the Resurrection in your life?

¹On Sunday morning, while it was still dark, Mary Magdalene came to the tomb and found that the stone had been rolled away from the entrance.

²She ran and found Simon Peter and the other disciple, the one whom Jesus loved. She said, "They have taken the Lord's body out of the tomb, and we don't know where they have put him!" ³Peter and the other disciple started out for the tomb.

⁴They were both running, but the other disciple outran Peter and reached the tomb first. ⁵He stooped and looked in and saw the linen wrappings lying there, but he didn't go in. ⁶Then Simon Peter arrived and went inside. He also noticed the linen wrappings lying there, ⁷while the cloth that had covered Jesus' head was folded up and lying apart from the other wrappings.

⁸Then the disciple who had reached the tomb first also went in, and he saw and believed—⁹for until then they still hadn't understood the Scriptures that said Jesus must rise from the dead. ¹⁰Then they went home.

~ John 20:1-10

A Witness of Jesus' Resurrection

After His resurrection Jesus appeared first of all to a woman – Mary Magdalene – and she immediately went to tell the disciples the good news. Although women were not highly esteemed in biblical times, they were of cardinal importance to Jesus. You are important to Him too.

[11]Mary was standing outside the tomb crying, and as she wept, she stooped and looked in. [12]She saw two white-robed angels, one sitting at the head and the other at the foot of the place where the body of Jesus had been lying.

[13]"Dear woman, why are you crying?" the angels asked her. "Because they have taken away my Lord," she replied, "and I don't know where they have put him." [14]She turned to leave and saw someone standing there. It was Jesus, but she didn't recognize him.

[15]"Dear woman, why are you crying?" Jesus asked her. "Who are you looking for?" She thought he was the gardener. "Sir," she said, "if you have taken him away, tell me where you have put him, and I will go and get him."

[16]"Mary!" Jesus said. She turned to him and cried out, "Rabboni!" (which is Hebrew for "Teacher").

[17]"Don't cling to me," Jesus said, "for I haven't yet ascended to the Father. But go find my brothers and tell them, 'I am ascending to my Father and your Father, to my God and your God.'" [18]Mary Magdalene found the disciples and told them, "I have seen the Lord!" Then she gave them his message.

~ John 20:11-18

You Are Sent by God

The first message Jesus proclaimed to His disciples after His resurrection was that He was sending them into the world as His Father had sent Him. Likewise, you are sent by God to proclaim the Good News to the world.

[19]That Sunday evening the disciples were meeting behind locked doors because they were afraid of the Jewish leaders. Suddenly, Jesus was standing there among them! "Peace be with you," he said.

[20]As he spoke, he showed them the wounds in his hands and his side. They were filled with joy when they saw the Lord! [21]Again he said, "Peace be with you. As the Father has sent me, so I am sending you."

[24]One of the twelve disciples, Thomas (nicknamed the Twin), was not with the others when Jesus came. [25]They told him, "We have seen the Lord!" But he replied, "I won't believe it unless I see the nail wounds in his hands, put my fingers into them, and place my hand into the wound in his side."

[26]Eight days later the disciples were together again, and this time Thomas was with them. The doors were locked; but suddenly, as before, Jesus was standing among them. "Peace be with you," he said. [27]Then he said to Thomas, "Put your finger here, and look at my hands. Put your hand into the wound in my side. Don't be faithless any longer. Believe!"

[28]"My Lord and my God!" Thomas exclaimed.

[29]Then Jesus told him, "You believe because you have seen me. Blessed are those who believe without seeing me."

~ John 20:19-21, 24-29

A Task for Peter – and for You!

Jesus asked Peter to show his love for Him by taking care of His followers and feeding them spiritual food. This instruction is still entrusted to every believer. Show your love for Jesus by taking care of His flock.

[15]After breakfast Jesus asked Simon Peter, "Simon son of John, do you love me more than these?"

"Yes, Lord," Peter replied, "you know I love you."

"Then feed my lambs," Jesus told him.

[16]Jesus repeated the question: "Simon son of John, do you love me?"

"Yes, Lord," Peter said, "you know I love you."

"Then take care of my sheep," Jesus said.

[17]A third time he asked him, "Simon son of John, do you love me?" Peter was hurt that Jesus asked the question a third time. He said, "Lord, you know everything. You know that I love you." Jesus said, "Then feed my sheep.

[18]"I tell you the truth, when you were young, you were able to do as you liked; you dressed yourself and went wherever you wanted to go. But when you are old, you will stretch out your hands, and others will dress you and take you where you don't want to go."

[19]Jesus said this to let him know by what kind of death he would glorify God. Then Jesus told him, "Follow me."

~ John 21:15-19

By the Power of the Spirit

Jesus promised His disciples that they would be baptized with the Holy Spirit. When that happened, they would receive power to be His witnesses to all the earth. The Holy Spirit also gives you power to witness to others.

¹In my first book I told you, Theophilus, about everything Jesus began to do and teach ²until the day he was taken up to heaven after giving his chosen apostles further instructions through the Holy Spirit.

³During the forty days after his crucifixion, he appeared to the apostles from time to time, and he proved to them in many ways that he was actually alive. And he talked to them about the Kingdom of God.

⁴Once when he was eating with them, he commanded them, "Do not leave Jerusalem until the Father sends you the gift he promised, as I told you before. ⁵John baptized with water, but in just a few days you will be baptized with the Holy Spirit."

⁶So when the apostles were with Jesus, they kept asking him, "Lord, has the time come for you to free Israel and restore our kingdom?" ⁷He replied, "The Father alone has the authority to set those dates and times, and they are not for you to know. ⁸But you will receive power when the Holy Spirit comes upon you. And you will be my witnesses, telling people about me everywhere—in Jerusalem, throughout Judea, in Samaria, and to the ends of the earth."

~ Acts 1:1-8

Jesus' Ascension

Jesus was taken up to heaven in a cloud while His disciples were watching. Two angels told them that Jesus, who has been taken from them into heaven, would come back for His children in the same way.

⁹After saying this, he was taken up into a cloud while they were watching, and they could no longer see him. ¹⁰As they strained to see him rising into heaven, two white-robed men suddenly stood among them.

¹¹"Men of Galilee," they said, "why are you standing here staring into heaven? Jesus has been taken from you into heaven, but someday he will return from heaven in the same way you saw him go!"

¹²Then the apostles returned to Jerusalem from the Mount of Olives, a distance of half a mile. ¹³When they arrived, they went to the upstairs room of the house where they were staying. Here are the names of those who were present: Peter, John, James, Andrew, Philip, Thomas, Bartholomew, Matthew, James (son of Alphaeus), Simon (the Zealot), and Judas (son of James).

¹⁴They all met together and were constantly united in prayer, along with Mary the mother of Jesus, several other women, and the brothers of Jesus.

~ Acts 1:9-14

The Outpouring of the Holy Spirit

On the first day of Pentecost, when all the believers were together, they were all filled with the Holy Spirit. Suddenly they could speak in tongues so that everyone could hear the gospel in their own language and understand it.

¹On the day of Pentecost all the believers were meeting together in one place. ²Suddenly, there was a sound from heaven like the roaring of a mighty windstorm, and it filled the house where they were sitting. ³Then, what looked like flames or tongues of fire appeared and settled on each of them. ⁴And everyone present was filled with the Holy Spirit and began speaking in other languages, as the Holy Spirit gave them this ability.

⁵At that time there were devout Jews from every nation living in Jerusalem. ⁶When they heard the loud noise, everyone came running, and they were bewildered to hear their own languages being spoken by the believers. ⁷They were completely amazed. "How can this be?" they exclaimed. "These people are all from Galilee, ⁸and yet we hear them speaking in our own native languages!

⁹"Here we are—Parthians, Medes, Elamites, people from Mesopotamia, Judea, Cappadocia, Pontus, the province of Asia, ¹⁰Phrygia, Pamphylia, Egypt, and the areas of Libya around Cyrene, visitors from Rome ¹¹(both Jews and converts to Judaism), Cretans, and Arabs. And we all hear these people speaking in our own languages about the wonderful things God has done!" ¹²They stood there amazed and perplexed. "What can this mean?" they asked each other. ¹³But others in the crowd ridiculed them, saying, "They're just drunk, that's all!"

~ Acts 2:1-13

Peter Addresses the Crowds

Peter confirmed that the Holy Spirit has been poured out on God's children, and told them of Jesus who rose from the grave. He encouraged everybody to repent and be baptized so that their sins could be forgiven, and so that they could receive the gift of the Holy Spirit.

[29]"Dear brothers, think about this! You can be sure that the patriarch David wasn't referring to himself, for he died and was buried, and his tomb is still here among us. [30]But he was a prophet, and he knew God had promised with an oath that one of David's own descendants would sit on his throne.

[31]"David was looking into the future and speaking of the Messiah's resurrection. He was saying that God would not leave him among the dead or allow his body to rot in the grave. [32]God raised Jesus from the dead, and we are all witnesses of this.

[33]"Now he is exalted to the place of highest honor in heaven, at God's right hand. And the Father, as he had promised, gave him the Holy Spirit to pour out upon us, just as you see and hear today. [34]For David himself never ascended into heaven, yet he said, 'The LORD said to my Lord, "Sit in the place of honor at my right hand [35]until I humble your enemies, making them a footstool under your feet."'

[36]"So let everyone in Israel know for certain that God has made this Jesus, whom you crucified, to be both Lord and Messiah!"

~ Acts 2:29-36

October

Follow Their Example

On the first day of Pentecost Jesus used Peter in such a powerful way that 3,000 people came to believe in Jesus and became members of the church. These believers shared their money and possessions with each other and praised God continuously. The Lord added new believers to the church every day.

37Peter's words pierced their hearts, and they said to him and to the other apostles, "Brothers, what should we do?" 38Peter replied, "Each of you must repent of your sins and turn to God, and be baptized in the name of Jesus Christ for the forgiveness of your sins. Then you will receive the gift of the Holy Spirit. 39This promise is to you, and to your children, and even to the Gentiles—all who have been called by the Lord our God."

40Then Peter continued preaching for a long time, strongly urging all his listeners, "Save yourselves from this crooked generation!"

41Those who believed what Peter said were baptized and added to the church that day—about 3,000 in all. 42All the believers devoted themselves to the apostles' teaching, and to fellowship, and to sharing in meals (including the Lord's Supper), and to prayer.

44And all the believers met together in one place and shared everything they had. 45They sold their property and possessions and shared the money with those in need. 46They worshiped together at the Temple each day, met in homes for the Lord's Supper, and shared their meals with great joy and generosity—47all the while praising God and enjoying the goodwill of all the people. And each day the Lord added to their fellowship those who were being saved.

~ Acts 2:37-42, 44-47

Impossible to Keep Quiet

The important members of the Jewish council forbade Peter and John to speak about Jesus any longer, but these two proclaimed that they could not help but witness about their experiences. They also said that they could not be more obedient to people than to God.

[8]Then Peter, filled with the Holy Spirit, said to them, "Rulers and elders of our people, [9]are we being questioned today because we've done a good deed for a crippled man? Do you want to know how he was healed? [10]Let me clearly state to all of you and to all the people of Israel that he was healed by the powerful name of Jesus Christ the Nazarene, the man you crucified but whom God raised from the dead.

[12]"There is salvation in no one else! God has given no other name under heaven by which we must be saved." [13]The members of the council were amazed when they saw the boldness of Peter and John, for they could see that they were ordinary men with no special training in the Scriptures. They also recognized them as men who had been with Jesus.

[14]But since they could see the man who had been healed standing right there among them, there was nothing the council could say. [15]So they ordered Peter and John out of the council chamber and conferred among themselves.

[18]So they called the apostles back in and commanded them never again to speak or teach in the name of Jesus. [19]But Peter and John replied, "Do you think God wants us to obey you rather than him? [20]We cannot stop telling about everything we have seen and heard."

~ Acts 4:8-10, 12-15, 18-20

Speak the Truth

When Ananias and Sapphira sold a piece of land and then lied about the selling price, they were both punished by death. This might sound like an undue punishment, but God wants to emphasize the importance of honesty. Always speak the truth!

[1]There was a certain man named Ananias who, with his wife, Sapphira, sold some property. [2]He brought part of the money to the apostles, claiming it was the full amount. With his wife's consent, he kept the rest. [3]Then Peter said, "Ananias, why have you let Satan fill your heart? You lied to the Holy Spirit, and you kept some of the money for yourself.

[4]"The property was yours to sell or not sell, as you wished. And after selling it, the money was also yours to give away. How could you do a thing like this? You weren't lying to us but to God!" [5]As soon as Ananias heard these words, he fell to the floor and died. Everyone who heard about it was terrified.

[6]Then some young men got up, wrapped him in a sheet, and took him out and buried him. [7]About three hours later his wife came in, not knowing what had happened. [8]Peter asked her, "Was this the price you and your husband received for your land?"

"Yes," she replied, "that was the price."

[9]And Peter said, "How could the two of you even think of conspiring to test the Spirit of the Lord like this? The young men who buried your husband are just outside the door, and they will carry you out, too." [10]Instantly, she fell to the floor and died. When the young men came in and saw that she was dead, they carried her out and buried her beside her husband. [11]Great fear gripped the entire church and everyone else who heard what had happened.

~ Acts 5:1-11

Saul's Calling

Saul, an eager persecutor of Christians, met with God on the road to Damascus. He was blind for three days before God healed his sight and sent Ananias to him to tell him that he has been specially chosen to proclaim the gospel to the Gentiles.

³As he was approaching Damascus on this mission, a light from heaven suddenly shone down around him. ⁴He fell to the ground and heard a voice saying to him, "Saul! Saul! Why are you persecuting me?"

⁵"Who are you, lord?" Saul asked. And the voice replied, "I am Jesus, the one you are persecuting! ⁶Now get up and go into the city, and you will be told what you must do."

¹⁰Now there was a believer in Damascus named Ananias. The Lord spoke to him in a vision, calling, "Ananias!"

"Yes, Lord!" he replied. ¹¹The Lord said, "Go over to Straight Street, to the house of Judas. When you get there, ask for a man from Tarsus named Saul. He is praying to me right now. ¹²I have shown him a vision of a man named Ananias coming in and laying hands on him so he can see again."

¹³"But Lord," exclaimed Ananias, "I've heard many people talk about the terrible things this man has done to the believers in Jerusalem! ¹⁴And he is authorized by the leading priests to arrest everyone who calls upon your name."

¹⁵But the Lord said, "Go, for Saul is my chosen instrument to take my message to the Gentiles and to kings, as well as to the people of Israel. ¹⁶And I will show him how much he must suffer for my name's sake."

~ Acts 9:3-6, 10-16

A Kind and Good Woman

When Tabitha, a widow who was always busy helping others, died, her friends called Peter and asked him to make her alive again – which he did. What would people say about you? Are you always doing good to others?

[36]There was a believer in Joppa named Tabitha (which in Greek is Dorcas). She was always doing kind things for others and helping the poor. [37]About this time she became ill and died. Her body was washed for burial and laid in an upstairs room.

[38]But the believers had heard that Peter was nearby at Lydda, so they sent two men to beg him, "Please come as soon as possible!"

[39]So Peter returned with them; and as soon as he arrived, they took him to the upstairs room. The room was filled with widows who were weeping and showing him the coats and other clothes Dorcas had made for them.

[40]But Peter asked them all to leave the room; then he knelt and prayed. Turning to the body he said, "Get up, Tabitha." And she opened her eyes! When she saw Peter, she sat up! [41]He gave her his hand and helped her up. Then he called in the widows and all the believers, and he presented her to them alive.

[42]The news spread through the whole town, and many believed in the Lord. [43]And Peter stayed a long time in Joppa, living with Simon, a tanner of hides.

~ Acts 9:36-43

Hymns of Praise in Prison

When Paul and Silas landed in jail even though they were innocent, they started to sing hymns of praise instead of moan about their lot. Then there was such a violent earthquake that the foundations of the prison were shaken. At once all the prison doors flew open, and everybody's chains came loose. Paul shared the gospel with the jailer, and he and his family were baptized.

[23]They were severely beaten, and then they were thrown into prison. The jailer was ordered to make sure they didn't escape. [24]So the jailer put them into the inner dungeon and clamped their feet in the stocks. [25]Around midnight Paul and Silas were praying and singing hymns to God, and the other prisoners were listening.

[26]Suddenly, there was a massive earthquake, and the prison was shaken to its foundations. All the doors immediately flew open, and the chains of every prisoner fell off! [27]The jailer woke up to see the prison doors wide open. He assumed the prisoners had escaped, so he drew his sword to kill himself.

[28]But Paul shouted to him, "Stop! Don't kill yourself! We are all here!" [29]The jailer called for lights and ran to the dungeon and fell down trembling before Paul and Silas. [30]Then he brought them out and asked, "Sirs, what must I do to be saved?" [31]They replied, "Believe in the Lord Jesus and you will be saved, along with everyone in your household."

[32]And they shared the word of the Lord with him and with all who lived in his household. [33]Even at that hour of the night, the jailer cared for them and washed their wounds. Then he and everyone in his household were immediately baptized.

~ Acts 16:23-33

The Creator God

Paul explained to the people of Athens who God is: He is the Creator God who gives life to every living thing. We must long for Him because through Him we live and breathe and have our being. We are His offspring. Do you know and worship this God?

²²So Paul, standing before the council, addressed them as follows: "Men of Athens, I notice that you are very religious in every way, ²³for as I was walking along I saw your many shrines. And one of your altars had this inscription on it: 'To an Unknown God.' This God, whom you worship without knowing, is the one I'm telling you about.

²⁴"He is the God who made the world and everything in it. Since he is Lord of heaven and earth, he doesn't live in man-made temples, ²⁵and human hands can't serve his needs—for he has no needs. He himself gives life and breath to everything, and he satisfies every need.

²⁶"From one man he created all the nations throughout the whole earth. He decided beforehand when they should rise and fall, and he determined their boundaries. ²⁷His purpose was for the nations to seek after God and perhaps feel their way toward him and find him—though he is not far from any one of us.

²⁸"For in him we live and move and exist. As some of your own poets have said, 'We are his offspring.' ²⁹And since this is true, we shouldn't think of God as an idol designed by craftsmen from gold or silver or stone."

~ Acts 17:22-29

Paul's Life Calling

When the Jews refused to listen to Paul's message about Jesus, he said that he would take the gospel to the Gentiles, and that they would listen to him. You are part of God's people through Jesus, and thus His message of salvation is for you too.

²³So a time was set, and on that day a large number of people came to Paul's lodging. He explained and testified about the Kingdom of God and tried to persuade them about Jesus from the Scriptures. Using the law of Moses and the books of the prophets, he spoke to them from morning until evening.

²⁴Some were persuaded by the things he said, but others did not believe. ²⁵And after they had argued back and forth among themselves, they left with this final word from Paul: "The Holy Spirit was right when he said to your ancestors through Isaiah the prophet, ²⁶'Go and say to this people: When you hear what I say, you will not understand. When you see what I do, you will not comprehend. ²⁷For the hearts of these people are hardened, and their ears cannot hear, and they have closed their eyes—so their eyes cannot see, and their ears cannot hear, and their hearts cannot understand, and they cannot turn to me and let me heal them.'

²⁸"So I want you to know that this salvation from God has also been offered to the Gentiles, and they will accept it." ³⁰For the next two years, Paul lived in Rome at his own expense. He welcomed all who visited him, ³¹boldly proclaiming the Kingdom of God and teaching about the Lord Jesus Christ. And no one tried to stop him.

~ Acts 28:23-31

We Are All Sinners

All people are sinners – there is not even one who is without sin. From birth we have been stained with sin, and we cannot be freed from sin by only obeying the Law. There is another way!

⁹Well then, should we conclude that we Jews are better than others? No, not at all, for we have already shown that all people, whether Jews or Gentiles, are under the power of sin. ¹⁰As the Scriptures say, "No one is righteous—not even one. ¹¹No one is truly wise; no one is seeking God. ¹²All have turned away; all have become useless. No one does good, not a single one. ¹³"Their talk is foul, like the stench from an open grave. Their tongues are filled with lies. Snake venom drips from their lips.

¹⁴"Their mouths are full of cursing and bitterness. ¹⁵They rush to commit murder. ¹⁶Destruction and misery always follow them. ¹⁷They don't know where to find peace. ¹⁸They have no fear of God at all."

¹⁹Obviously, the law applies to those to whom it was given, for its purpose is to keep people from having excuses, and to show that the entire world is guilty before God. ²⁰For no one can ever be made right with God by doing what the law commands. The law simply shows us how sinful we are.

~ Romans 3:9-20

God's Solution

God frees us from sin when we trust in Him to forgive our sins. Jesus has brought reconciliation between God and us through His death on the cross to all who believe. It's the only way to escape God's punishment.

23For everyone has sinned; we all fall short of God's glorious standard. 24Yet God, with undeserved kindness, declares that we are righteous. He did this through Christ Jesus when he freed us from the penalty for our sins.

25For God presented Jesus as the sacrifice for sin. People are made right with God when they believe that Jesus sacrificed his life, shedding his blood. This sacrifice shows that God was being fair when he held back and did not punish those who sinned in times past, 26for he was looking ahead and including them in what he would do in this present time. God did this to demonstrate his righteousness, for he himself is fair and just, and he declares sinners to be right in his sight when they believe in Jesus.

27Can we boast, then, that we have done anything to be accepted by God? No, because our acquittal is not based on obeying the law. It is based on faith. 28So we are made right with God through faith and not by obeying the law. 29After all, is God the God of the Jews only? Isn't he also the God of the Gentiles? Of course he is.

30There is only one God, and he makes people right with himself only by faith, whether they are Jews or Gentiles. 31Well then, if we emphasize faith, does this mean that we can forget about the law? Of course not! In fact, only when we have faith do we truly fulfill the law.

~ Romans 3:23-31

What a Privilege to Be a Christian!

When Jesus paid the ransom with His blood for our sins, He also established peace between sinful people and a holy God. Now God's grace is freely available to you – you can even call Him your own personal Friend.

¹Therefore, since we have been made right in God's sight by faith, we have peace with God because of what Jesus Christ our Lord has done for us. ²Because of our faith, Christ has brought us into this place of undeserved privilege where we now stand, and we confidently and joyfully look forward to sharing God's glory.

⁵And this hope will not lead to disappointment. For we know how dearly God loves us, because he has given us the Holy Spirit to fill our hearts with his love. ⁶When we were utterly helpless, Christ came at just the right time and died for us sinners.

⁷Now, most people would not be willing to die for an upright person, though someone might perhaps be willing to die for a person who is especially good. ⁸But God showed his great love for us by sending Christ to die for us while we were still sinners. ⁹And since we have been made right in God's sight by the blood of Christ, he will certainly save us from God's condemnation.

¹⁰For since our friendship with God was restored by the death of his Son while we were still his enemies, we will certainly be saved through the life of his Son. ¹¹So now we can rejoice in our wonderful new relationship with God because our Lord Jesus Christ has made us friends of God.

~ Romans 5:1-2, 5-11

Live for God

People who believe in Jesus are free from the control of sin and can live for God because they are one with Jesus. Be available to God and live a life that is dedicated to Him. His gift of grace and mercy to you is eternal life.

[9]We are sure of this because Christ was raised from the dead, and he will never die again. Death no longer has any power over him. [10]When he died, he died once to break the power of sin. But now that he lives, he lives for the glory of God.

[11]So you also should consider yourselves to be dead to the power of sin and alive to God through Christ Jesus. [12]Do not let sin control the way you live; do not give in to sinful desires.

[13]Do not let any part of your body become an instrument of evil to serve sin. Instead, give yourselves completely to God, for you were dead, but now you have new life. So use your whole body as an instrument to do what is right for the glory of God. [14]Sin is no longer your master, for you no longer live under the requirements of the law. Instead, you live under the freedom of God's grace.

[18]Now you are free from your slavery to sin, and you have become slaves to righteous living. [19]Because of the weakness of your human nature, I am using the illustration of slavery to help you understand all this. Previously, you let yourselves be slaves to impurity and lawlessness, which led ever deeper into sin. Now you must give yourselves to be slaves to righteous living so that you will become holy.

~ Romans 6:9-14, 18-19

The Spirit Sets You Free

The Holy Spirit sets you free from the grip of sin that leads to death. From now on the Spirit should guide your life. Focus your thoughts on God, and give control of your entire life to Him.

⁵Those who are dominated by the sinful nature think about sinful things, but those who are controlled by the Holy Spirit think about things that please the Spirit. ⁶So letting your sinful nature control your mind leads to death. But letting the Spirit control your mind leads to life and peace.

⁷For the sinful nature is always hostile to God. It never did obey God's laws, and it never will. ⁸That's why those who are still under the control of their sinful nature can never please God.

⁹But you are not controlled by your sinful nature. You are controlled by the Spirit if you have the Spirit of God living in you. (And remember that those who do not have the Spirit of Christ living in them do not belong to him at all.)

¹⁰And Christ lives within you, so even though your body will die because of sin, the Spirit gives you life because you have been made right with God. ¹¹The Spirit of God, who raised Jesus from the dead, lives in you. And just as God raised Christ Jesus from the dead, he will give life to your mortal bodies by this same Spirit living within you.

~ Romans 8:5-11

Children and Heirs

The Holy Spirit in you confirms that you are a child of God. And if you are God's child, you are also an heir, and you share together with Jesus in God's immeasurable riches and glory.

[12]Therefore, dear brothers and sisters, you have no obligation to do what your sinful nature urges you to do. [13]For if you live by its dictates, you will die. But if through the power of the Spirit you put to death the deeds of your sinful nature, you will live. [14]For all who are led by the Spirit of God are children of God.

[15]So you have not received a spirit that makes you fearful slaves. Instead, you received God's Spirit when he adopted you as his own children. Now we call him, "Abba, Father." [16]For his Spirit joins with our spirit to affirm that we are God's children.

[17]And since we are his children, we are his heirs. In fact, together with Christ we are heirs of God's glory. But if we are to share his glory, we must also share his suffering.

~ Romans 8:12-17

God Works Everything Out

At the moment, creation is caught up in a meaning-less cycle of adversity and God's children are suf-fering. But our earthly trouble will one day come to an end, and we know that in all things God works everything together for the good of those who love Him.

[18]Yet what we suffer now is nothing compared to the glory he will reveal to us later. [20]Against its will, all creation was subjected to God's curse. But with eager hope, [21]the creation looks forward to the day when it will join God's children in glorious freedom from death and decay. [22]For we know that all creation has been groaning as in the pains of childbirth right up to the present time. [23]And we believers also groan, even though we have the Holy Spirit within us as a foretaste of future glory, for we long for our bodies to be released from sin and suffering. We, too, wait with eager hope for the day when God will give us our full rights as his adopted children.

[24]We were given this hope when we were saved. (If we already have something, we don't need to hope for it. [25]But if we look forward to something we don't yet have, we must wait patiently and confidently.) [26]And the Holy Spirit helps us in our weakness. For example, we don't know what God wants us to pray for. But the Holy Spirit prays for us with groanings that cannot be expressed in words. [27]And the Father who knows all hearts knows what the Spirit is saying, for the Spirit pleads for us believers in harmony with God's own will. [28]And we know that God causes everything to work together for the good of those who love God and are called according to his purpose for them.

~ Romans 8:18, 20-28

Nothing Can Separate You from God's Love

In a beautiful song of praise, Paul proclaimed that nothing on earth or in heaven could ever separate him from God's love. God has shown you this love by giving His Son as a sacrifice for us all. If He is for you, who can ever be against you?

³¹What shall we say about such wonderful things as these? If God is for us, who can ever be against us? ³²Since he did not spare even his own Son but gave him up for us all, won't he also give us everything else?

³³Who dares accuse us whom God has chosen for his own? No one—for God himself has given us right standing with himself. ³⁴Who then will condemn us? No one—for Christ Jesus died for us and was raised to life for us, and he is sitting in the place of honor at God's right hand, pleading for us. ³⁵Can anything ever separate us from Christ's love? Does it mean he no longer loves us if we have trouble or calamity, or are persecuted, or hungry, or destitute, or in danger, or threatened with death? ³⁶(As the Scriptures say, "For your sake we are killed every day; we are being slaughtered like sheep.") ³⁷No, despite all these things, overwhelming victory is ours through Christ, who loved us.

³⁸And I am convinced that nothing can ever separate us from God's love. Neither death nor life, neither angels nor demons, neither our fears for today nor our worries about tomorrow—not even the powers of hell can separate us from God's love. ³⁹No power in the sky above or in the earth below—indeed, nothing in all creation will ever be able to separate us from the love of God that is revealed in Christ Jesus our Lord.

~ Romans 8:31-39

Give Your Life to God

When we think of all the things that God has done for us, we ought to give our lives to Him as living sacrifices, holy and pleasing in His sight. We must allow God to renew our minds. Only then will we be acceptable in His sight.

¹And so, dear brothers and sisters, I plead with you to give your bodies to God because of all he has done for you. Let them be a living and holy sacrifice—the kind he will find acceptable. This is truly the way to worship him.

²Don't copy the behavior and customs of this world, but let God transform you into a new person by changing the way you think. Then you will learn to know God's will for you, which is good and pleasing and perfect.

⁴Just as our bodies have many parts and each part has a special function, ⁵so it is with Christ's body. We are many parts of one body, and we all belong to each other.

⁶In his grace, God has given us different gifts for doing certain things well. So if God has given you the ability to prophesy, speak out with as much faith as God has given you. ⁷If your gift is serving others, serve them well. If you are a teacher, teach well. ⁸If your gift is to encourage others, be encouraging. If it is giving, give generously. If God has given you leadership ability, take the responsibility seriously. And if you have a gift for showing kindness to others, do it gladly.

~ Romans 12:1-2, 4-8

Be Enthusiastic!

Paul gave us guidelines on how a Christian should live. Never be lacking in zeal and fervor when serving the Lord, but be joyful in everything. Care for your fellow believers in love and live in harmony with others.

[9]Don't just pretend to love others. Really love them. Hate what is wrong. Hold tightly to what is good. [10]Love each other with genuine affection, and take delight in honoring each other. [11]Never be lazy, but work hard and serve the Lord enthusiastically.

[12]Rejoice in our confident hope. Be patient in trouble, and keep on praying. [13]When God's people are in need, be ready to help them. Always be eager to practice hospitality.

[14]Bless those who persecute you. Don't curse them; pray that God will bless them. [15]Be happy with those who are happy, and weep with those who weep. [16]Live in harmony with each other. Don't be too proud to enjoy the company of ordinary people. And don't think you know it all!

[17]Never pay back evil with more evil. Do things in such a way that everyone can see you are honorable.

~ Romans 12:9-17

Think Like Jesus

God's Spirit alone knows His deepest thoughts: Through Christ's death on the cross you are free from sin and receive God's promise that you will one day live forever with Him. You can only understand these things if you learn to think like Jesus does.

¹⁰But it was to us that God revealed these things by his Spirit. For his Spirit searches out everything and shows us God's deep secrets. ¹¹No one can know a person's thoughts except that person's own spirit, and no one can know God's thoughts except God's own Spirit. ¹²And we have received God's Spirit (not the world's spirit), so we can know the wonderful things God has freely given us.

¹³When we tell you these things, we do not use words that come from human wisdom. Instead, we speak words given to us by the Spirit, using the Spirit's words to explain spiritual truths. ¹⁴But people who aren't spiritual can't receive these truths from God's Spirit. It all sounds foolish to them and they can't understand it, for only those who are spiritual can understand what the Spirit means.

¹⁵Those who are spiritual can evaluate all things, but they themselves cannot be evaluated by others. ¹⁶For, "Who can know the Lord's thoughts? Who knows enough to teach him?" But we understand these things, for we have the mind of Christ.

~ 1 Corinthians 2:10-16

God's Temple

Each child of God is a temple in which the Spirit of God dwells. God's temple is sacred and you are that temple. If anybody destroys God's temple, God will destroy him. Because you belong to Christ and Christ belongs to God, you should live a holy life.

[16]Don't you realize that all of you together are the temple of God and that the Spirit of God lives in you? [17]God will destroy anyone who destroys this temple. For God's temple is holy, and you are that temple.

[18]Stop deceiving yourselves. If you think you are wise by this world's standards, you need to become a fool to be truly wise. [19]For the wisdom of this world is foolishness to God. As the Scriptures say, "He traps the wise in the snare of their own cleverness."

[20]And again, "The LORD knows the thoughts of the wise; he knows they are worthless."

[21]So don't boast about following a particular human leader. For everything belongs to you—[22]whether Paul or Apollos or Peter, or the world, or life and death, or the present and the future. Everything belongs to you, [23]and you belong to Christ, and Christ belongs to God.

~ 1 Corinthians 3:16-23

Bought at a Price

Our bodies are not meant for sexual immorality. Therefore, avoid sexual sins because your body is part of Christ. You were bought at a high price – because of that you should glorify God with your body.

¹²You say, "I am allowed to do anything"—but not everything is good for you. And even though "I am allowed to do anything," I must not become a slave to anything. ¹³You say, "Food was made for the stomach, and the stomach for food." (This is true, though someday God will do away with both of them.) But you can't say that our bodies were made for sexual immorality. They were made for the Lord, and the Lord cares about our bodies. ¹⁴And God will raise us from the dead by his power, just as he raised our Lord from the dead.

¹⁵Don't you realize that your bodies are actually parts of Christ? Should a man take his body, which is part of Christ, and join it to a prostitute? Never! ¹⁶And don't you realize that if a man joins himself to a prostitute, he becomes one body with her? For the Scriptures say, "The two are united into one." ¹⁷But the person who is joined to the Lord is one spirit with him.

¹⁸Run from sexual sin! No other sin so clearly affects the body as this one does. For sexual immorality is a sin against your own body. ¹⁹Don't you realize that your body is the temple of the Holy Spirit, who lives in you and was given to you by God? You do not belong to yourself, ²⁰for God bought you with a high price. So you must honor God with your body.

~ 1 Corinthians 6:12-20

Perfect Love

To love like Jesus is the most important characteristic: your love should be patient and kind, it should not boast or be jealous or keep a record of wrongs. What shall remain until the end is faith, hope and love. But the greatest of these is love.

[1]If I could speak all the languages of earth and of angels, but didn't love others, I would only be a noisy gong or a clanging cymbal. [2]If I had the gift of prophecy, and if I understood all of God's secret plans and possessed all knowledge, and if I had such faith that I could move mountains, but didn't love others, I would be nothing. [3]If I gave everything I have to the poor and even sacrificed my body, I could boast about it; but if I didn't love others, I would have gained nothing.

[4]Love is patient and kind. Love is not jealous or boastful or proud [5]or rude. It does not demand its own way. It is not irritable, and it keeps no record of being wronged. [6]It does not rejoice about injustice but rejoices whenever the truth wins out. [7]Love never gives up, never loses faith, is always hopeful, and endures through every circumstance.

[8]Prophecy and speaking in unknown languages and special knowledge will become useless. But love will last forever! [9]Now our knowledge is partial and incomplete, and even the gift of prophecy reveals only part of the whole picture! [10]But when the time of perfection comes, these partial things will become useless. [11]When I was a child, I spoke and thought and reasoned as a child. But when I grew up, I put away childish things.

[13]Three things will last forever—faith, hope, and love—and the greatest of these is love.

~ 1 Corinthians 13:1-11, 13

Victory over Death

One day all believers will be raised from the dead to live in glory. You will get a new body that will never perish. With Christ's resurrection from the grave He conquered death forever so that you can live with Him for all eternity.

⁵⁰What I am saying, dear brothers and sisters, is that our physical bodies cannot inherit the Kingdom of God. These dying bodies cannot inherit what will last forever.

⁵¹But let me reveal to you a wonderful secret. We will not all die, but we will all be transformed! ⁵²It will happen in a moment, in the blink of an eye, when the last trumpet is blown. For when the trumpet sounds, those who have died will be raised to live forever. And we who are living will also be transformed. ⁵³For our dying bodies must be transformed into bodies that will never die; our mortal bodies must be transformed into immortal bodies.

⁵⁴Then, when our dying bodies have been transformed into bodies that will never die, this Scripture will be fulfilled: "Death is swallowed up in victory. ⁵⁵O death, where is your victory? O death, where is your sting?"

~ 1 Corinthians 15:50-55

Suffering Produces Trust

God comforts us in our troubles so that we can comfort others in their suffering. When you experience times of hardship you can trust God. He is the only one who can deliver you from deadly peril.

[3]All praise to God, the Father of our Lord Jesus Christ. God is our merciful Father and the source of all comfort. [4]He comforts us in all our troubles so that we can comfort others. When they are troubled, we will be able to give them the same comfort God has given us. [5]For the more we suffer for Christ, the more God will shower us with his comfort through Christ.

[6]Even when we are weighed down with troubles, it is for your comfort and salvation! For when we ourselves are comforted, we will certainly comfort you. Then you can patiently endure the same things we suffer. [7]We are confident that as you share in our sufferings, you will also share in the comfort God gives us.

[8]We think you ought to know, dear brothers and sisters, about the trouble we went through in the province of Asia. We were crushed and overwhelmed beyond our ability to endure, and we thought we would never live through it. [9]In fact, we expected to die. But as a result, we stopped relying on ourselves and learned to rely only on God, who raises the dead. [10]And he did rescue us from mortal danger, and he will rescue us again. We have placed our confidence in him, and he will continue to rescue us.

~ 2 Corinthians 1:3-10

Mirrors of God's Glory

God's children should be mirrors that reflect His glory. We must constantly change in order to become more like Jesus in our thoughts and deeds, so that His glory in us can increase daily. The Holy Spirit in us will help us.

3 [18]So all of us who have had that veil removed can see and reflect the glory of the Lord. And the Lord—who is the Spirit—makes us more and more like him as we are changed into his glorious image.

4 [1]Therefore, since God in his mercy has given us this new way, we never give up. [2]We reject all shameful deeds and underhanded methods. We don't try to trick anyone or distort the word of God. We tell the truth before God, and all who are honest know this.

[3]If the Good News we preach is hidden behind a veil, it is hidden only from people who are perishing. [4]Satan, who is the god of this world, has blinded the minds of those who don't believe. They are unable to see the glorious light of the Good News. They don't understand this message about the glory of Christ, who is the exact likeness of God.

[5]You see, we don't go around preaching about ourselves. We preach that Jesus Christ is Lord, and we ourselves are your servants for Jesus' sake. [6]For God, who said, "Let there be light in the darkness," has made this light shine in our hearts so we could know the glory of God that is seen in the face of Jesus Christ.

~ 2 Corinthians 3:18-4:6

Eternal Glory

If you believe in Jesus you can know for sure that your earthly suffering will pass. Even more than that, your light and momentary troubles are achieving for you eternal glory that far outweighs everything.

[1]Therefore, since God in his mercy has given us this new way, we never give up.

[11]Yes, we live under constant danger of death because we serve Jesus, so that the life of Jesus will be evident in our dying bodies. [12]So we live in the face of death, but this has resulted in eternal life for you. [13]But we continue to preach because we have the same kind of faith the psalmist had when he said, "I believed in God, so I spoke." [14]We know that God, who raised the Lord Jesus, will also raise us with Jesus and present us to himself together with you. [15]All of this is for your benefit. And as God's grace reaches more and more people, there will be great thanksgiving, and God will receive more and more glory.

[16]That is why we never give up. Though our bodies are dying, our spirits are being renewed every day. [17]For our present troubles are small and won't last very long. Yet they produce for us a glory that vastly outweighs them and will last forever! [18]So we don't look at the troubles we can see now; rather, we fix our gaze on things that cannot be seen. For the things we see now will soon be gone, but the things we cannot see will last forever.

~ 2 Corinthians 4:1, 11-18

An Eternal House in Heaven

Your life on earth is nothing more than an earthly tent. You have a permanent heavenly dwelling – a house that will stand forever because it is not built by human hands. For this reason you can always have courage.

[1]For we know that when this earthly tent we live in is taken down (that is, when we die and leave this earthly body), we will have a house in heaven, an eternal body made for us by God himself and not by human hands. [2]We grow weary in our present bodies, and we long to put on our heavenly bodies like new clothing. [3]For we will put on heavenly bodies; we will not be spirits without bodies.

[4]While we live in these earthly bodies, we groan and sigh, but it's not that we want to die and get rid of these bodies that clothe us. Rather, we want to put on our new bodies so that these dying bodies will be swallowed up by life. [5]God himself has prepared us for this, and as a guarantee he has given us his Holy Spirit.

[6]So we are always confident, even though we know that as long as we live in these bodies we are not at home with the Lord. [7]For we live by believing and not by seeing. [8]Yes, we are fully confident, and we would rather be away from these earthly bodies, for then we will be at home with the Lord. [9]So whether we are here in this body or away from this body, our goal is to please him. [10]For we must all stand before Christ to be judged. We will each receive whatever we deserve for the good or evil we have done in this earthly body.

~ 2 Corinthians 5:1-10

An Ambassador of Jesus' Love

Jesus came to earth to reconcile God and people. To fulfill this purpose God let His Son die in your place. You should proclaim this message of salvation to other people on earth and be an ambassador; a representative of God.

5 [18]And all of this is a gift from God, who brought us back to himself through Christ. And God has given us this task of reconciling people to him. [19]For God was in Christ, reconciling the world to himself, no longer counting people's sins against them. And he gave us this wonderful message of reconciliation.

[20]So we are Christ's ambassadors; God is making his appeal through us. We speak for Christ when we plead, "Come back to God!" [21]For God made Christ, who never sinned, to be the offering for our sin, so that we could be made right with God through Christ.

6 [1]As God's partners, we beg you not to accept this marvelous gift of God's kindness and then ignore it. [2]For God says, "At just the right time, I heard you. On the day of salvation, I helped you." Indeed, the "right time" is now. Today is the day of salvation.

~ 2 Corinthians 5:18-6:2

Live with Your Thorn

Like all people, Paul had something in his life that tormented him. He prayed that God would take it away, but He didn't. He offered Paul His grace instead, and His power in weakness. God wants to do this for you too.

[1]This boasting will do no good, but I must go on. I will reluctantly tell about visions and revelations from the Lord. [2]I was caught up to the third heaven fourteen years ago. Whether I was in my body or out of my body, I don't know—only God knows. [3]Yes, only God knows whether I was in my body or outside my body. But I do know [4]that I was caught up to paradise and heard things so astounding that they cannot be expressed in words, things no human is allowed to tell.

[5]That experience is worth boasting about, but I'm not going to do it. I will boast only about my weaknesses. [6]If I wanted to boast, I would be no fool in doing so, because I would be telling the truth. But I won't do it, because I don't want anyone to give me credit beyond what they can see in my life or hear in my message, [7]even though I have received such wonderful revelations from God. So to keep me from becoming proud, I was given a thorn in my flesh, a messenger from Satan to torment me and keep me from becoming proud.

[8]Three different times I begged the Lord to take it away. [9]Each time he said, "My grace is all you need. My power works best in weakness." So now I am glad to boast about my weaknesses, so that the power of Christ can work through me. [10]That's why I take pleasure in my weaknesses, and in the insults, hardships, persecutions, and troubles that I suffer for Christ. For when I am weak, then I am strong.

~ 2 Corinthians 12:1-10

Jesus Lives in You!

You will never have a fulfilling relationship with God only by obeying His Law. God's children are, in fact, dead to the Law. You were crucified with Christ, and should now live for Him. In truth you don't live any longer, Christ Himself lives in you.

15"You and I are Jews by birth, not 'sinners' like the Gentiles. 16Yet we know that a person is made right with God by faith in Jesus Christ, not by obeying the law. And we have believed in Christ Jesus, so that we might be made right with God because of our faith in Christ, not because we have obeyed the law. For no one will ever be made right with God by obeying the law."

17But suppose we seek to be made right with God through faith in Christ and then we are found guilty because we have abandoned the law. Would that mean Christ has led us into sin? Absolutely not! 18Rather, I am a sinner if I rebuild the old system of law I already tore down. 19For when I tried to keep the law, it condemned me. So I died to the law—I stopped trying to meet all its requirements—so that I might live for God. 20My old self has been crucified with Christ. It is no longer I who live, but Christ lives in me. So I live in this earthly body by trusting in the Son of God, who loved me and gave himself for me.

21I do not treat the grace of God as meaningless. For if keeping the law could make us right with God, then there was no need for Christ to die.

~ Galatians 2:15-21

The Fruit of the Spirit

The fruit of the Spirit should be clearly visible in the lives of God's children. These fruits are love, joy, peace, patience, kindness, goodness, faithfulness, gentleness, and self-control. Since we live by the Spirit, we should follow the Spirit's leading in every part of our lives.

[15]But if you are always biting and devouring one another, watch out! Beware of destroying one another.

[16]So I say, let the Holy Spirit guide your lives. Then you won't be doing what your sinful nature craves. [17]The sinful nature wants to do evil, which is just the opposite of what the Spirit wants. And the Spirit gives us desires that are the opposite of what the sinful nature desires. These two forces are constantly fighting each other, so you are not free to carry out your good intentions. [18]But when you are directed by the Spirit, you are not under obligation to the law of Moses.

[19]When you follow the desires of your sinful nature, the results are very clear: sexual immorality, impurity, lustful pleasures, [20]idolatry, sorcery, hostility, quarreling, jealousy, outbursts of anger, selfish ambition, dissension, division, [21]envy, drunkenness, wild parties, and other sins like these. Let me tell you again, as I have before, that anyone living that sort of life will not inherit the Kingdom of God. [22]But the fruit of the Spirit is love, joy, peace, patience, kindness, goodness, faithfulness, [23]gentleness and self-control. Against such things there is no law.

~ Galatians 5:15-23

November

Free Spiritual Gifts!

Through His death on the cross Jesus made God's spiritual gifts available to you – for free. You only have to confess your sins, and God promises to forgive them based on what Jesus did for you. God also gives us the Holy Spirit as a guarantee that all His promises will come true.

[3]All praise to God, the Father of our Lord Jesus Christ, who has blessed us with every spiritual blessing in the heavenly realms because we are united with Christ. [4]Even before he made the world, God loved us and chose us in Christ to be holy and without fault in his eyes. [5]God decided in advance to adopt us into his own family by bringing us to himself through Jesus Christ. This is what he wanted to do, and it gave him great pleasure.

[6]So we praise God for the glorious grace he has poured out on us who belong to his dear Son. [7]He is so rich in kindness and grace that he purchased our freedom with the blood of his Son and forgave our sins. [8]He has showered his kindness on us, along with all wisdom and understanding. [9]God has now revealed to us his mysterious plan regarding Christ, a plan to fulfill his own good pleasure.

[12]God's purpose was that we Jews who were the first to trust in Christ would bring praise and glory to God. [13]And now you Gentiles have also heard the truth, the Good News that God saves you. And when you believed in Christ, he identified you as his own by giving you the Holy Spirit, whom he promised long ago.

[14]The Spirit is God's guarantee that he will give us the inheritance he promised and that he has purchased us to be his own people. He did this so we would praise and glorify him.

~ Ephesians 1:3-9, 12-14

Life-Changing Prayers

Paul prayed for the people in Ephesus that they may know the hope to which God has called them, the riches of His glorious inheritance in the saints, and His incomparably great power for everyone who believes. Make these prayers part of your prayer life as you pray for others.

1 [15]Ever since I first heard of your strong faith in the Lord Jesus and your love for God's people everywhere, [16]I have not stopped thanking God for you. I pray for you constantly, [17]asking God, the glorious Father of our Lord Jesus Christ, to give you spiritual wisdom and insight so that you might grow in your knowledge of God. [18]I pray that your hearts will be flooded with light so that you can understand the confident hope he has given to those he called—his holy people who are his rich and glorious inheritance. [19]I also pray that you will understand the incredible greatness of God's power for us who believe him.

3 [14]When I think of all this, I fall to my knees and pray to the Father, [15]the Creator of everything in heaven and on earth. [16]I pray that from his glorious, unlimited resources he will empower you with inner strength through his Spirit. [17]Then Christ will make his home in your hearts as you trust in him. Your roots will grow down into God's love and keep you strong. [18]And may you have the power to understand, as all God's people should, how wide, how long, how high, and how deep his love is. [19]May you experience the love of Christ, though it is too great to understand fully. Then you will be made complete with all the fullness of life and power that comes from God.

[20]Now all glory to God, who is able, through his mighty power at work within us, to accomplish infinitely more than we might ask or think.

~ Ephesians 1:15-19; 3:14-20

The Work of God's Hands

God has made us alive with Jesus. Through His undeserved goodness He saved us and gave us faith
as a gift. You are God's handiwork. He made you in
a very special way to live out the good purpose for
which He has created you – right where you are!

[1]Once you were dead because of your disobedience and your
many sins. [2]You used to live in sin, just like the rest of the world,
obeying the devil—the commander of the powers in the unseen
world. He is the spirit at work in the hearts of those who refuse
to obey God. [3]All of us used to live that way, following the pas-
sionate desires and inclinations of our sinful nature. By our very
nature we were subject to God's anger, just like everyone else.

[4]But God is so rich in mercy, and he loved us so much, [5]that
even though we were dead because of our sins, he gave us life
when he raised Christ from the dead. (It is only by God's grace
that you have been saved!) [6]For he raised us from the dead
along with Christ and seated us with him in the heavenly realms
because we are united with Christ Jesus. [7]So God can point to
us in all future ages as examples of the incredible wealth of his
grace and kindness toward us, as shown in all he has done for
us who are united with Christ Jesus.

[8]God saved you by his grace when you believed. And you
can't take credit for this; it is a gift from God. [9]Salvation is not
a reward for the good things we have done, so none of us can
boast about it. [10]For we are God's masterpiece. He has created
us anew in Christ Jesus, so we can do the good things he
planned for us long ago.

~ Ephesians 2:1-10

United with Christ

Through Christ's death on the cross, we are united with Him. By dying for our sins, He broke down the wall that separated us from God. We are now reconciled with God and other people.

¹²In those days you were living apart from Christ. You lived in this world without God and without hope. ¹³But now you have been united with Christ Jesus. Once you were far away from God, but now you have been brought near to him through the blood of Christ.

¹⁴For Christ himself has brought peace to us. He united Jews and Gentiles into one people when, in his own body on the cross, he broke down the wall of hostility that separated us. ¹⁵He did this by ending the system of law with its commandments and regulations. He made peace between Jews and Gentiles by creating in himself one new people from the two groups. ¹⁶Together as one body, Christ reconciled both groups to God by means of his death on the cross, and our hostility toward each other was put to death.

¹⁷He brought this Good News of peace to you Gentiles who were far away from him, and peace to the Jews who were near. ¹⁸Now all of us can come to the Father through the same Holy Spirit because of what Christ has done for us.

¹⁹So now you Gentiles are no longer strangers and foreigners. You are citizens along with all of God's holy people. You are members of God's family. ²⁰Together, we are his house, built on the foundation of the apostles and the prophets. And the cornerstone is Christ Jesus himself. ²¹We are carefully joined together in him, becoming a holy temple for the Lord. ²²Through him you Gentiles are also being made part of this dwelling where God lives by his Spirit.

~ Ephesians 2:12-22

A Christian Lifestyle

Because you belong to God, you should live a humble and peaceful life. You should speak the truth in love and grow in all circumstances to be more like Christ. Put on your new nature, created to be like God. Ask the Holy Spirit to help you.

[1]Therefore I, a prisoner for serving the Lord, beg you to lead a life worthy of your calling, for you have been called by God. [2]Always be humble and gentle. Be patient with each other, making allowance for each other's faults because of your love. [3]Make every effort to keep yourselves united in the Spirit, binding yourselves together with peace. [4]For there is one body and one Spirit, just as you have been called to one glorious hope for the future. [5]There is one Lord, one faith, one baptism, [6]and one God and Father, who is over all and in all and living through all. [7]However, he has given each one of us a special gift through the generosity of Christ.

[13]This will continue until we all come to such unity in our faith and knowledge of God's Son that we will be mature in the Lord, measuring up to the full and complete standard of Christ. [14]Then we will no longer be immature like children. We won't be tossed and blown about by every wind of new teaching. We will not be influenced when people try to trick us with lies so clever they sound like the truth. [15]Instead, we will speak the truth in love, growing in every way more and more like Christ, who is the head of his body, the church.

[23]Instead, let the Spirit renew your thoughts and attitudes. [24]Put on your new nature, created to be like God—truly righteous and holy.

~ Ephesians 4:1-7, 13-15, 23-24

Living in the Light

God wants us to live in His light. We must stay away from sexual immorality, impurity and greed, and we should expose evil deeds. Use every opportunity to be filled with the Holy Spirit – sing God's praises and thank Him for everything.

¹Imitate God, therefore, in everything you do, because you are his dear children. ²Live a life filled with love, following the example of Christ. He loved us and offered himself as a sacrifice for us, a pleasing aroma to God.

³Let there be no sexual immorality, impurity, or greed among you. Such sins have no place among God's people. ⁴Obscene stories, foolish talk, and coarse jokes—these are not for you. Instead, let there be thankfulness to God. ⁵You can be sure that no immoral, impure, or greedy person will inherit the Kingdom of Christ and of God. For a greedy person is an idolater, worshiping the things of this world.

⁸For once you were full of darkness, but now you have light from the Lord. So live as people of light! ⁹For this light within you produces only what is good and right and true. ¹⁰Carefully determine what pleases the Lord. ¹¹Take no part in the worthless deeds of evil and darkness; instead, expose them.

¹⁵So be careful how you live. Don't live like fools, but like those who are wise. ¹⁶Make the most of every opportunity in these evil days. ¹⁷Don't act thoughtlessly, but understand what the Lord wants you to do. ¹⁸Don't be drunk with wine, because that will ruin your life. Instead, be filled with the Holy Spirit, ¹⁹singing psalms and hymns and spiritual songs among yourselves, and making music to the Lord in your hearts.

~ Ephesians 5:1-5, 8-11, 15-19

God's Armor

Everyone who wants to stand firm against the Evil One must wear God's armor. The Holy Spirit will teach you how to put it on and take action. Pray in the Spirit always, and find strength in your relationship with the Lord.

[10]A final word: Be strong in the Lord and in his mighty power. [11]Put on all of God's armor so that you will be able to stand firm against all strategies of the devil. [12]For we are not fighting against flesh-and-blood enemies, but against evil rulers and authorities of the unseen world, against mighty powers in this dark world, and against evil spirits in the heavenly places.

[13]Therefore, put on every piece of God's armor so you will be able to resist the enemy in the time of evil. Then after the battle you will still be standing firm. [14]Stand your ground, putting on the belt of truth and the body armor of God's righteousness. [15]For shoes, put on the peace that comes from the Good News so that you will be fully prepared. [16]In addition to all of these, hold up the shield of faith to stop the fiery arrows of the devil. [17]Put on salvation as your helmet, and take the sword of the Spirit, which is the word of God.

[18]Pray in the Spirit at all times and on every occasion. Stay alert and be persistent in your prayers for all believers everywhere.

~ Ephesians 6:10-18

God's Work in You Must Come to Completion

Paul prayed that the good work God started within each of His children would come to completion, and that the love of the Philippians for each other would increase and that they would live holy and blameless lives. Ask God to make this prayer true in your life.

³Every time I think of you, I give thanks to my God. ⁴Whenever I pray, I make my requests for all of you with joy, ⁵for you have been my partners in spreading the Good News about Christ from the time you first heard it until now. ⁶And I am certain that God, who began the good work within you, will continue his work until it is finally finished on the day when Christ Jesus returns.

⁹I pray that your love will overflow more and more, and that you will keep on growing in knowledge and understanding. ¹⁰For I want you to understand what really matters, so that you may live pure and blameless lives until the day of Christ's return. ¹¹May you always be filled with the fruit of your salvation—the righteous character produced in your life by Jesus Christ—for this will bring much glory and praise to God.

~ Philippians 1:3-6; 9-11

Reflect God's Good News

It is essential for Christians to portray characteristics like agreeing wholeheartedly with each other, loving one another, and working together with one mind and purpose. When your lifestyle reflects your faith, it shows that you are ready for Christ to return.

1 [27]Above all, you must live as citizens of heaven, conducting yourselves in a manner worthy of the Good News about Christ. Then, whether I come and see you again or only hear about you, I will know that you are standing together with one spirit and one purpose, fighting together for the faith, which is the Good News. [28]Don't be intimidated in any way by your enemies. This will be a sign to them that they are going to be destroyed, but that you are going to be saved, even by God himself. [29]For you have been given not only the privilege of trusting in Christ but also the privilege of suffering for him. [30]We are in this struggle together. You have seen my struggle in the past, and you know that I am still in the midst of it.

2 [1]Is there any encouragement from belonging to Christ? Any comfort from his love? Any fellowship together in the Spirit? Are your hearts tender and compassionate? [2]Then make me truly happy by agreeing wholeheartedly with each other, loving one another, and working together with one mind and purpose. [3]Don't be selfish; don't try to impress others. Be humble, thinking of others as better than yourselves. [4]Don't look out only for your own interests, but take an interest in others, too.

[12]Dear friends, you always followed my instructions when I was with you. And now that I am away, it is even more important. Work hard to show the results of your salvation, obeying God with deep reverence and fear. [13]For God is working in you, giving you the desire and the power to do what pleases him.

~ Philippians 1:27-2:4, 12-13

A Song about the Son

Jesus existed before anything was created and is supreme over all creation. Through Him God created everything in the heavenly realms and on earth. God made peace with everything in heaven and on earth by means of Christ's blood on the cross.

[11]We also pray that you will be strengthened with all his glorious power so you will have all the endurance and patience you need. May you be filled with joy, [12]always thanking the Father. He has enabled you to share in the inheritance that belongs to his people, who live in the light. [13]For he has rescued us from the kingdom of darkness and transferred us into the Kingdom of his dear Son, [14]who purchased our freedom and forgave our sins.

[15]Christ is the visible image of the invisible God. He existed before anything was created and is supreme over all creation, [16]for through him God created everything in the heavenly realms and on earth. He made the things we can see and the things we can't see—such as thrones, kingdoms, rulers, and authorities in the unseen world. Everything was created through him and for him. [17]He existed before anything else, and he holds all creation together. [18]Christ is also the head of the church, which is his body. He is the beginning, supreme over all who rise from the dead. So he is first in everything. [19]For God in all his fullness was pleased to live in Christ, [20]and through him God reconciled everything to himself. He made peace with everything in heaven and on earth by means of Christ's blood on the cross.

~ Colossians 1:11-20

Live the New Life!

You have been raised to new life with Christ, and therefore your thoughts should be fixed on heavenly things. Rid your life of old, sinful deeds and put on your new nature. Be renewed as you learn to know your Creator and become more like Him.

¹Since you have been raised to new life with Christ, set your sights on the realities of heaven, where Christ sits in the place of honor at God's right hand. ²Think about the things of heaven, not the things of earth.

⁵So put to death the sinful, earthly things lurking within you. Have nothing to do with sexual immorality, impurity, lust, and evil desires. Don't be greedy, for a greedy person is an idolater, worshiping the things of this world. ⁶Because of these sins, the anger of God is coming. ⁷You used to do these things when your life was still part of this world. ⁸But now is the time to get rid of anger, rage, malicious behavior, slander, and dirty language. ⁹Don't lie to each other, for you have stripped off your old sinful nature and all its wicked deeds. ¹⁰Put on your new nature, and be renewed as you learn to know your Creator and become like him. ¹¹In this new life, it doesn't matter if you are a Jew or a Gentile, circumcised or uncircumcised, barbaric, uncivilized, slave, or free. Christ is all that matters, and he lives in all of us.

¹²Since God chose you to be the holy people he loves, you must clothe yourselves with tenderhearted mercy, kindness, humility, gentleness, and patience. ¹³Make allowance for each other's faults, and forgive anyone who offends you. Remember, the Lord forgave you, so you must forgive others.

~ Colossians 3:1-2, 5-13

Christ Is Visible in Your Relationships

The most important characteristic God wants to see in you is love that ties everything together in perfect unity. Your faith should be reflected in your relationships with other people: wives must submit to their husbands, husbands must love their wives, and children must obey their parents.

3 [14]Above all, clothe yourselves with love, which binds us all together in perfect harmony.

[16]Let the message about Christ, in all its richness, fill your lives. Teach and counsel each other with all the wisdom he gives. Sing psalms and hymns and spiritual songs to God with thankful hearts.

[18]Wives, submit to your husbands, as is fitting for those who belong to the Lord. [19]Husbands, love your wives and never treat them harshly. [20]Children, always obey your parents, for this pleases the Lord. [21]Fathers, do not aggravate your children, or they will become discouraged. [22]Slaves, obey your earthly masters in everything you do. Try to please them all the time, not just when they are watching you. Serve them sincerely because of your reverent fear of the Lord. [23]Work willingly at whatever you do, as though you were working for the Lord rather than for people. [24]Remember that the Lord will give you an inheritance as your reward, and that the Master you are serving is Christ. [25]But if you do what is wrong, you will be paid back for the wrong you have done. For God has no favorites.

4 [1]Masters, be just and fair to your slaves. Remember that you also have a Master—in heaven.

[5]Live wisely among those who are not believers, and make the most of every opportunity.

~ Colossians 3:14, 16, 18-4:1, 5

Live to Glorify God

If you belong to God, you should live in a way that pleases Him. It is God's will that you should be devoted to Him, keep yourself free from sexual sin, and stay pure. God will teach you how to love others, live a peaceful life and work with your hands.

[1]Finally, dear brothers and sisters, we urge you in the name of the Lord Jesus to live in a way that pleases God, as we have taught you. You live this way already, and we encourage you to do so even more. [2]For you remember what we taught you by the authority of the Lord Jesus.

[3]God's will is for you to be holy, so stay away from all sexual sin. [4]Then each of you will control his own body and live in holiness and honor—[5]not in lustful passion like the pagans who do not know God and his ways. [6]Never harm or cheat a Christian brother in this matter by violating his wife, for the Lord avenges all such sins, as we have solemnly warned you before. [7]God has called us to live holy lives, not impure lives. [8]Therefore, anyone who refuses to live by these rules is not disobeying human teaching but is rejecting God, who gives his Holy Spirit to you.

[9]But we don't need to write to you about the importance of loving each other, for God himself has taught you to love one another. [10]Indeed, you already show your love for all the believers throughout Macedonia. Even so, dear brothers and sisters, we urge you to love them even more. [11]Make it your goal to live a quiet life, minding your own business and working with your hands, just as we instructed you before.

~ 1 Thessalonians 4:1-11

Expect the Second Coming

The Lord will return unexpectedly, like a thief in the night. Make sure you are not caught sleeping. You should stay alert and clearheaded. Expect the Second Coming every day, protected by the armor of faith and love.

[1]Now concerning how and when all this will happen, dear brothers and sisters, we don't really need to write you. [2]For you know quite well that the day of the Lord's return will come unexpectedly, like a thief in the night. [3]When people are saying, "Everything is peaceful and secure," then disaster will fall on them as suddenly as a pregnant woman's labor pains begin. And there will be no escape.

[4]But you aren't in the dark about these things, dear brothers and sisters, and you won't be surprised when the day of the Lord comes like a thief. [5]For you are all children of the light and of the day; we don't belong to darkness and night. [6]So be on your guard, not asleep like the others. Stay alert and be clearheaded. [7]Night is the time when people sleep and drinkers get drunk. [8]But let us who live in the light be clearheaded, protected by the armor of faith and love, and wearing as our helmet the confidence of our salvation.

[9]For God chose to save us through our Lord Jesus Christ, not to pour out his anger on us. [10]Christ died for us so that, whether we are dead or alive when he returns, we can live with him forever. [11]So encourage each other and build each other up, just as you are already doing.

~ 1 Thessalonians 5:1-11

What God Expects from You

It is God's will that all His children live in perfect harmony together. God expects of you as a Christian to always be joyful, to never stop praying, and be thankful in all circumstances.

¹²Dear brothers and sisters, honor those who are your leaders in the Lord's work. They work hard among you and give you spiritual guidance. ¹³Show them great respect and wholehearted love because of their work. And live peacefully with each other.

¹⁴Brothers and sisters, we urge you to warn those who are lazy. Encourage those who are timid. Take tender care of those who are weak. Be patient with everyone. ¹⁵See that no one pays back evil for evil, but always try to do good to each other and to all people.

¹⁶Always be joyful. ¹⁷Never stop praying. ¹⁸Be thankful in all circumstances, for this is God's will for you who belong to Christ Jesus. ¹⁹Do not stifle the Holy Spirit. ²⁰Do not scoff at prophecies, ²¹but test everything that is said. Hold on to what is good. ²²Stay away from every kind of evil.

²³Now may the God of peace make you holy in every way, and may your whole spirit and soul and body be kept blameless until our Lord Jesus Christ comes again. ²⁴God will make this happen, for he who calls you is faithful.

~ 1 Thessalonians 5:12-24

Persevere in Suffering

When you, as a Christian, experience hardships and are able to persevere and keep your faith, God will use this suffering to show His justice and to make you worthy of His kingdom, for which you are suffering.

[3]Dear brothers and sisters, we can't help but thank God for you, because your faith is flourishing and your love for one another is growing. [4]We proudly tell God's other churches about your endurance and faithfulness in all the persecutions and hardships you are suffering. [5]And God will use this persecution to show his justice and to make you worthy of his Kingdom, for which you are suffering. [6]In his justice he will pay back those who persecute you.

[7]And God will provide rest for you who are being persecuted and also for us when the Lord Jesus appears from heaven. He will come with his mighty angels, [8]in flaming fire, bringing judgment on those who don't know God and on those who refuse to obey the Good News of our Lord Jesus. [9]They will be punished with eternal destruction, forever separated from the Lord and from his glorious power. [10]When he comes on that day, he will receive glory from his holy people—praise from all who believe. And this includes you, for you believed what we told you about him.

[11]So we keep on praying for you, asking our God to enable you to live a life worthy of his call. May he give you the power to accomplish all the good things your faith prompts you to do.

~ 2 Thessalonians 1:3-11

Pray for People in Authority

It is God's will that we pray for all people, especially for people in positions of authority. Make it your goal to pray for the government and church leaders of your country so that peace will reign supreme again.

[1] I urge you, first of all, to pray for all people. Ask God to help them; intercede on their behalf, and give thanks for them. [2] Pray this way for kings and all who are in authority so that we can live peaceful and quiet lives marked by godliness and dignity.

[3] This is good and pleases God our Savior, [4] who wants everyone to be saved and to understand the truth. [5] For there is only one God and one Mediator who can reconcile God and humanity—the man Christ Jesus. [6] He gave his life to purchase freedom for everyone. This is the message God gave to the world at just the right time. [7] And I have been chosen as a preacher and apostle to teach the Gentiles this message about faith and truth. I'm not exaggerating—just telling the truth.

[8] In every place of worship, I want men to pray with holy hands lifted up to God, free from anger and controversy. [9] And I want women to be modest in their appearance. They should wear decent and appropriate clothing and not draw attention to themselves by the way they fix their hair or by wearing gold or pearls or expensive clothes. [10] For women who claim to be devoted to God should make themselves attractive by the good things they do.

[15] But women will be saved through childbearing, assuming they continue to live in faith, love, holiness, and modesty.

~ 1 Timothy 2:1-10, 15

Spiritual Fitness

Many people exercise in the gym for hours to become physically fit. Spiritual fitness, however, is much more important. Practice hard to become spiritually fit by developing your spiritual gifts through prayer, Bible reading and living close to God.

[6]If you explain these things to the brothers and sisters, Timothy, you will be a worthy servant of Christ Jesus, one who is nourished by the message of faith and the good teaching you have followed.

[7]Do not waste time arguing over godless ideas and old wives' tales. Instead, train yourself to be godly. [8]"Physical training is good, but training for godliness is much better, promising benefits in this life and in the life to come."

[9]This is a trustworthy saying, and everyone should accept it. [10]This is why we work hard and continue to struggle, for our hope is in the living God, who is the Savior of all people and particularly of all believers.

[11]Teach these things and insist that everyone learn them.

~ 1 Timothy 4:6-11

True Wealth

True godliness plus contentment equals great wealth. Rich people shouldn't put their trust in their money. They should be rich in good works and generous to those in need, always willing to share with others. Do you share God's gifts with others to show your thankfulness to God?

[6]Yet true godliness with contentment is itself great wealth. [7]After all, we brought nothing with us when we came into the world, and we can't take anything with us when we leave it. [8]So if we have enough food and clothing, let us be content. [9]But people who long to be rich fall into temptation and are trapped by many foolish and harmful desires that plunge them into ruin and destruction. [10]For the love of money is the root of all kinds of evil. And some people, craving money, have wandered from the true faith and pierced themselves with many sorrows.

[11]But you, Timothy, are a man of God; so run from all these evil things. Pursue righteousness and a godly life, along with faith, love, perseverance, and gentleness. [12]Fight the good fight for the true faith. Hold tightly to the eternal life to which God has called you, which you have confessed so well before many witnesses.

[17]Teach those who are rich in this world not to be proud and not to trust in their money, which is so unreliable. Their trust should be in God, who richly gives us all we need for our enjoyment. [18]Tell them to use their money to do good. They should be rich in good works and generous to those in need, always being ready to share with others. [19]By doing this they will be storing up their treasure as a good foundation for the future so that they may experience true life.

~ 1 Timothy 6:6-12, 17-19

Power, Love and Self-Discipline

You should develop the spiritual gift God gave you, because God didn't give His children a spirit of fear and timidity, but of power, love, and self-discipline. Always be ready to tell others about God and share His grace with them.

³Timothy, I thank God for you—the God I serve with a clear conscience, just as my ancestors did. Night and day I constantly remember you in my prayers. ⁴I long to see you again, for I remember your tears as we parted. And I will be filled with joy when we are together again.

⁵I remember your genuine faith, for you share the faith that first filled your grandmother Lois and your mother, Eunice. And I know that same faith continues strong in you. ⁶This is why I remind you to fan into flames the spiritual gift God gave you when I laid my hands on you. ⁷For God has not given us a spirit of fear and timidity, but of power, love, and self-discipline.

⁸So never be ashamed to tell others about our Lord. And don't be ashamed of me, either, even though I'm in prison for him. With the strength God gives you, be ready to suffer with me for the sake of the Good News. ⁹For God saved us and called us to live a holy life. He did this, not because we deserved it, but because that was his plan from before the beginning of time—to show us his grace through Christ Jesus. ¹⁰And now he has made all of this plain to us by the appearing of Christ Jesus, our Savior. He broke the power of death and illuminated the way to life and immortality through the Good News.

~ 2 Timothy 1:3-10

What the Bible Does

God gives us His Word to study it and to gain insight into the salvation that comes by trusting in Christ Jesus. The whole Bible is inspired by God and is useful to teach us what is true and to make us realize what is wrong in our lives.

[10]But you, Timothy, certainly know what I teach, and how I live, and what my purpose in life is. You know my faith, my patience, my love, and my endurance. [11]You know how much persecution and suffering I have endured. You know all about how I was persecuted in Antioch, Iconium, and Lystra—but the Lord rescued me from all of it. [12]Yes, and everyone who wants to live a godly life in Christ Jesus will suffer persecution. [13]But evil people and impostors will flourish. They will deceive others and will themselves be deceived.

[14]But you must remain faithful to the things you have been taught. You know they are true, for you know you can trust those who taught you. [15]You have been taught the holy Scriptures from childhood, and they have given you the wisdom to receive the salvation that comes by trusting in Christ Jesus. [16]All Scripture is inspired by God and is useful to teach us what is true and to make us realize what is wrong in our lives. It corrects us when we are wrong and teaches us to do what is right. [17]God uses it to prepare and equip his people to do every good work.

~ 2 Timothy 3:10-17

The Christian's Instruction

Paul gave Timothy a few commands each Christian must follow: We must preach the Word of God, patiently correct and encourage other people, and not be afraid to suffer persecution for Christ.

[1]I solemnly urge you in the presence of God and Christ Jesus, who will someday judge the living and the dead when he appears to set up his Kingdom: [2]Preach the word of God. Be prepared, whether the time is favorable or not. Patiently correct, rebuke, and encourage your people with good teaching.

[3]For a time is coming when people will no longer listen to sound and wholesome teaching. They will follow their own desires and will look for teachers who will tell them whatever their itching ears want to hear. [4]They will reject the truth and chase after myths. [5]But you should keep a clear mind in every situation. Don't be afraid of suffering for the Lord. Work at telling others the Good News, and fully carry out the ministry God has given you.

[6]As for me, my life has already been poured out as an offering to God. The time of my death is near. [7]I have fought the good fight, I have finished the race, and I have remained faithful. [8]And now the prize awaits me—the crown of righteousness, which the Lord, the righteous Judge, will give me on the day of his return. And the prize is not just for me but for all who eagerly look forward to his appearing.

~ 2 Timothy 4:1-8

Saved by Grace

God saves you, not because of what you have done, but because of His grace and mercy. He gives you His Holy Spirit as Helper, and forgives your sins because of what Jesus has done. He sets you free so that eternal life can be yours!

[1]Remind the believers to submit to the government and its officers. They should be obedient, always ready to do what is good. [2]They must not slander anyone and must avoid quarreling. Instead, they should be gentle and show true humility to everyone. [3]Once we, too, were foolish and disobedient. We were misled and became slaves to many lusts and pleasures. Our lives were full of evil and envy, and we hated each other.

[4]But—"When God our Savior revealed his kindness and love, [5]he saved us, not because of the righteous things we had done, but because of his mercy. He washed away our sins, giving us a new birth and new life through the Holy Spirit.

[6]"He generously poured out the Spirit upon us through Jesus Christ our Savior. [7]Because of his grace he declared us righteous and gave us confidence that we will inherit eternal life." [8]This is a trustworthy saying, and I want you to insist on these teachings so that all who trust in God will devote themselves to doing good. These teachings are good and beneficial for everyone.

~ Titus 3:1-8

God Speaks through His Son

In Old Testament times God often spoke to His people through prophets, but now He speaks to everyone through His Son. Jesus reflects God's glory, and was made in His likeness and image. Through His crucifixion He paid the full price for our sin.

[1]Long ago God spoke many times and in many ways to our ancestors through the prophets. [2]And now in these final days, he has spoken to us through his Son. God promised everything to the Son as an inheritance, and through the Son he created the universe.

[3]The Son radiates God's own glory and expresses the very character of God, and he sustains everything by the mighty power of his command. When he had cleansed us from our sins, he sat down in the place of honor at the right hand of the majestic God in heaven. [4]This shows that the Son is far greater than the angels, just as the name God gave him is greater than their names.

[5]For God never said to any angel what he said to Jesus: "You are my Son. Today I have become your Father." God also said, "I will be his Father, and he will be my Son."

[6]And when he brought his firstborn Son into the world, God said, "Let all of God's angels worship him."

~ Hebrews 1:1-6

Family of Jesus

If Jesus purifies your sins, then God is your Father, and Jesus calls all believers His brothers and sisters! Through Christ's redemptive work you are God's child, family of Jesus and part of His heavenly glory.

⁶For in one place the Scriptures say, "What are mere mortals that you should think about them, or a son of man that you should care for him? ⁷Yet you made them only a little lower than the angels and crowned them with glory and honor. ⁸You gave them authority over all things." Now when it says "all things," it means nothing is left out. But we have not yet seen all things put under their authority.

⁹What we do see is Jesus, who was given a position "a little lower than the angels"; and because he suffered death for us, he is now "crowned with glory and honor." Yes, by God's grace, Jesus tasted death for everyone. ¹⁰God, for whom and through whom everything was made, chose to bring many children into glory. And it was only right that he should make Jesus, through his suffering, a perfect leader, fit to bring them into their salvation.

¹¹So now Jesus and the ones he makes holy have the same Father. That is why Jesus is not ashamed to call them his brothers and sisters. ¹²For he said to God, "I will proclaim your name to my brothers and sisters. I will praise you among your assembled people."

~ Hebrews 2:6-12

God's Word Gives Life

God's Word is alive and powerful. It is sharper than any double-edged sword and cuts between joint and marrow. It exposes our innermost thoughts and desires. Nothing in all creation is hidden from God. He is the One to whom we are accountable.

3[7]That is why the Holy Spirit says, "Today when you hear his voice, [8]don't harden your hearts as Israel did when they rebelled, when they tested me in the wilderness."

[12]Be careful then, dear brothers and sisters. Make sure that your own hearts are not evil and unbelieving, turning you away from the living God. [13]You must warn each other every day, while it is still "today," so that none of you will be deceived by sin and hardened against God.

4[12]For the word of God is alive and powerful. It is sharper than the sharpest two-edged sword, cutting between soul and spirit, between joint and marrow. It exposes our innermost thoughts and desires. [13]Nothing in all creation is hidden from God. Everything is naked and exposed before his eyes, and he is the one to whom we are accountable.

~ Hebrews 3:7-8, 12-13, 4:12-13

Jesus, Your High Priest

Jesus plays the role of the High Priest between you and God. He understands our weaknesses, for He faced all of the same tests we do. Because of what Jesus has done for us, we can come boldly to the throne of our gracious God. There we will receive His mercy, and we will find grace to help us when we need it.

4 ¹⁴So then, since we have a great High Priest who has entered heaven, Jesus the Son of God, let us hold firmly to what we believe. ¹⁵This High Priest of ours understands our weaknesses, for he faced all of the same testings we do, yet he did not sin. ¹⁶So let us come boldly to the throne of our gracious God. There we will receive his mercy, and we will find grace to help us when we need it most.

5 ¹Every high priest is a man chosen to represent other people in their dealings with God. He presents their gifts to God and offers sacrifices for their sins. ²And he is able to deal gently with ignorant and wayward people because he himself is subject to the same weaknesses. ³That is why he must offer sacrifices for his own sins as well as theirs.

⁴And no one can become a high priest simply because he wants such an honor. He must be called by God for this work, just as Aaron was. ⁵That is why Christ did not honor himself by assuming he could become High Priest. No, he was chosen by God, who said to him, "You are my Son. Today I have become your Father."

⁶And in another passage God said to him, "You are a priest forever in the order of Melchizedek."

~ Hebrews 4:14-5:6

You Need Faith to Please God

Faith is the assurance we have that the things we cannot see will actually happen. If you don't believe this, you can't please God. If you want to pray to God you must believe that He exists and that He will reward you.

[1] Faith is the confidence that what we hope for will actually happen; it gives us assurance about things we cannot see. [2] Through their faith, the people in days of old earned a good reputation.

[3] By faith we understand that the entire universe was formed at God's command, that what we now see did not come from anything that can be seen.

[4] It was by faith that Abel brought a more acceptable offering to God than Cain did. Abel's offering gave evidence that he was a righteous man, and God showed his approval of his gifts. Although Abel is long dead, he still speaks to us by his example of faith.

[5] It was by faith that Enoch was taken up to heaven without dying—"he disappeared, because God took him." For before he was taken up, he was known as a person who pleased God. [6] And it is impossible to please God without faith. Anyone who wants to come to him must believe that God exists and that he rewards those who sincerely seek him.

~ Hebrews 11:1-6

The Race of Faith

All believers are busy running a race of faith. In order to run this race with perseverance, you need to throw off everything that hinders you, especially the sin that so easily entangles you, so that you can run the race with endurance. Our eyes must be fixed on Jesus, the Champion who initiates and perfects our faith.

¹Therefore, since we are surrounded by such a huge crowd of witnesses to the life of faith, let us strip off every weight that slows us down, especially the sin that so easily trips us up. And let us run with endurance the race God has set before us. ²We do this by keeping our eyes on Jesus, the champion who initiates and perfects our faith. Because of the joy awaiting him, he endured the cross, disregarding its shame. Now he is seated in the place of honor beside God's throne.

³Think of all the hostility he endured from sinful people; then you won't become weary and give up. ⁴After all, you have not yet given your lives in your struggle against sin. ⁵And have you forgotten the encouraging words God spoke to you as his children? He said, "My child, don't make light of the LORD's discipline, and don't give up when he corrects you. ⁶For the LORD disciplines those he loves, and he punishes each one he accepts as his child."

~ Hebrews 12:1-6

Guidelines for a Christian Life

As Christians you should love one another, show hospitality to others and be faithful to your marriage partner. God is your strength; you need not be afraid. Your life should be a continual sacrifice of praise. This is the kind of offering God wants.

¹Keep on loving each other as brothers and sisters. ²Don't forget to show hospitality to strangers, for some who have done this have entertained angels without realizing it! ³Remember those in prison, as if you were there yourself. Remember also those being mistreated, as if you felt their pain in your own bodies.

⁴Give honor to marriage, and remain faithful to one another in marriage. God will surely judge people who are immoral and those who commit adultery.

⁵Don't love money; be satisfied with what you have. For God has said, "I will never fail you. I will never abandon you." ⁶So we can say with confidence, "The LORD is my helper, so I will have no fear. What can mere people do to me?"

¹⁵Therefore, let us offer through Jesus a continual sacrifice of praise to God, proclaiming our allegiance to his name. ¹⁶And don't forget to do good and to share with those in need. These are the sacrifices that please God.

~ Hebrews 13:1-6; 15-16

December

Rejoice in Suffering

God's children can rejoice in their trials because these trials not only test their faith, but also develop perseverance. When you persevere in times of trial God will give you life.

[2]Dear brothers and sisters, when troubles come your way, consider it an opportunity for great joy. [3]For you know that when your faith is tested, your endurance has a chance to grow. [4]So let it grow, for when your endurance is fully developed, you will be perfect and complete, needing nothing.

[5]If you need wisdom, ask our generous God, and he will give it to you. He will not rebuke you for asking. [6]But when you ask him, be sure that your faith is in God alone. Do not waver, for a person with divided loyalty is as unsettled as a wave of the sea that is blown and tossed by the wind. [7]Such people should not expect to receive anything from the Lord.

[12]God blesses those who patiently endure testing and temptation. Afterward they will receive the crown of life that God has promised to those who love him.

~ James 1:2-7, 12

Don't Just Listen – Act!

God's people must be willing to listen, think before they speak and not become easily angered. Be a woman who does what the Word says, and not only listens to it. Then you can expect God's blessings on your life.

[19]Understand this, my dear brothers and sisters: You must all be quick to listen, slow to speak, and slow to get angry. [20]Human anger does not produce the righteousness God desires. [21]So get rid of all the filth and evil in your lives, and humbly accept the word God has planted in your hearts, for it has the power to save your souls.

[22]But don't just listen to God's word. You must do what it says. Otherwise, you are only fooling yourselves. [23]For if you listen to the word and don't obey, it is like glancing at your face in a mirror. [24]You see yourself, walk away, and forget what you look like. [25]But if you look carefully into the perfect law that sets you free, and if you do what it says and don't forget what you heard, then God will bless you for doing it.

[26]If you claim to be religious but don't control your tongue, you are fooling yourself, and your religion is worthless.

~ James 1:19-26

Faith Alone Is Not Enough

We must have faith, but faith on its own is not enough. The faith of God's children must be seen through their deeds. As a body without a spirit is dead, so faith without deeds is dead.

[14]What good is it, dear brothers and sisters, if you say you have faith but don't show it by your actions? Can that kind of faith save anyone? [15]Suppose you see a brother or sister who has no food or clothing, [16]and you say, "Good-bye and have a good day; stay warm and eat well"—but then you don't give that person any food or clothing. What good does that do?

[17]So you see, faith by itself isn't enough. Unless it produces good deeds, it is dead and useless. [18]Now someone may argue, "Some people have faith; others have good deeds." But I say, "How can you show me your faith if you don't have good deeds? I will show you my faith by my good deeds."

[19]You say you have faith, for you believe that there is one God. Good for you! Even the demons believe this, and they tremble in terror. [20]How foolish! Can't you see that faith without good deeds is useless?

[21]Don't you remember that our ancestor Abraham was shown to be right with God by his actions when he offered his son Isaac on the altar? [22]You see, his faith and his actions worked together. His actions made his faith complete.

[26]Just as the body is dead without breath, so also faith is dead without good works.

~ James 2:14-22, 26

Guard Your Tongue

Women's tongues tend to get them into big trouble!
If you are able to guard your tongue, you will also be
able to control your whole body. Ask God to help you
tame your tongue.

¹Dear brothers and sisters, not many of you should become
teachers in the church, for we who teach will be judged more
strictly. ²Indeed, we all make many mistakes. For if we could
control our tongues, we would be perfect and could also control
ourselves in every other way.

³We can make a large horse go wherever we want by means
of a small bit in its mouth. ⁴And a small rudder makes a huge
ship turn wherever the pilot chooses to go, even though the
winds are strong. ⁵In the same way, the tongue is a small thing
that makes grand speeches. But a tiny spark can set a great
forest on fire. ⁶And the tongue is a flame of fire. It is a whole
world of wickedness, corrupting your entire body. It can set your
whole life on fire, for it is set on fire by hell itself.

⁷People can tame all kinds of animals, birds, reptiles, and
fish, ⁸but no one can tame the tongue. It is restless and evil, full
of deadly poison. ⁹Sometimes it praises our Lord and Father,
and sometimes it curses those who have been made in the
image of God. ¹⁰And so blessing and cursing come pouring
out of the same mouth. Surely, my brothers and sisters, this
is not right! ¹¹Does a spring of water bubble out with both fresh
water and bitter water? ¹²Does a fig tree produce olives, or a
grapevine produce figs? No, and you can't draw fresh water
from a salty spring.

~ James 3:1-12

Prayers with Wrong Motives

Don't pray to God with wrong and impure motives for your own benefit, He will not answer such selfish requests. God hates pride. But when your life is surrendered to God and you draw near to Him sincerely, He will draw near to you too.

[1]What is causing the quarrels and fights among you? Don't they come from the evil desires at war within you? [2]You want what you don't have, so you scheme and kill to get it. You are jealous of what others have, but you can't get it, so you fight and wage war to take it away from them. Yet you don't have what you want because you don't ask God for it. [3]And even when you ask, you don't get it because your motives are all wrong—you want only what will give you pleasure.

[7]So humble yourselves before God. Resist the devil, and he will flee from you. [8]Come close to God, and God will come close to you. Wash your hands, you sinners; purify your hearts, for your loyalty is divided between God and the world. [9]Let there be tears for what you have done. Let there be sorrow and deep grief. Let there be sadness instead of laughter, and gloom instead of joy. [10]Humble yourselves before the Lord, and he will lift you up in honor.

~ James 4:1-3, 7-10

The Christian Wife

Peter laid down a few guidelines that some feminists struggle with. Wives must submit to their husbands and accept their authority, and we must have a quiet and gentle spirit. Furthermore, we must be sympathetic, compassionate and humble, and strive for peace.

[1]In the same way, you wives must accept the authority of your husbands. Then, even if some refuse to obey the Good News, your godly lives will speak to them without any words. They will be won over [2]by observing your pure and reverent lives.

[3]Don't be concerned about the outward beauty of fancy hairstyles, expensive jewelry, or beautiful clothes. [4]You should clothe yourselves instead with the beauty that comes from within, the unfading beauty of a gentle and quiet spirit, which is so precious to God. [5]This is how the holy women of old made themselves beautiful. They trusted God and accepted the authority of their husbands. [6]For instance, Sarah obeyed her husband, Abraham, and called him her master. You are her daughters when you do what is right without fear of what your husbands might do.

[7]In the same way, you husbands must give honor to your wives. Treat your wife with understanding as you live together. She may be weaker than you are, but she is your equal partner in God's gift of new life. Treat her as you should so your prayers will not be hindered.

[8]Finally, all of you should be of one mind. Sympathize with each other. Love each other as brothers and sisters. Be tenderhearted, and keep a humble attitude. [9]Don't repay evil for evil. Don't retaliate with insults when people insult you. Instead, pay them back with a blessing. That is what God has called you to do, and he will bless you for it.

~ 1 Peter 3:1-9

Expect Suffering

That you will experience trials and suffering on earth, is a fact. But be glad about your suffering, because in this way you participate in the suffering of Christ. After you have suffered God will restore you and make you strong, firm and steadfast.

4¹²Dear friends, don't be surprised at the fiery trials you are going through, as if something strange were happening to you. ¹³Instead, be very glad—for these trials make you partners with Christ in his suffering, so that you will have the wonderful joy of seeing his glory when it is revealed to all the world.

¹⁴So be happy when you are insulted for being a Christian, for then the glorious Spirit of God rests upon you. ¹⁵If you suffer, however, it must not be for murder, stealing, making trouble, or prying into other people's affairs. ¹⁶But it is no shame to suffer for being a Christian. Praise God for the privilege of being called by his name! ¹⁷For the time has come for judgment, and it must begin with God's household. And if judgment begins with us, what terrible fate awaits those who have never obeyed God's Good News? ¹⁸And also, "If the righteous are barely saved, what will happen to godless sinners?"

¹⁹So if you are suffering in a manner that pleases God, keep on doing what is right, and trust your lives to the God who created you, for he will never fail you.

5¹⁰In his kindness God called you to share in his eternal glory by means of Christ Jesus. So after you have suffered a little while, he will restore, support, and strengthen you, and he will place you on a firm foundation.

~ 1 Peter 4:12-19; 5:10

Prove That God Has Called and Chosen You

God has made you new, and your lifestyle should reflect this. You must make a concerted effort to show to others with your life that you are personally chosen and called by God and that you belong to Him.

[5]In view of all this, make every effort to respond to God's promises. Supplement your faith with a generous provision of moral excellence, and moral excellence with knowledge, [6]and knowledge with self-control, and self-control with patient endurance, and patient endurance with godliness, [7]and godliness with brotherly affection, and brotherly affection with love for everyone.

[8]The more you grow like this, the more productive and useful you will be in your knowledge of our Lord Jesus Christ. [9]But those who fail to develop in this way are shortsighted or blind, forgetting that they have been cleansed from their old sins. [10]So, dear brothers and sisters, work hard to prove that you really are among those God has called and chosen. Do these things, and you will never fall away. [11]Then God will give you a grand entrance into the eternal Kingdom of our Lord and Savior Jesus Christ.

~ 2 Peter 1:5-11

God's Perspective on Time

God's perspective and our perspective on time are completely different. For God one day is like a thousand years, and a thousand years like a day. That Jesus is lingering before He returns is evidence that He is granting you more opportunities to come to faith in Him. Have you used it?

[8]But you must not forget this one thing, dear friends: A day is like a thousand years to the Lord, and a thousand years is like a day. [9]The Lord isn't really being slow about his promise, as some people think. No, he is being patient for your sake. He does not want anyone to be destroyed, but wants everyone to repent. [10]But the day of the Lord will come as unexpectedly as a thief. Then the heavens will pass away with a terrible noise, and the very elements themselves will disappear in fire, and the earth and everything on it will be found to deserve judgment.

[11]Since everything around us is going to be destroyed like this, what holy and godly lives you should live, [12]looking forward to the day of God and hurrying it along. On that day, he will set the heavens on fire, and the elements will melt away in the flames. [13]But we are looking forward to the new heavens and new earth he has promised, a world filled with God's righteousness.

[14]And so, dear friends, while you are waiting for these things to happen, make every effort to be found living peaceful lives that are pure and blameless in his sight. [15]And remember, our Lord's patience gives people time to be saved.

~ 2 Peter 3:8-15

Live in the Light!

Because God is light, His children should also live in the light. But we are all sinners – we must be willing to confess our sins. God is faithful and just and will forgive your sins through the blood of Jesus Christ.

[5]This is the message we heard from Jesus and now declare to you: God is light, and there is no darkness in him at all. [6]So we are lying if we say we have fellowship with God but go on living in spiritual darkness; we are not practicing the truth.

[7]But if we are living in the light, as God is in the light, then we have fellowship with each other, and the blood of Jesus, his Son, cleanses us from all sin.

[8]If we claim we have no sin, we are only fooling ourselves and not living in the truth. [9]But if we confess our sins to him, he is faithful and just to forgive us our sins and to cleanse us from all wickedness. [10]If we claim we have not sinned, we are calling God a liar and showing that his word has no place in our hearts.

~ 1 John 1:5-10

Jesus Is Your Helper

Each time you sin, Jesus wants to be your Helper. He has already paid in full for the sins of the whole world. If you have an intimate relationship with Him, you ought to live like He lives. You should love other people with a sincere heart.

¹My dear children, I am writing this to you so that you will not sin. But if anyone does sin, we have an advocate who pleads our case before the Father. He is Jesus Christ, the one who is truly righteous. ²He himself is the sacrifice that atones for our sins—and not only our sins but the sins of all the world.

³And we can be sure that we know him if we obey his commandments. ⁴If someone claims, "I know God," but doesn't obey God's commandments, that person is a liar and is not living in the truth. ⁵But those who obey God's word truly show how completely they love him. That is how we know we are living in him. ⁶Those who say they live in God should live their lives as Jesus did.

⁷Dear friends, I am not writing a new commandment for you; rather it is an old one you have had from the very beginning. This old commandment—to love one another—is the same message you heard before. ⁸Yet it is also new. Jesus lived the truth of this commandment, and you also are living it. For the darkness is disappearing, and the true light is already shining. ⁹If anyone claims, "I am living in the light," but hates a Christian brother or sister, that person is still living in darkness.

¹⁰Anyone who loves another brother or sister is living in the light and does not cause others to stumble.

~ 1 John 2:1-10

Do Not Love the Things of the World

When you love the things of the world, you do not love God enough. Acknowledge Jesus as the Son of God, then you will also have the Father and eternal life. Don't wait any longer before you deepen your relationship with God.

¹⁵Do not love this world nor the things it offers you, for when you love the world, you do not have the love of the Father in you. ¹⁶For the world offers only a craving for physical pleasure, a craving for everything we see, and pride in our achievements and possessions. These are not from the Father, but are from this world. ¹⁷And this world is fading away, along with everything that people crave. But anyone who does what pleases God will live forever.

¹⁸Dear children, the last hour is here. You have heard that the Antichrist is coming, and already many such antichrists have appeared. From this we know that the last hour has come.

²³Anyone who denies the Son doesn't have the Father, either. But anyone who acknowledges the Son has the Father also. ²⁴So you must remain faithful to what you have been taught from the beginning. If you do, you will remain in fellowship with the Son and with the Father.

²⁸And now, dear children, remain in fellowship with Christ so that when he returns, you will be full of courage and not shrink back from him in shame. ²⁹Since we know that Christ is righteous, we also know that all who do what is right are God's children.

~ 1 John 2:15-18, 23-24, 28-29

Love Each Other

Jesus commands you to love other people like He loves you. When you do this, it will be impossible for you to see people suffering and not help them. Make sure that your love for others is not just lip service, but that it is evident through your actions.

¹¹This is the message you have heard from the beginning: We should love one another.

¹⁶We know what real love is because Jesus gave up his life for us. So we also ought to give up our lives for our brothers and sisters. ¹⁷If someone has enough money to live well and sees a brother or sister in need but shows no compassion—how can God's love be in that person?

¹⁸Dear children, let's not merely say that we love each other; let us show the truth by our actions. ¹⁹Our actions will show that we belong to the truth, so we will be confident when we stand before God. ²⁰Even if we feel guilty, God is greater than our feelings, and he knows everything.

²¹Dear friends, if we don't feel guilty, we can come to God with bold confidence. ²²And we will receive from him whatever we ask because we obey him and do the things that please him. ²³And this is his commandment: We must believe in the name of his Son, Jesus Christ, and love one another, just as he commanded us. ²⁴Those who obey God's commandments remain in fellowship with him, and he with them. And we know he lives in us because the Spirit he gave us lives in us.

~ 1 John 3:11, 16-24

True Love Comes from God

True love always comes from God and can only be acted out by God's children. God showed His love for us by sending His Son as an atoning sacrifice for our sins so that we can have eternal life. God loves you unto death; this is how you should love others.

⁷Dear friends, let us continue to love one another, for love comes from God. Anyone who loves is a child of God and knows God. ⁸But anyone who does not love does not know God, for God is love.

⁹God showed how much he loved us by sending his one and only Son into the world so that we might have eternal life through him. ¹⁰This is real love—not that we loved God, but that he loved us and sent his Son as a sacrifice to take away our sins.

¹¹Dear friends, since God loved us that much, we surely ought to love each other. ¹²No one has ever seen God. But if we love each other, God lives in us, and his love is brought to full expression in us. ¹³And God has given us his Spirit as proof that we live in him and he in us.

¹⁶We know how much God loves us, and we have put our trust in his love. God is love, and all who live in love live in God, and God lives in them. ¹⁷And as we live in God, our love grows more perfect. So we will not be afraid on the day of judgment, but we can face him with confidence because we live like Jesus here in this world. ¹⁸Such love has no fear, because perfect love expels all fear. If we are afraid, it is for fear of punishment, and this shows that we have not fully experienced his perfect love.

~ 1 John 4:7-13, 16-18

We Love Because God First Loved Us

We should love each other because God first loved us. And if you love God you should also love others unconditionally. In order to demonstrate your love for God you should be willing to obey His commands.

4 [19]We love each other because he loved us first. [20]If someone says, "I love God," but hates a Christian brother or sister, that person is a liar; for if we don't love people we can see, how can we love God, whom we cannot see? [21]And he has given us this command: Those who love God must also love their Christian brothers and sisters.

5 [1]Everyone who believes that Jesus is the Christ has become a child of God. And everyone who loves the Father loves his children, too. [2]We know we love God's children if we love God and obey his commandments. [3]Loving God means keeping his commandments, and his commandments are not burdensome. [4]For every child of God defeats this evil world, and we achieve this victory through our faith. [5]And who can win this battle against the world? Only those who believe that Jesus is the Son of God.

[11]And this is what God has testified: He has given us eternal life, and this life is in his Son. [12]Whoever has the Son has life; whoever does not have God's Son does not have life.

~ 1 John 4:19-5:5, 11-12

Love Requires Obedience

Love for God means to continue to live according to Jesus' commands and to obey Him. It also requires an intimate relationship with Jesus. Only then will you share in the Father and the Son.

¹This letter is from John, the elder. I am writing to the chosen lady and to her children, whom I love in the truth—as does everyone else who knows the truth—²because the truth lives in us and will be with us forever.

³Grace, mercy, and peace, which come from God the Father and from Jesus Christ—the Son of the Father—will continue to be with us who live in truth and love.

⁴How happy I was to meet some of your children and find them living according to the truth, just as the Father commanded.

⁵I am writing to remind you, dear friends, that we should love one another. This is not a new commandment, but one we have had from the beginning. ⁶Love means doing what God has commanded us, and he has commanded us to love one another, just as you heard from the beginning.

⁹Anyone who wanders away from this teaching has no relationship with God. But anyone who remains in the teaching of Christ has a relationship with both the Father and the Son.

~ 2 John 1-6, 9

What Does Your Testimonial Say?

John gave a very appreciative testimonial of Gaius. He is faithful in what he does and is willing to help other believers. How would your testimonial look if you had to receive one for being a believer?

¹This letter is from John, the elder. I am writing to Gaius, my dear friend, whom I love in the truth. ²Dear friend, I hope all is well with you and that you are as healthy in body as you are strong in spirit. ³Some of the traveling teachers recently returned and made me very happy by telling me about your faithfulness and that you are living according to the truth. ⁴I could have no greater joy than to hear that my children are following the truth.

⁵Dear friend, you are being faithful to God when you care for the traveling teachers who pass through, even though they are strangers to you. ⁶They have told the church here of your loving friendship. Please continue providing for such teachers in a manner that pleases God. ⁷For they are traveling for the Lord, and they accept nothing from people who are not believers. ⁸So we ourselves should support them so that we can be their partners as they teach the truth.

¹³I have much more to say to you, but I don't want to write it with pen and ink. ¹⁴For I hope to see you soon, and then we will talk face to face. ¹⁵Peace be with you. Your friends here send you their greetings. Please give my personal greetings to each of our friends there.

~ 3 John 1-8, 13-15

Build on the Foundation of Your Faith

God's children must continue to build on the foundation of their faith. This command is applicable to you too – therefore, continue to pray, live through the Holy Spirit, stay in God's love, and know that Jesus will give you eternal life.

[17]But you, my dear friends, must remember what the apostles of our Lord Jesus Christ said. [18]They told you that in the last times there would be scoffers whose purpose in life is to satisfy their ungodly desires. [19]These people are the ones who are creating divisions among you. They follow their natural instincts because they do not have God's Spirit in them.

[20]But you, dear friends, must build each other up in your most holy faith, pray in the power of the Holy Spirit, [21]and await the mercy of our Lord Jesus Christ, who will bring you eternal life. In this way, you will keep yourselves safe in God's love.

[22]And you must show mercy to those whose faith is wavering. [23]Rescue others by snatching them from the flames of judgment. Show mercy to still others, but do so with great caution, hating the sins that contaminate their lives.

[24]Now all glory to God, who is able to keep you from falling away and will bring you with great joy into his glorious presence without a single fault.

~ Jude 17-24

The Beginning and the End

When Jesus returns on the clouds, every eye will see Him. He is the Alpha and Omega, the First and the Last, the living God. He is the One who is, and was, and is to come. Therefore, do not fear.

¹This is a revelation from Jesus Christ, which God gave him to show his servants the events that must soon take place. He sent an angel to present this revelation to his servant John, ²who faithfully reported everything he saw. This is his report of the word of God and the testimony of Jesus Christ. ³God blesses the one who reads the words of this prophecy to the church, and he blesses all who listen to its message and obey what it says, for the time is near.

⁴This letter is from John to the seven churches in the province of Asia. Grace and peace to you from the one who is, who always was, and who is still to come; from the sevenfold Spirit before his throne; ⁵and from Jesus Christ. He is the faithful witness to these things, the first to rise from the dead, and the ruler of all the kings of the world. All glory to him who loves us and has freed us from our sins by shedding his blood for us.

⁷Look! He comes with the clouds of heaven. And everyone will see him—even those who pierced him. And all the nations of the world will mourn for him. Yes! Amen!

⁸"I am the Alpha and the Omega—the beginning and the end," says the Lord God. "I am the one who is, who always was, and who is still to come—the Almighty One."

¹⁷When I saw him, I fell at his feet as if I were dead. But he laid his right hand on me and said, "Don't be afraid! I am the First and the Last. ¹⁸I am the living one. I died, but look—I am alive forever and ever! And I hold the keys of death and the grave. ¹⁹Write down what you have seen—both the things that are now happening and the things that will happen."

~ Revelation 1:1-5, 7-8, 17-19

Do You Still Have Your First Love?

God knows everything about you. He knows when you're following the example of the church in Ephesus, and when you don't love Him quite like you used to. Repent, and do the things you did at first.

¹"Write this letter to the angel of the church in Ephesus. This is the message from the one who holds the seven stars in his right hand, the one who walks among the seven gold lampstands:

²"I know all the things you do. I have seen your hard work and your patient endurance. I know you don't tolerate evil people. You have examined the claims of those who say they are apostles but are not. You have discovered they are liars. ³You have patiently suffered for me without quitting.

⁴"But I have this complaint against you. You don't love me or each other as you did at first! ⁵Look how far you have fallen! Turn back to me and do the works you did at first. If you don't repent, I will come and remove your lampstand from its place among the churches. ⁶But this is in your favor: You hate the evil deeds of the Nicolaitans, just as I do.

⁷"Anyone with ears to hear must listen to the Spirit and understand what he is saying to the churches. To everyone who is victorious I will give fruit from the tree of life in the paradise of God."

~ Revelation 2:1-7

Be Spiritually Rich

Some believers are like the church in Smyrna – outwardly they are poor, but spiritually they are rich. When you suffer it often produces spiritual wealth because it teaches you to trust more in God. If you are faithful to the end, you will receive the crown of life.

8"Write this letter to the angel of the church in Smyrna. This is the message from the one who is the First and the Last, who was dead but is now alive:

9"I know about your suffering and your poverty—but you are rich! I know the blasphemy of those opposing you. They say they are Jews, but they are not, because their synagogue belongs to Satan. 10Don't be afraid of what you are about to suffer. The devil will throw some of you into prison to test you. You will suffer for ten days. But if you remain faithful even when facing death, I will give you the crown of life.

11"Anyone with ears to hear must listen to the Spirit and understand what he is saying to the churches. Whoever is victorious will not be harmed by the second death."

~ Revelation 2:8-11

Stay True and Faithful

If you can manage to be like the church in Pergamum who, despite worldly and negative circumstances, stayed true and loyal to Him, God will give you a new name in His kingdom.

[12]"Write this letter to the angel of the church in Pergamum. This is the message from the one with the sharp two-edged sword:

[13]"I know that you live in the city where Satan has his throne, yet you have remained loyal to me. You refused to deny me even when Antipas, my faithful witness, was martyred among you there in Satan's city.

[14]"But I have a few complaints against you. You tolerate some among you whose teaching is like that of Balaam, who showed Balak how to trip up the people of Israel. He taught them to sin by eating food offered to idols and by committing sexual sin. [15]In a similar way, you have some Nicolaitans among you who follow the same teaching. [16]Repent of your sin, or I will come to you suddenly and fight against them with the sword of my mouth.

[17]"Anyone with ears to hear must listen to the Spirit and understand what he is saying to the churches. To everyone who is victorious I will give some of the manna that has been hidden away in heaven. And I will give to each one a white stone, and on the stone will be engraved a new name that no one understands except the one who receives it."

~ Revelation 2:12-17

Hold on to Jesus!

The church in Thyatira had healthy faith, but there were a few people in the church who participated in sexual immorality. Nonetheless things there still improved. Be alert against the sexual norms of the world today and hold on to God's values.

18"Write this letter to the angel of the church in Thyatira. This is the message from the Son of God, whose eyes are like flames of fire, whose feet are like polished bronze:

19"I know all the things you do. I have seen your love, your faith, your service, and your patient endurance. And I can see your constant improvement in all these things.

20"But I have this complaint against you. You are permitting that woman—that Jezebel who calls herself a prophet—to lead my servants astray. She teaches them to commit sexual sin and to eat food offered to idols. 21I gave her time to repent, but she does not want to turn away from her immorality.

22"Therefore, I will throw her on a bed of suffering, and those who commit adultery with her will suffer greatly unless they repent and turn away from her evil deeds. 23I will strike her children dead. Then all the churches will know that I am the one who searches out the thoughts and intentions of every person. And I will give to each of you whatever you deserve.

24"But I also have a message for the rest of you in Thyatira who have not followed this false teaching ('deeper truths,' as they call them—depths of Satan, actually). I will ask nothing more of you 25except that you hold tightly to what you have until I come. 26To all who are victorious, who obey me to the very end, To them I will give authority over all the nations."

~ Revelation 2:18-26

Life or Death?

Sardis had the reputation of being alive, but they were spiritually dead. Be careful that this is not true of you. The names of those who overcome will never be blotted out from the Book of Life. Christ Himself guarantees your heavenly inheritance.

[1]"Write this letter to the angel of the church in Sardis. This is the message from the one who has the sevenfold Spirit of God and the seven stars: "I know all the things you do, and that you have a reputation for being alive—but you are dead. [2]Wake up! Strengthen what little remains, for even what is left is almost dead. I find that your actions do not meet the requirements of my God. [3]Go back to what you heard and believed at first; hold to it firmly. Repent and turn to me again. If you don't wake up, I will come to you suddenly, as unexpected as a thief.

[4]"Yet there are some in the church in Sardis who have not soiled their clothes with evil. They will walk with me in white, for they are worthy. [5]All who are victorious will be clothed in white. I will never erase their names from the Book of Life, but I will announce before my Father and his angels that they are mine.

[6]"Anyone with ears to hear must listen to the Spirit and understand what he is saying to the churches."

~ Revelation 3:1-6

God Stands at the Door and Knocks

God stands at the door of your heart and knocks. If you hear His voice and open the door, He will come in and be with you. Don't wait any longer before you open the door of your life to Him.

[14]"Write this letter to the angel of the church in Laodicea. This is the message from the one who is the Amen—the faithful and true witness, the beginning of God's new creation:

[15]"I know all the things you do, that you are neither hot nor cold. I wish that you were one or the other! [16]But since you are like lukewarm water, neither hot nor cold, I will spit you out of my mouth! [17]You say, 'I am rich. I have everything I want. I don't need a thing!' And you don't realize that you are wretched and miserable and poor and blind and naked. [18]So I advise you to buy gold from me—gold that has been purified by fire. Then you will be rich. Also buy white garments from me so you will not be shamed by your nakedness, and ointment for your eyes so you will be able to see. [19]I correct and discipline everyone I love. So be diligent and turn from your indifference.

[20]"Look! I stand at the door and knock. If you hear my voice and open the door, I will come in, and we will share a meal together as friends. [21]Those who are victorious will sit with me on my throne, just as I was victorious and sat with my Father on his throne.

[22]"Anyone with ears to hear must listen to the Spirit and understand what he is saying to the churches."

~ Revelation 3:14-22

Worship in Heaven

John saw how God was being worshiped in the heavenly throne room by twenty-four elders and four living creatures. They worshiped Him day and night. God is worthy to be praised – bow before Him daily in worship.

[1]Then as I looked, I saw a door standing open in heaven, and the same voice I had heard before spoke to me like a trumpet blast. The voice said, "Come up here, and I will show you what must happen after this." [2]And instantly I was in the Spirit, and I saw a throne in heaven and someone sitting on it. [3]The one sitting on the throne was as brilliant as gemstones—like jasper and carnelian. And the glow of an emerald circled his throne like a rainbow. [4]Twenty-four thrones surrounded him, and twenty-four elders sat on them. They were all clothed in white and had gold crowns on their heads.

[6]In front of the throne was a shiny sea of glass, sparkling like crystal. In the center and around the throne were four living beings, each covered with eyes, front and back.

[8]Each of these living beings had six wings, and their wings were covered all over with eyes, inside and out. Day after day and night after night they keep on saying, "Holy, holy, holy is the Lord God, the Almighty—the one who always was, who is, and who is still to come."

[9]Whenever the living beings give glory and honor and thanks to the one sitting on the throne (the one who lives forever and ever), [10]the twenty-four elders fall down and worship the one sitting on the throne (the one who lives forever and ever). And they lay their crowns before the throne and say, [11]"You are worthy, O Lord our God, to receive glory and honor and power. For you created all things, and they exist because you created what you pleased."

~ Revelation 4:1-4, 6, 8-11

The Lamb That Was Slain

Jesus, the Lamb of God, is the only One worthy to break the seals and open the heavenly scroll. He is the Lamb who was slain, and with His blood He purchased people for God. To Him be glory and honor.

¹Then I saw a scroll in the right hand of the one who was sitting on the throne. There was writing on the inside and the outside of the scroll, and it was sealed with seven seals. ²And I saw a strong angel, who shouted with a loud voice: "Who is worthy to break the seals on this scroll and open it?" ³But no one in heaven or on earth or under the earth was able to open the scroll and read it.

⁴Then I began to weep bitterly because no one was found worthy to open the scroll and read it. ⁵But one of the twenty-four elders said to me, "Stop weeping! Look, the Lion of the tribe of Judah, the heir to David's throne, has won the victory. He is worthy to open the scroll and its seven seals."

⁶Then I saw a Lamb that looked as if it had been slaughtered, but it was now standing between the throne and the four living beings and among the twenty-four elders. He had seven horns and seven eyes, which represent the sevenfold Spirit of God that is sent out into every part of the earth. ⁷He stepped forward and took the scroll from the right hand of the one sitting on the throne. ⁸And when he took the scroll, the four living beings and the twenty-four elders fell down before the Lamb. Each one had a harp, and they held gold bowls filled with incense, which are the prayers of God's people.

⁹And they sang a new song with these words: "You are worthy to take the scroll and break its seals and open it. For you were slaughtered, and your blood has ransomed people for God from every tribe and language and people and nation."

~ Revelation 5:1-9

The Wedding Supper of the Lamb

All who are invited to the wedding feast of the Lamb are truly blessed. If you have accepted Jesus as your Savior then you are invited and can already look forward to the feast of the Lamb. God's words are true indeed.

[5]And from the throne came a voice that said, "Praise our God, all his servants, all who fear him, from the least to the greatest."

[6]Then I heard again what sounded like the shout of a vast crowd or the roar of mighty ocean waves or the crash of loud thunder: "Praise the LORD! For the Lord our God, the Almighty, reigns. [7]Let us be glad and rejoice, and let us give honor to him. For the time has come for the wedding feast of the Lamb, and his bride has prepared herself. [8]She has been given the finest of pure white linen to wear." For the fine linen represents the good deeds of God's holy people.

[9]And the angel said to me, "Write this: Blessed are those who are invited to the wedding feast of the Lamb." And he added, "These are true words that come from God."

[10]Then I fell down at his feet to worship him, but he said, "No, don't worship me. I am a servant of God, just like you and your brothers and sisters who testify about their faith in Jesus. Worship only God. For the essence of prophecy is to give a clear witness for Jesus."

~ Revelation 19:5-10

A New Heaven and a New Earth

God is preparing a new heaven and a new earth for His children. There God will be with us forever; no more death or mourning or crying or pain. For the old order of things has passed away. Everything is made new!

¹Then I saw a new heaven and a new earth, for the old heaven and the old earth had disappeared. And the sea was also gone. ²And I saw the holy city, the new Jerusalem, coming down from God out of heaven like a bride beautifully dressed for her husband.

³I heard a loud shout from the throne, saying, "Look, God's home is now among his people! He will live with them, and they will be his people. God himself will be with them. ⁴He will wipe every tear from their eyes, and there will be no more death or sorrow or crying or pain. All these things are gone forever."

⁵And the one sitting on the throne said, "Look, I am making everything new!" And then he said to me, "Write this down, for what I tell you is trustworthy and true." ⁶And he also said, "It is finished! I am the Alpha and the Omega—the Beginning and the End. To all who are thirsty I will give freely from the springs of the water of life. ⁷All who are victorious will inherit all these blessings, and I will be their God, and they will be my children."

~ Revelation 21:1-7

With God as Your Light

God's city of gold with gates of pearls will have no temple and need no sun or moon to shine on it; for the glory of God gives it light, and the Lamb is its lamp. Only the people whose names are written in the Book of Life will be able to live in the city. Make sure your name is there!

[19]The wall of the city was built on foundation stones inlaid with twelve precious stones: the first was jasper, the second sapphire, the third agate, the fourth emerald, [20]the fifth onyx, the sixth carnelian, the seventh chrysolite, the eighth beryl, the ninth topaz, the tenth chrysoprase, the eleventh jacinth, the twelfth amethyst.

[21]The twelve gates were made of pearls—each gate from a single pearl! And the main street was pure gold, as clear as glass.

[22]I saw no temple in the city, for the Lord God Almighty and the Lamb are its temple. [23]And the city has no need of sun or moon, for the glory of God illuminates the city, and the Lamb is its light. [24]The nations will walk in its light, and the kings of the world will enter the city in all their glory. [25]Its gates will never be closed at the end of day because there is no night there.

[26]And all the nations will bring their glory and honor into the city. [27]Nothing evil will be allowed to enter, nor anyone who practices shameful idolatry and dishonesty—but only those whose names are written in the Lamb's Book of Life.

~ Revelation 21:19-27

Jesus Is Coming Soon!

Jesus is the Alpha and Omega, the First and the Last, the Beginning and the End. He said Himself that He is coming soon. He is coming to take you to be with Him forever. Are you ready?

[7]"Look, I am coming soon! Blessed are those who obey the words of prophecy written in this book."

[8]I, John, am the one who heard and saw all these things. And when I heard and saw them, I fell down to worship at the feet of the angel who showed them to me. [9]But he said, "No, don't worship me. I am a servant of God, just like you and your brothers the prophets, as well as all who obey what is written in this book. Worship only God!"

[10]Then he instructed me, "Do not seal up the prophetic words in this book, for the time is near."

[12]"Look, I am coming soon, bringing my reward with me to repay all people according to their deeds."

[17]The Spirit and the bride say, "Come." Let anyone who hears this say, "Come." Let anyone who is thirsty come. Let anyone who desires drink freely from the water of life.

[20]He who is the faithful witness to all these things says, "Yes, I am coming soon!" Amen! Come, Lord Jesus! [21]May the grace of the Lord Jesus be with God's holy people.

~ Revelation 22:7-10, 12, 17, 20-21

Scripture Index